FEMINISM IN A TRADITIONAL SOCIETY

SHAKTI BOOKS is devoted solely to publishing studies on Women. The aim of the several series under this imprint is to provide documentation, analyses, interpretive comment and research findings on all aspects of the various issues related to women, from the standpoint of anthropology, sociology, history, politics, economics and social history. Emphasis will be placed on the Third World experience and contributions invited from academicians, professionals with field experience, social scientists and scholars. In those areas of social concern where formal data are scanty or unavailable, informal but fully authenticated studies will be considered as part of a holistic treatment of a complex and, in many ways, still undefined subject.

SHAKTI intends to publish a body of work, multidisciplinary and unaffected by bias, that will serve as resource material and as a reference point for further enquiry.

The following series are in preparation :

   I. WOMEN IN SOCIETY

  II. WOMEN IN POVERTY

 III. WOMEN IN DEVELOPMENT

 IV. WOMEN IN THE THIRD WORLD : Socio-Cultural Perspectives

WOMEN IN SOCIETY

FEMINISM IN A TRADITIONAL SOCIETY
Women of the Manipur Valley

Manjusri Chaki-Sircar

SHAKTI BOOKS

Distributed By
ADVENT BOOKS
141 East 44 Street
New York, NY 10017

SHAKTI BOOKS
a division of
Vikas Publishing House Pvt Ltd
Regd. Office: 5 Ansari Road, New Delhi 110002
H. O. Vikas House, 20/4 Industrial Area, Sahibabad 201010
Distt. Ghaziabad, U.P. (India)

ISBN 0-7069-1967-X

1V2SDP19

Printed at Central Electric Press, 80-D, Kamla Nagar, Delhi–110007 (India)

In memory of my father
the late Nanigopal Chaki
and
to my husband
Dr Parbati Kumar Sircar

Preface

Can feminism survive in a society where there is a strong influence of Hindu patriarchy? The present study of Meitei women of the Manipur Valley in north-eastern India focuses on the basis of feminism i.e., women's individual self-reliance and sisterhood or collective solidarity, in a society under strong Brahmanic influence.

In Indian societies women still have extremely limited options to extend their role outside the domestic domain. There is rarely any scope for women to act as a collective body. Among some lower socio-economic communities women enjoy considerable freedom outside their homes, but they too are often subjected to pressures from high-caste ideology and male domination. Today, average educated women, working and non-working, face continuous discrimination stemming from a patriarchal culture and its appurtenant sexual preference for male children, prejudice towards daughters' inheritance rights, and unequal access to job-oriented education and professional fields. They face especial discrimination in marriage where the portent of dowry casts its lurid shadow. The traditionalism of the marriage custom often blurs the issue of sexual equality and intersexual harmony.

In this atmosphere, a legacy of Hindu patriarchy, where the issue of women's rights is in perpetual pendancy, this study of Meitei women may expose some new aspects to extend the scope of our cultural horizon. In spite of the strong ideological impact of Hindu Brahmans, Meitei women have retained their vital roles in the public sphere, the dissonance with Brahmanism being particularly evident in their unaffected contact and interaction with Meitei men.

This book is based on anthropological field research conducted in 1977-78 for approximately one year in the urban and rural communities of the Manipur Valley, focusing on women's traditional sex roles and the changes evidenced. While dealing with women's roles, I try to focus on Meitei cultural values, which greatly differ from the Brahmanic ideology of mainstream Indian culture. The study thus projects the issue of the inherent conflict between the two cultures—Brahmanic Hinduism and traditional Meiteism—which have been in confrontation over the past two hundred years.

This study analyzes women's roles in the ritual and non-ritual spheres of Meitei society in Manipur. *Lai Harouba*, a principal ritual of the indigenous pre-Hindu faith (which presently coexists with Hinduism) serves as the major ethnographic focus for this account of traditional Meitei sex roles as interpreted and evaluated in the context of contemporary Meitei society, especially in its political, economic, social, and religious spheres. *Lai Harouba*, it is argued, represents the traditional socio-moral world of the Meitei, a world based on a mutual partnership and respect between the sexes.

Two major historical events—a devastating male depopulation resulting from protracted warfare (which was ended by the Indo-Burmese Treaty of 1826), and the advent of colonial rule in 1892—have had a considerable impact on Meitei sex roles and social relationships. While the depopulation of males expanded women's economic roles, it also promoted polygyny. Subsequently, the development of a transportation network under colonial auspices enabled these women to extend their trading activities throughout and beyond Manipur. Meanwhile, under royal patronage and supported by immigrant Brahmans, the Meitei have undergone a massive process of Sanskritization since the early eighteenth century; the neo-Hinduism thus created helping to enrich Meitei religious and cultural life, especially its ethnic traditions of music, dance, and ritual. However, while Meitei society may be viewed as a field of conflict and compromise between two diametrically opposing forces—the process of Sanskritization and the resistance to it from the indigenous tradition—because of the strong position of Meitei women in the extra-domestic world, Sanskritization here (unlike in many Indian societies) largely failed in curtailing the role of women vis-a-vis men.

Meitei women make crucial economic contributions and hold a distinctive position in social, religious, and political life. Outside of subsistence, the Meitei economy provides two major avenues for women's autonomy—the weaving industry and trade—which remain exclusively in the female domain. Within an overall patrilineal framework women are thus able to develop a power base and a group solidarity, strengthened by various women's organizations. Women's collective power in the political arena, hitherto a male domain, was made evident during the "women's wars" (*Nupi-lan*) in 1904 and 1939, against colonial policies.

Nevertheless, the Meitei are a patrilineal society with an inherent social ideology of male superiority. This notion of male superiority, however, does not entail actual female subordination, a situation whose ambiguity causes conflict and tension between the sexes. *Lai Harouba* attempts to resolve this inherent social-structural contradiction. It promotes idealized sex role models and stresses intersexual harmony. It recognizes two contrasting models for women: the primary role as mother, wife, and daughter, and the alternative or nonconformist role of the woman as priestess. The recognition of ordinary women's economic contribution and the acceptance of nonconformist women as priestesses in their society's core religious ritual indicate the extraordinary position women are accorded in Meitei culture. In Meitei society men and women perform their assigned roles in complementary spheres. Women's collective power thus emerges as an integral part of the patrilineal system; it provides moral backing to that system, rather than a subculture of opposition to it.

The "Meitei-ization" of Manipuri society in modern times—a re-emphasizing of non-Hindu cultural traits—has diminished the political power of the Brahmans. As a result, women have become increasingly prominent in the Hindu religious sphere. A resurgence of *Lai Harouba* as the embodiment of Meitei cultural identity has recently occurred. It has served to reassert traditional Meitei values vis-a-vis the ascendancy of Sanskritized culture.

Does this indicate that the Meitei are shifting toward their pre-Hindu ideology with more enhanced social freedom for women and intersexual harmony? Or, is it that the visible manifestation of ethnicity in *Lai Harouba* ritual is only a statement of their political awareness? Is it too late to liberate the chauvinistic attitude of the Hinduized Meitei males?

This study raises some of these questions and brings up some revealing aspects of sex roles and social relationships in a changing society, which are not only unexpected in South Asia, but also unusual in the ethnographic terrain of anthropological literature.

MANJUSRI CHAKI-SIRCAR

Acknowledgements

I would like first to express my deep gratitude to Professors
Alexander Alland, Jr., Conrad M. Arensberg, Daisy Hilse Dwyer
and Clive Kessler, members of my advisory committee in the
Department of Anthropology, Columbia University.

Professor Alland inspired me immensely to study Meitei society
from the very beginning of my student days in the Department.
Throughout my stay at Columbia University and my writing period,
he showed constant interest in my research and gave much of his
valuable time, providing critical judgement, penetrating comments,
and scholarly insight.   Professor Arensberg was very kind in patiently
offering sound advice whenever I needed it.   His teaching gave me
an interest in the comparative study of South Asian cultures and
a cross-cultural perspective on social organizations. Professor
Dwyer created in me a real incentive for the study of sex roles, and
this eventually led to my study of them in Meitei society.   She
helped me a great deal to clarify my approach to an analysis of the
sex roles of Meitei women.   Professor Kessler's academic influence
took me in the direction of rituals and encouraged me to research
those of Meitei society.   I benefited from his remarks drawing
parallels between Meitei and Southeast Asian societies.   I also
benefited greatly from my student years which furnished me with a
background of South Asian and African cultures provided by
Professors Morton Klass and Elliot Skinner, respectively.

I am grateful to the Indian Council of Social Science Research
for a Research Fellowship which met part of my field expenses.
My deep gratitude goes to Maharajkumari Binodini Devi, my hostess
in the capital, and to Dr Waripokpom Bhagirath Singh and his
wife, Gamghini Devi, of Nambol. Whatever little I have
accomplished I could not have done without their constant support.
My two assistants, Saibam Biswabhanu Devi of Imphal and

Laishram Ibemhal Devi of Nambol, worked with me with real commitment. The latter also assisted me throughout my writing period with regular correspondence and sincere support.

I would also like to express appreciation towards several Meitei scholars: Dr Ch Buddhi Singh, anthropologist at the Jawaharlal Nehru Centre for Post Graduate Studies at Imphal, who gave his valuable time to discussions on my fieldwork and suggested important leads to my understanding of his own culture; Pundit N. Khelchandra, who helped me with his scholarly background in Meitei history; and Professor Sanamani Yambem, who with his generous correspondence filled in some important gaps in my data on Meitei history; he was also kind enough to provide me with his own field research data on the night patrollers of Manipur.

I wish to thank Professor H. Ranbir Singh, Director of the Jawaharlal Nehru Centre for Post Graduate Studies, and to Th Joychandra Singh for their administrative support. Of the many who kindly contributed to my work directly or indirectly, and some who made my stay in Manipur a joyous experience, I shall mention only a few: R K Achobi Sana, Mr S Tombi Singh, Sm Promodini Devi, Pundit Kulachandra Singh, Ima Rajani Maibi, Rajo Maibi, Kumar Maibi, Ima Rebati Maibi, Amar Maibi, Professor N Nilkanta Singh, Sm Tondon Devi, Dr Y Satyabati Devi, Dr N Bino Devi, Pundit O Bhogendra Singh, Mr Devendra Singh of Moirang, Th Birchandra Singh of Utlou, Dr Kunjabihari Singh and his wife of Nambol, Mr Daoji Sharma, and Mr L Debeswar Singh and his family of Lampok. There are others too numerous to mention by name.

My deepest thanks go to the large number of women of the Valley I met, who shared their joys and sorrows with their *mayang* (North Indian—foreigner) sister.

I would also like to mention Dr Renuka Biswas, Prof. Shanu Lahiri and Dr. Moni Nag who very kindly offered me support in my endeavours and to thank L. Somi Roy and Daoji Sharma, for the use of their photographs.

Lastly, I greatly acknowledge my deep indebtedness to my revered parents, my father the late Nanigopal Chaki, and my mother Smt. Charubala Chaki, and my family of birth, who provided moral support and inspiration for me to develop both aesthetic and academic interest in life, which was further supported by my own family, especially during my second time round in graduate studies; my husband, Professor Parbati Kumar Sircar; and Ranjabati, my daughter, who was patient enough to edit the manuscript. My thanks also to Irma Garlick for her help in the last-mentioned. I would also like to thank Felix J Carneiro for typing the manuscript.

Contents

1
Introduction

For this anthropologist, a native Bengali Hindu middle-class woman, the first encounter with Meitei society was overwhelming in its unexpected contrast with other Indian societies. Particularly was this so in the ubiquitous presence of women in the public domain and the mode of intersex behaviour in various social situations.

On my first day in Manipur in November, 1977 I was looking for a suitable place to live in. In the house of my prospective landlady (an established entrepreneur) in Uripok *Leikai* (ward), Imphal, my companions (a princess of Manipur and a common man) and I were offered a tray of western and local cigarettes (*biris*). The women and men lighted one another's cigarettes. The old lady asked me several questions, e.g. "Are you a divorcee?" "Do you have a son?" "What do you do to make a living?"

On the first evening in my new home, the landlady's daughter-in-law, Laxmipriya (45) was helping me fix a mosquito net. As we went about our task, she explained her situation to me. "Sister, I live with my mother-in-law, along with my son, daughter-in-law, and two daughters. My mother-in-law threw her son [her husband] out because he brought home a new wife." "She threw her son out and asked you to stay with her?" I asked in surprise. "Yes, Sister," she replied. "My mother-in-law and I work together with many, many weavers. We do not want a strange woman among us. My mother-in-law got very annoyed at her son's irresponsible behaviour. It was very sad. But now I am happy—my son got married only last month. In a way I am relieved that he is out of the household. He used to drink all the time."

A few days later I went to visit some women weavers in Wankhai *Leikai*. As we (a young woman assistant and myself) got down from the rickshaw, we were greeted by two well-groomed women with *chandan* marks[1], in their early thirties. On their way home, they stopped at a thatched-roof roadside café run by a woman in her forties. Several men and women lounged around, having tea and snacks. One of the women introduced me as a *mayang*[2] (foreigner or North Indian). She whispered the word *mayang* and added, "She is quite different from others. She likes us. She wears Meitei dress and tries hard to speak our language. She is going to write a book on Meitei women." The café was a rendezvous for both sexes. Men and women chatted in a relaxed comfortable atmosphere and smoked *biris*. A brother of one of the two women was the husband of the owner of the café. He sat next to me and treated me to tea and several snacks. He was curious about my visit and asked, "Where do you come from?" "Are you a *mou* (married) or a *laishabi* (unmarried)?" "How much money do you make?" "Do you have children?"

Later we visited the house of one of the women. It was a well-maintained thatched-roof, mud house with a huge wooden door and windows. On one side of the porch was a hand loom with half-finished silk fabric. There were two thread-winding wheels and several bobbins of thread scattered near the loom and a basketful of patterns drawn on paper. The courtyard was clean with a *tulsi*, a basil plant on a small earthen mound, a must for all Hindu Vaisnavite homes and a very familiar feature in Bengal. She said that she was the third wife of a man who visited her every weekend. She had no children, so she had adopted her brother's son. She was very close to the other woman, a divorcee with three children, who had left her husband when he brought home another wife and had come, with her three children, to live with her parents. They helped her build a small house in their compound. The anecdotes were related in good humour, with the women joking about irresponsible men running after women. The second woman introduced me to several of her female relatives. After being treated to a delicious hot lunch, we spent the afternoon visiting different homes in the neighbourhood.

[1]*Chandan* or sandalwood paste or a paste made out of yellow clay, used to decorate the nose, forehead and throat with fine lines, is a sign of Vaisnavite Hindu faith among orthodox Vaisnavas in India.

[2]*Mayang*, meaning North Indian, has become a rather derogatory term at present, because of an anti-Indian political mood in the last few years. When children addressed me as a *mayang nupi* (foreigner woman), mothers felt very embarrassed and asked them to call me *Ine* (father's sister, or aunt).

Every house had one or more looms, with young girls (some looked thirteen or fourteen) and women making varieties of fabrics and mosquito nets. In the courtyards, bundles of brilliantly-coloured thread were hung from clothes-lines to dry and fences were draped with freshly dyed cloths or threads. The weavers took a break to chat with us, and some left their work and joined our team. A group of wide-eyed, giggling children followed us everywhere.

We were joined by the goldsmith's wife, who took us to her husband's shop. The goldsmith greeted me with a warm smile. His wife turned to his assistant, a man in his forties, and said teasingly, "Look at him. He must be near fifty and still a bachelor ..." The man looked away, very embarrassed, with eyes cast down, and attempted to concentrate on his work. Other women and children giggled at the teasing.

Travelling by bus, I observed streams of women carrying loads of fish, vegetables, cloth, fabrics, rice, and other merchandise. Women helped each other unload huge baskets and boxes. On the street, many young women rode their bicycles to school or to work. I visited Khwarimbond bazaar, the main market, Laxmi bazaar, the cloth market, Kwakeithel bazaar, and Senjamei bazaar—everywhere I went, I found hundreds of women traders in tin-roofed or brick-built sheds. In the market, there were no children in sight, not even babies tied to women's backs. At every street corner there was a small roadside bazaar run by women vendors. There were no coolies anywhere.

In a few days I was to realize that I was in a very different society from the one I was familiar with in India. During my ten-month sojourn, I was to become more and more convinced that Meitei society was unusual not only in the pervasive role of women in the socio-economic sphere, but also in women's role in religion in a patrilineal society. In fact, the progressive revelation of the very nature of the male-female relationship in a so-called Hinduized or Sanskritized (Srinivas 1952, 1971, 1976) society like the Meitei was rather like an adventure into the unexpected.

PREVIOUS STUDIES

There is a body of literature written by colonial administrators between 1835 and 1913 which gives valuable accounts of the social, political and religious customs of nineteenth century Meitei society. The colonial writers were impressed by the contribution of women in

Meitei society and have not failed to express their admiration; but they do not offer any detailed information on this aspect. On the women's important role in the economy, Dunn (1975 (1886) : 17) states, "Most of the work of the country, except the heaviest, is performed by them [women], and they are consequently the mainstay of the family circle. All marketing is done by women, all work of buying and selling in public, and the carrying to and fro of the articles to be sold; whilst at home they are busily employed in weaving and spinning." Johnstone (1896:134) supports Dunn's view and says, "Women are the great traders, and many walk miles in the morning, and buy things in the more distant bazaars to sell again in the capital in the evening. It was not considered etiquette for men too often to frequent the bazaars. Crowds of hillmen visit bazaars." Hodson (1908, reprinted in 1975:23) goes further to state, "The women hold a high and free position in Manipur, all the internal trade and exchange of the produce of the country being managed by them."

Concerning religion, Hodson (*Ibid* :109) states, "Side by side with the Brahman, there exist the priests and priestesses of the animistic faith who are called *maibas* and *maibis*." He adds another curious piece of information (*Ibid*: 62) : "The *Maibi Loishang* (the council of the *maibis*) corresponds to the *Maiba Loishang* and is the college of the *maibis*." On women's prominence in religious ceremonies of Lai Harouba, we find McCullock's description (McCullock in Hodson, *Ibid*: 104): "The worship consists in a number of married women and unmarried girls led by a priestess, accompanied by a party of men and boys in dresses of former times, dancing and singing and performing various evolutions in the holy presence." On women's participation in public dance performances, he says, " . . . all girls whose position is at all respectable learn to dance, for in Manipur the dancing profession is often a road to royal dignity and is not despised in any way as is the case in India" (*Ibid* : 23)[3].

There are several pieces of tantalizing information here—women's pervasive role in trade, the presence of the priestesses on par with the Brahmans, "a college of the *maibis*, " men and women participating

[3]At present, classical Indian dancing is a prestigious performing art for women in India. It has been accepted among the modern educated class in cities as an expression of their awareness of and pride in the ancient heritage of Indian culture. Despite the revival of this ancient art, women's dancing in public is mostly limited to the urban areas (Chaki-Sircar, 1971, 1977).

together in a religious ritual in public. Should this not suffice to arouse immense curiosity in an anthropologist familiar with South Asian societies? Yet, strangely enough, there is no further writing on Meitei women until 1958. Lightfoot (1958) gives a description of parts of Lai Harouba very similar to what had been provided by Shakespeare about half a century earlier (Shakespeare 1913: 428).

More recently, Meitei authors have written about their history, culture and literature, but these display a significant lack of attention to the role of women, of such specific concern to foreign writers. Some of the comments even betray an antipathy towards women. About women's economic role, for example: ". . . weaving is the second common profession which is practised more out of the people's sentiments for it than for its profit which is negligible in the present context" (N. Tombi Singh, 1975:47). About women's political role: "The Manipuri male folk considered it below their dignity to do so [i.e., to engage in non-violent collective protests as the market women had done]. So they left it to the females." [L. Iboongohal Singh, 1963:45] Sometimes the Hinduized value of the writer distorted the social reality: "It is considered by many that there is a widow or second marriage amongst the Hindu Manipur community. It is far from being true. A female can be married only once but a male can marry a hundred times." (*Ibid* :90.) However, younger scholars, like historian Sanamani Yambem, offer a valuable perspective on women's socio-political role in their studies on the *Nupi-lan* (women's war) (Yambem, 1976) and the recent study on the night patrollers of Manipur (Yambem, 1978).[4] Anthropologist Ch. Buddhi Singh (1972, 1973) furnishes some valuable facts on women's socio-economic role in Meitei society in his field research on the fishing economy of a lacustrine community. All of these studies certainly gave direction to my own research.

MEITEI WOMEN AND SOUTH ASIAN SOCIETY

The preceding facts reflect the distinctive nature of the role of women in Meitei culture in comparison with other South Asian societies. In Dube's study (1956:174-175) in a social microcosm of a single village in Telengana we find a pattern of women's sex roles which can be found in many other communities of the larger Indian society. He presents a model of women in four socio-economic strata.

[4]Unpublished research data.

At the highest level, women have a leisurely life with domestic help. They live a secluded life observing the rule of purdah (veil) and making absolutely no economic contribution to the family. Their men are land owners who engage people to work in their fields. On the next level, we find common peasants who work their fields without any outside help. Their women also live in seclusion, partaking of domestic chores but making no other economic contribution to the family. On the third level, he places the poor low-caste farmers who work on their family land along with their women. These women sometimes also work for wages in other people's fields and go to the market. On the lowest level are the untouchable and tribal people, the poorest of all. These women never expect to be provided for by their husbands and always work for their living.

Karve's study (1965) of regional socio-structural differences shows how subtly the life style of women differs from one part of India to another and also from one socio-economic level to another. This wide variation is illustrated by the available data on women from many studies. These include work on North Indian societies (O. Lewis, 1955; Marriott, 1955), on Central Indian Hindu or Muslim societies (Mayer, 1960; Jacobson, 1973, 1977), on the matrilineal Nayar and the patrilineal Southern Hindu (Gough, 1955, 1974), on the Lingayat and Havik Brahman of the South (Harper, 1964, 1969), on Himalayan Hindus (Berreman, 1966) and Himalayan Nepalese (Jones & Jones, 1976; Andors, 1976; Bennett n.d.), on Bengali middle class women (Roy, 1975), and on tribal women (Fuchs, 1968 on the Gond; S. Roy, 1912 on the Munda; Furer-Haimendorf, 1962, 1967 on the Naga; Orans, 1965 on the Santal, etc). From a review of the major literature on women in South Asia one consistent pattern emerges: the higher the socio-economic level of a group, the closer it is to the ideal Sanskritized life style for women. For example, among the Limbu (Jones & Jones, 1976), lower caste women have relative freedom to select marriage partners, to divorce, and to remarry (in the case of divorcees and widows). They contribute a major share of the family income. But the high caste Nepalese Hindu women do not enjoy any of this liberty. They have to adhere to the high-caste rules of Hindu society, e.g., strict segregation of the sexes, exclusion of women from the economic sphere, prohibition of divorce and of re-marriage for widows, seclusion of women from the public, and so on. Ulrich's study (1975) of a South Indian village in Karnataka shows this gap between the behaviour models of the

Havik Brahman women and the Sudra caste Divaru women. Traits like the self-effacement and submissiveness of the Havik women (who accept their husbands as personal gods) are absent among the Divaru women. On the contrary, a Divaru woman enjoys an egalitarian relationship with her husband and can even criticize him in public.[5]

Meitei society has gone through a massive process of Sanskritization over the past two hundred years, but has not yet accepted any of the common traits of women of upper-caste Indian societies or others which have Sanskritized their life style toward an upper-caste model (Epstein, 1973; Sinha, 1971; Mandelbaum, 1970; Bailey, 1957).[6] A trait shared by almost all Indian societies is the division of religious labour between the sexes; but Meitei women co-operate with men in public rituals almost on an equal footing. There is no opportunity for professional priesthood for women in the formal religious system of Hinduism, whereas women are ordained as religious specialists and priests in the traditional Meitei religious organization.

Meitei women are not only major economic contributors (in both subsistence and trade); they also have a considerable voice in the political sphere. Until the colonial period there was a separate women's court with formal jural authority vested in women.

In fact, an analogy to Meitei women in other Indian societies was hard to find. We cannot expect the upper-caste "Sanskritized" behaviour model to prevail among the socially free Meitei women, nor can we equate them with any of the low-caste or tribal communities in India. Meitei women's socio-economic behaviour is to some extent similar to that of women in some Southeast Asian societies of Burma, Java, and Malaysia. The similarity is striking in the areas of potential economic freedom for women, marital instability, and the pattern of matrifocal households.

[5]The gap between the life styles of women in the upper and lower classes had been noted in the early literature of the colonial writers. Risley (1915:186-87) states, for example, "Among the lower caste women are much more of a power than they are among the higher; they assert themselves on a variety of public occasions, and in many cases they have secured themselves the right to initiate proceedings for divorce."

[6]Srinivas states, "Sankritization is the process by which a 'low' Hindu caste, or tribal or other group, changes its customs, ritual, ideology and way of life in the direction of a high, and frequently 'twice-born', caste." (1971:6).

In socio-economic and political areas, Meitei women can sometimes be compared with those of some West African societies, such
as the Igbo, Nupe, and Yoruba of Nigeria, the Ga, Akan, and Ashanti
of Ghana, the Mende of Sierra Leone, where they have important
roles not only in the subsistence economy but also in marketing and
trade. In both cases, women belong to a wider, extradomestic world,
exerting political power that arises out of their socio-economic
network in the market associations (Awe, 1977 on the Yoruba; Van
Allen, 1976 on the Igbo; Okonjo, 1976 on the Igbo; Nadel, 1970
on the Nupe; Lewis, 1977 on the Ivorian; Robertson, 1976 on the
Ga; Ifeka-Moller, 1975; Sanday, 1974). When I observed the pervasive prominence of women in important ritual performances and
the presence of women priests in the central religious organization,
I recognized a rather unusual quality of Meitei culture found perhaps nowhere else in the patriarchal systems of Brahmanic India,
Buddhist Burma, Islamized Malaysia or traditional Africa.

Intersexual dependence in the economy, a complementary and
a considerable egalitarian relationship of the sexes in the socio-
religious sphere, women's potential autonomy both socially and
economically, and their high ritual status are distinctive characteris-
tics of the Meitei among South Asian cultures. But all of these traits
coexist with an ideology of socio-structural superiority of men.
However, despite the socio-structural superiority of the male, Meitei
ideology does not undermine the female role. There is no polarity
of the sexes. Women's collective power has a recognized status in
different cultural areas. Such an apparent contradiction indeed poses
a problem for an anthropologist. This study does not promise to
solve this problem, but probably will unveil some facts still unknown
in the ethnographic terrain.

LAI HAROUBA RITUAL: STABILITY AND PERSISTENCE OF MEITEI CULTURAL TRAITS

I became particularly interested in Lai Harouba, a prime ritual of
the ancient Meitei religion performed annually from five days to one
month by almost all the villages in the Valley. Although Hindu culture has swept through the Valley in exuberant and aesthetic grandeur,
the traditional religion of the Meitei has held its own and co-exists
with the Hindu religious system in a mutually exclusive way. I
focus on the basic cultural arenas of Meitei society: political, economic, social and religious. In Lai Harouba I observed the sex role

models as represented in the ritual repertoire. I have concentrated basically on the persistent character of certain traditional cultural traits especially in women's sex roles and how these have been preserved and reinforced in the Lai Harouba ritual.

Since mass Hinduization two hundred years ago, the Meitei have been living in a rapidly changing society. But even prior to that, in the fifteenth century, warfare with neighbouring states commenced, continuing for four centuries. During the last sixty years of this period, male population was considerably reduced. However, peace came in 1826 with the signing of the Indo-Burmese Treaty. British colonization started in 1892, bringing with it a measure of modernization which has accelerated since World War II. The merging of Manipur with the nation state of India (1972) freed people from traditional state control with respect to several social and cultural institutions. Where I discuss the process of change, especially "Sanskritization," I refer to the trend of "Meiteiization" as an expression of "de-Sanskritization." De-Sanskritization in several Indian communities has had the political motivation of achieving some of the advantages offered by the Indian government to the scheduled caste communities (Sinha, 1971 on the Bhumija; Srivastava, 1966 on the Johar Bhotia in Mandelbaum, 1970; Lynch, 1969 on the Jatav of Agra; Patwardhan, 1973 on the Mahar Buddhist in Maharashtra; Orans, 1965 on the Santal).[7] De-Sanskritization here aims more at secular progress and modernization (higher education and job facilities) than at the so-called ritual status of the upper caste.

Among the Meitei, the movement towards, de-Sanskritization (which I term Meiteiization) rose from a deeper conflict between Meitei cultural identity and the dominance of an alien (Indian Hindu) cultural model. The process of Meiteiization is particularly significant to me for its growing force in the Lai Harouba ritual. For the past few decades, there has been a greatly regenerated appeal for Lai Harouba among the people.

I was impressed by two important aspects of Meitei culture.

First, that Lai Harouba although an ancient ritual, still represents the Meitei cultural ethos, and expresses a spirit of mutual res-

[7]However, the Agra Jatav and the Mahar Buddhists rejected the entire social framework of the Hindu caste structure and adopted Buddhism to recover from their degraded untouchable status in Hindu society (Lynch, 1969; Patwardhan, 1973). An anti-Hindu consciousness developed into a new political identity for gaining secular privileges in modern India.

pect, companionship, and cooperation between the sexes in a joyous celebration of life.

The ritual model is an idealized version of the intersexual relationship of an ancient society. The fossilised forms may not directly reflect disharmony found in the present society but the ceremony still sustains and reaffirms the fundamental principle of sex role morals which is profound in the social and economic relationships of the sexes today.

Secondly, the sex role ideology of Meitei society is very different from that of Hindu society, which promotes the patriarchal model of male supremacy. In the Manipur Valley, the process of Sanskritization failed to work in the socio-economic and religious areas because of the vital presence of female power, which may be described as a kind of feminism. This can be recognized in women's individual self-reliance and collective solidarity. Here feminism does not entail a sub-culture or anti-male attitude but exists as a moral support to the male, an integral part of the social system. Thus Hinduism has been absorbed into the ethnic culture, and there is a pervasive and distinctive role for women in the public sphere, viz. political, economic, social and religious, found perhaps nowhere else in India.

This study is arranged in seven chapters.

In Chapter I, I describe my field site, with a brief geographical background of the Manipur Valley and its people.

In Chapter II, the focus is on women's role in the political context. I offer a brief account of the political position of a rural man and his direct link with the central state organization and show that, though in a peripheral position, women still have a considerable political voice.

Chapter III shows the basic division of labour between the sexes in the economic structure of the society and highlights the crucial importance of women in subsistence, in the weaving industry, and in trade.

Chapter IV delineates Meitei social organization, giving an account of the principle of patriliny, the formation of clan and lineage, the system of marriage, the rules of divorce and polygyny, the household structure, and the abduction of women.

Chapter V emphasizes the unusual prominence of women in the Meitei religious world. Two traditions of religious life are discussed: Vaisnavite Hinduism and ancient *Lai* worship. In the first, we see that the upper-caste ideology of Indian culture has had to accommodate itself to the public prominence of Meitei women in key roles of Meitei religious rituals.

Chapter VI presents a detailed record of my observations of the Lai Harouba ritual. In order to focus on the ritual status of women in relation to their social position, this chapter is especially important for its ethnographic reference.

Chapter VII starts with an ethnographic analysis to demonstrate the stability and persistence of the traditional Meitei cultural ethos. Two distinct aspects of Meitei women's sex roles are highlighted: firstly, the vital importance of women's role in Meitei society, which could not be diminished by the pressure of Sanskritization, and secondly, the coexistence of Meitei women's power with a social ideology of male domination.

With this perspective on the social position of women, I analyze the ritual repertoire of Lai Harouba and show that it not only reaffirms the traditional ethos, but also represents the socio-moral world of the Meitei.

METHODOLOGY

I collected case histories, interviewed people, gathered information from male and female informants of varied social backgrounds, and gained knowledge from my daily encounters with Meitei people in different social situations. Out of respect for their confidences and in order to preserve their anonymity, I use pseudonyms for all my informants and for my study villages in presenting my findings in this study.

Being a woman, I faced the usual problem of not having full research access to the opposite sex. But as a visitor in a rural society I was fortunate in not being treated as an outsider. Soon I found that certain men acted as my elder or younger brothers, uncles, or nephews. A visit by my husband and frequent visits by my daughter offered me a legitimate standing in the social framework of the rural society. Fictive kin terms helped me tremendously to be at ease with the people and removed any possible tension or suspicion that might have arisen from the presence of a "mayang" enquirer.

I worked with the assistance of two young Meitei women in their twenties. One lived in the capital. The other, my constant companion, L. Ibemhal Devi, was the daughter of a village *maiba* (shaman, medicine man) and elder sister of a *maibi* (woman priest). Members of her family (cultivators, weavers, shopkeepers, a primary school teacher, students, and a trader in the bazaar) gave me a full and initial introduction to Meitei rural life. In my fieldsite, Nambol, my host, Dr. Waripokom Bhagirath Singh, a Meitei social leader, his wife, Gambhini Devi, a nursery school teacher, and their family took a special interest in my work and supported me almost as a team in different undertakings like the making of sketches, maps, and the collection of data.   In the capital, Imphal, my hostess was Maharajkumari Binodini Devi, a celebrated writer. She spent many hours translating ancient Meitei texts for me, and introduced me to the complex organization of the royal temple and its hierarchical religio-political atmosphere. Through her I met several pundits, *maibas* and *maibis* (women priests) who were attached to the royal offices. Thus I was fortunate to have access to and contact with a veritable cross-section—members of the uppermost stratum of the society as well as with common cultivators and traders of the rural area.

After a two-month period in Imphal, I concentrated my work in the rural area for the succeeding eight months. Some years ago, I had received professional instruction in Manipuri Vaisnavite and Lai Harouba dancing from Meitei gurus in Calcutta. This background helped me a great deal towards warm acceptance at Lai Harouba ceremonies. Incidentally, I was the first *mayang* to have participated in the ritual dances of Lai Harouba in the Nambol area. Two established *maibis*, Ima Rajani Maibi and Yumsam Maibi, enthusiastically taught me some of their esoteric dances, and I cherish that knowledge and my close contact with these women.

My assistants and I collected 135 case histories of women as an opportunity sample. Out of these, forty-two were from Sample Village 2, where a population of 364 lived in sixty-six households. I took time to verify my data with the help of my male and female informants. The women were most cooperative and often opened their hearts to this stranger.

In attempting to collect case studies of men, I was confronted with some real difficulties, as they tended to talk more about their achievements than their personal life. I had to accept the limitations of my data in this respect. I interviewed pundits, *maibas*, *penakhongbas* (instrumentalists)—all men—and gathered whatever information I possibly could from my daily discussion with male informants.

Since I often focus on the conflicting aspects of male/female social relationships, there is a danger of assuming that Meitei family and social life is always chaotic. On the contrary, I felt a joyous atmosphere pervading everyday life. An individual lives in a rather secure community and kin group based on mutual cooperation and dependence. A Bengali upper-caste woman visiting Manipur asked me, "Why do the women always appear so cheerful here? It seems that they really take care of themselves and always look so well groomed, with fresh flowers and *chandan* mark. Everywhere, in the bazaar, on the street and at home, they always seem to be enjoying themselves." Her sentiments are mine.

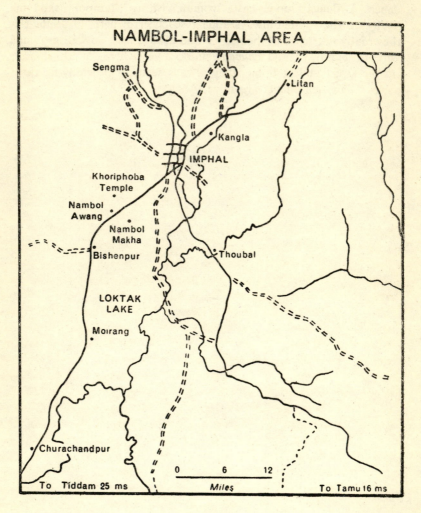

NAMBOL-IMPHAL AREA

Sengma

Litan

Kangla

IMPHAL

Khoriphoba
Temple

Nambol
Awang

Nambol
Makha

Bishenpur

Thoubal

LOKTAK
LAKE

Moirang

Churachandpur

To Tiddam 25 ms

0   6   12

Miles

To Tamu 16 ms

FIGURE 1

2
The Setting

The lower Himalayan ranges at the far eastern border of India cradle the beautiful green fertile valley of Manipur, the homeland of the Meitei. Manipur is bounded by Nagaland in the north, Burma in the east, Mizoram in the south, and Assam in the west.

Extending from latitudes 23°13′ north to 25°68′ north and longitudes 93°03′ east to 94°78′ east, Manipur covers an area of 22,356 square miles, with two distinct natural regions, the Valley and the surrounding hills. The Valley occupies only about one-tenth of the total area and is at an average elevation of 2,500 feet above sea level.

One can reach Manipur by road from Assam through Nagaland. The National Highway (No. 39), the Indo-Burma Road, runs from Assam through Dimapur and Kohima to the state capital of Manipur, Imphal, and terminates at Moreh, a market town at the border of Burma, about 107 km from Imphal. The New Cachar Road runs west from Imphal to Jiribam at the border with Assam. There is no railroad in Manipur. The nearest railhead is at Dimapur, in Assam, about 213 km from Imphal. There is a daily bus service between Dimapur and Imphal. At present there is a regular airflight from Calcutta to Imphal via Silchar and Gauhati in Assam.

The Manipur Valley is a fertile plain surrounded by mountain ranges. The northern hills are higher than the southern ones. The highest peak is Kobru rising 800 feet above the Valley in the north. The Valley slopes down gradually to the south and reaches Loktak Lake, the largest natural lake of Manipur. The lake is fed partly by rainfall and partly by streams and rivers. The terrain of hill ranges extends as part of the southern continuation of the Naga hills leading to Burma, and encircles the Valley plain.

From Lake Loktak the land rises on all sides up to the foot of the surrounding hills. The hills are drained by numerous streams flowing down to the lower valley. The streams develop into major rivers which drain the Valley.

The monsoon season usually starts between late May and June, when moist southwesterly winds bring heavy torrential rains which decrease between late August and September. During the next month, there are only a few showers and from October to late November, the air cools with the advent of cold northerly winds and a decrease in temperature in the next two months. Then comes a dry season lasting from February to late April, reaching its peak in March.

The climate of the Valley is moderated because of its elevation. During the cold months, minimum temperatures can be as low as 0°C, whereas during the summer months maximum temperatures can rise to 40°C.

The hill communities practice terrace cultivation, and 80 percent of the plainland of the Valley is under cultivation for growing wet rice, which is dependent on the monsoon cycle.

Most of the plainland gets one crop a year, except for a few places like Kakching, where a modern irrigation system makes double cropping possible. The Census report of 1951 refers to the abundance of crop and unwillingness of the Meitei to outmigrate from their fertile land to gain a livelihood. Although population has doubled since then, in my study area, people appear to be much better off than in the villages in the rest of India. Beggars are conspicuous by their absence in the urban and rural market centres.

The 1971 Census records a population of 1,027,253 in Manipur state, of which two-thirds are the plains people, the Meitei. There has been a steady rise in population since 1826 with females outnumbering males. (Ansari, 1976:36). Regular Census data are available since 1901. These show that again from 1901 to 1961, females outnumbered males. In the 1961 Census, the population was 7,80,037 with 50.4 percent female and 49.6 percent male. But in the 1971 Census, males outnumbered females: for every 1,000 males, there were 980 females. The presence of a large number of immigrant traders and army men is partly responsible for this reversal.

A phenomenal rise in population took place in the period between 1951 and 1971, during which the Valley population almost doubled. The main reason for this was a reduction in the death rate following the introduction of modern health care.

Manipur at present has the full status of a state in the Indian administration. At present there are 60 members in the State Assembly, elected by the people. There is a common High Court and a common Governor for the five regional states: Assam, Manipur, Meghalaya, Nagaland, and Tripura.

Manipuri belongs to the Tibeto-Burman group of languages. At present this is the official state language and taught at the graduate level in the University, as well as being the lingua franca of the state.

The present script of Manipuri was borrowed from Bengali two hundred years ago, which can be found in ancient books and palm-leaf scriptures. Currently there is a movement to reinstate the original Meitei script.

Manipuri has had highly developed literature since ancient times, dating back to the third century A.D. (K S Moirangthem 1970:37). The royal chronicle traces history from A.D. 33.

IMPHAL

Imphal, the capital city, is the centre of major economic and religious activities. There are two important bazaars in Imphal, Thangal and Paona, with a large number of stores run by North Indian (*mayang*) businessmen who deal mostly with out of state imported goods and with exports of local produce as well as numerous small shops everywhere run by both Meitei males and females (often as mixed teams). However the largest internal market in Imphal, the Khwarimbond bazaar[8] or Sana Keithel and several other important bazaars, e.g. Laxmi bazaar, Senjamei bazaar, Kwakeithel, etc., are all run by women. Women traders still control the local agricultural produce and woven products. Hundreds of women traders commute daily by public transport from a distance to attend to commercial transactions in the capital; the bazaars thus provide a vibrant socio-economic world for a large number of women living inside and outside the capital.

The main Hindu shrine in Imphal is the royal temple of Sri Govindaji adjacent to the royal palace.[9] It has been the centre of Hindu religious activity over the past two hundred years.

[8]Khwarimbond bazaar was established by King Khagemba in the sixteenth century.

[9]The present temple was built by Maharaja Churachand after the British occupied the former palace and the temple site and converted the area into army cantonment. However, during the past two hundred years, because of political pressure, the site of the royal temple moved from place to place along with the change of the palace site.

FIELDSITES

During the first two months of my stay in Imphal, I visited several possible sites for intensive field research. I wanted to be close to a market centre in a rural environment, to be able to observe the socio-economic structure in a traditional set-up. I did not want to be too far from Imphal, so that I could observe the socio-economic and religious networks of women in urban centres extending towards the interior of the Valley. Finally, I found Nambol, which provided me with an encouraging setting for my work. The next eight months of my study I concentrated mainly on Nambol, though I kept close contact with the markets and religious centres of the capital.

Nambol, a rural market centre, is situated on the banks of the River Nambol, about 14 kms. southwest of Imphal on a National Highway, the Tidim road. According to a Census of 1976, there are 6,880 people (male: 3,435; female: 3,445) in the eight-village administrative district of Nambol township. Out of the eight villages, there is a Kabui Naga village on a hillock with only sixty-five people.[10] The other seven villages are populated exclusively by the Meitei, with a few Brahmans, excepting Nambol *Makha* (south) and Nambol *Awang* (north).

Nambol Makha and Nambol Awang are two villages on the two sides of the Tidim road with a small population of North Indians residing in only two rows of houses.

My host village, Nambol Awang, is the centre for the educational, religious, economic, and political activities of the villages under Nambol administration and of several other villages in the surrounding area as well. As people living in the surrounding villages often identify themselves with Nambol, it was hard to define a social boundary for the Nambol area.

Nambol was of great interest to me for various reasons. First, the bazaar is the nucleus of a large economic network of the local women traders and traders from different areas of the Valley. During World War II, the largest women's market, Khwarimbond bazaar at Imphal, was closed, and Nambol bazaar sprang up as an important centre of trade. Second, an important temple of the ancient Meitei religion is situated on the Khoriphoba hillock at Nambol Awang about one-third of a mile from Nambol bazaar. Third, Nambol has been experiencing increased modernization since the end of World War II with

[10]Night census report I gathered from the administrative office of Nambol in March, 1978.

the introduction of public transport, schools and colleges, movie houses and roadside hotels. Thus it illustrates the changing pattern of a society accommodating the advent of modern facilities. Fourth, the surrounding rural area has a symbiotic relationship with Nambol and this gave me an opportunity to observe the village socio-economic structure in a traditional framework.

My host at Nambol Awang suggested village 1 which I name Radhagram, an adjacent village (about two kms. from Nambol bazaar) with a population of 1,797 (1971 census) as an interesting model of women's economic role. As any work got under way, I gradually realized that my sample village 1 had a relatively advanced economy (an attribute gained during the past fifteen years) which was not typical of the villages of the surrounding areas. I chose another smaller village adjacent to Radhagram (population : 364). My field assistant came from the second village—a fact that helped me a great deal towards establishing rapport within a short time. The other village which I name Thambalkhul, is two kms. past Radhagram, adjacent to Tidim road.

Nambol became a centre of Hindu Vaisnavite activities during the latter half of the last century. The othre villages followed Nambol's example. Today, within Radhagram there are seven Brahman households flanking a temple and *mandapa* (a community hall adjacent to the temple and devoted to socio-religious activities). In Thambalkhul a Brahman (now eighty years old) came to reside only thirty-six years ago. He was given land and a contribution from the community. He officiates at the Vaisnavite rituals in Thambalkhul and also for an adjacent village which still lacks a Brahman. While both villages have their own religious ceremonies, the villagers still look up to Nambol for important ritual ceremonies and festivals.

In Nambol I came across highly literate old men in their seventies and eighties, which was unusual in the surrounding villages. At present in Nambol township alone there are fourteen lower primary schools (for boys and girls), two girls' high schools, two boys' schools, one college, and two small Hindi schools.

The advent of modern education has ushered in a rapid rise of literacy among both sexes during the past thirty years. A number of students commute to Imphal daily to attend the colleges and the Jawaharlal Nehru University. However, I found that in the villages, girls, on reaching their mid-teens, suddenly cease to pursue their education, a point to be discussed later.

HOUSES

A striking aspect of the rural settlements is the well-maintained appearance of the homes and the cleanliness of the inhabitants. The floors of the traditional homes are plastered with clay-water daily, to give a hard, cemented look. Dark clay from the bottom of the pond is used with a touch of indigo to paint the walls. Three different types of grass are used for the roof thatch, varying in cost. The cost of a home swings from Rs. 10,000 for an all-wooden structure to Rs 5,000 for a bamboo structure. The ceilings of most homes are decorated with exquisite lattice work of woven bamboo and wood-work. The main entrance door, usually very impressive and large, is made of *uningthou* (king of the trees) timber, or teak. The windows are made entirely of wood. The compound is bound by bamboo groves, flowery plants and silver oaks. Most houses have a small pond (*pukhri*) adjacent to the yard for their supply of water.

Household furnishing is rather simple. In the front parlour (*mangol*), several mats are provided for visitors. Two beds, one cabinet with a glass door and an almirah, invariably found in most homes, are the best examples of high class carpentry and inlay work of the local craftsmen. These articles of furniture are usually given as dowry.

The most common utensils for eating (plates, bowls, tumblers and jugs) are made of bell metal crafted by Meitei smiths. Cooking pots are of brass or burnt clay. Firewood and paddy husk are the most common cooking fuels.

The Meitei take two large meals a day consisting of rice, pulses, vegetables, some fish (often dried), and mixed vegetable salads. Lily roots, fruits and nuts are eaten as snacks. Small roadside stalls serving hot snacks and tea are run by women and serve as social meeting places.

PEOPLE AND SOCIETY

The Meitei are known to have originated from the Sino-Tibetan language family of peoples (Roy, 1974; B.H. Hodgson, 1853 in Hodson, 1908, reprinted 1975:10). Successive invasions from Chinese, Shan, Burmese, and neighbouring states as well as from India have left permanent marks on the population. Indian immigrants, especially the Brahmans, forged their way in to Manipur and have been coming since the 15th century. Manipuri legends also indicate inter-marriage between the plains Meitei and the Nagas of the surrounding hills.

Historians (Roy, 1974 and others) believe that the settlement of the Valley is about two thousand years old, although there is no accurate chronology until the eighth century A.D.

There are five groups of people living in the Manipur plains : (*i*) the Brahmans, (*ii*) the Meitei, (*iii*) the Pangan (Meitei Muslim), (*iv*) the Kabui Naga and (*v*) the Mayang (the North Indian or foreigner).

The Brahmans

The Brahmans started to come to Manipur in the fifteenth century, serving as agents of Hinduization. From the eighteenth century onward, starting in the period of the King Garib Niwaz (1709-1748), who first adopted the Hindu Vaisnavite faith as a state religion, a large number of Brahmans have emigrated to Manipur from different parts of North India. Although the majority of the Brahmans came from Bengal and Assam, many others in the past two hundred years also found their way to the Valley from faraway places like Kashmir, Gujarat, Banaras, Punjab, Mathura, Orissa, Prayag, Kanpur, etc. (L.I. Singh, 1963). They had special prerogatives. There were thirty-two divisions among them, each with specific duties assigned by the King.

The Meitei

The Meitei can be subdivided into three groups: the Meitei Kshatriya, the Meitei RK (Raj Kumar and Raj Kumari), and the Meitei Loi.

The Meitei Kshatriya and the RKs both belong to the autochthonous people of the Valley, who donned the sacred thread of the Hindu caste from the Brahmans and claimed the Kshatriya caste status. Both the Meitei Kshatriya and the RK belong to seven exogamous clan groups.

The RKs, the descendants of the male members of the royal family known as Raj Kumars (princes) and Raj Kumaris (princesses), are not actually the children of the king. The Meitei kings in the past married many wives and the Meitei of royal blood swelled in number. King Bhagyachandra (1764-1798) had ninety-two wives.[11]

---

[11]The status of the Brahman was held so high during the period of King Bhagyachandra that when a Brahman criminal was executed by mistake, the King looked upon the incident as his own sin. He abdicated his throne and left on pilgrimage as a penance.

It is known that until the time of King Charoirengba (1697-1709) the number of RKs was very small. When the later kings began to indulge in uninhibited polygamy possibly under the influence of Hinduism, their descendants formed a distinct community with a privileged status. Men and women born in such families still precede their names with "RK". Till the dislocation of society with the onset of British rule, the RKs enjoyed special privileges in the exclusive use of certain types of dress and in the holding of political power through occupying royal offices.

The immediate children of the Maharaja are addressed as Maharajkumar and Maharajkumari, in short, MK, and they indeed enjoy the highest status among the royal descendants. Like the Brahman, the RK does not touch the plough.

The Loi have a fallen or outcaste status, but they originally belonged to the Meitei community. In the past, criminals stigmatised by the commission of grave offences were exiled to different Loi communities. Many communities, still existent, live deprived of the social status of having *lugun* (sacred thread of Hindu high caste) and are denied a place in the Hindu religious system.[12]

Many of the Lois became skilled tanners, agriculturists and wine distillers, since these occupations were discarded by the neo-Vaisnavites. Gradually some members of the communities became rich enough to donate large sums of money to reinstate themselves among local Brahmans. A former Loi village in Nambol area has adopted a Hinduized name for the village and now receives help from a Brahman from the adjacent village, Thambalkhul to organize Hinduized ceremonies.

The residents of this community distill wine and some persist with their old habits of rearing pigs, a lifestyle condemned by the Hinduized people of other villages.

The Pangan

The Pangan are Meitei Muslims who were brought to Manipur

---

[12]I visited Kwatha, an isolated Loi village in a hilly jungle about three kms. in the interior from the Indo-Burma Road, thirteen kms. from Moreh, a town at the India-Burma border. There are about 150 very poor residents struggling hard on unfertile hilly land without any other resource for their livelihood. They have to walk down to Moreh to buy salt. The older people wore Vaisnavite *chandan* mark and tulsibead (beads made from basil wood, another Vaisnavite mark). They rear pigs and use old-fashioned looms. A Christian church is being built inside the village by the missionaries and the young children have all been baptized.

as captives in 1606 from Cachar district of Assam during the time of King Khagemba.[13] They eventually married Meitei women, adopted fourteen family names with Meitei endings, became naturalized, and conversant with the Meitei language, too.

The Kabui Naga

Of all the Naga, only the Kabui Naga communities live in the plain. In the past, the Kabui Naga accepted the King's offer of menial jobs and because of their servility to the Meitei kings, they were considered of low status by the rest of the proud hill Naga communities. The Meitei consider them as aliens in Meitei society.

Some of the Kabui Naga communities in the urban area have acquired wealth through wine distillation. Many have also attained higher education. Although belonging to the Christian church, the Kabui Naga retain a great deal of their traditional religious rituals and festivals in their affluent urban neighbourhoods. In rural areas, until recently, they were precluded from owning land. In Nambol, the Kabui Naga village on a hillock is the poorest of all the settlements and it is without any resource of paddy land on the plain.

A typical village in Nambol area is comprised almost entirely of Meiteis with only one or a very few Brahman households. During my fieldwork I did not meet any Loi or Naga engaged in social, economic or religious activities in the villages. Only at the Nambol bazaar did I find four Kabui Naga men and women working as porters and cleaners.

In Radhagram, out of 256 households, 244 belong to the Meitei, seven to the Brahman, and three to the RK. In Thambalkhul, out of sixty-six households, sixty-one belong to the Meitei, one to the Brahman, and four to the RK.

CASTE

In the pre-Vaisnavite period, the Meitei lived in a more or less egalitarian society except for the presence of the outcaste Loi. But over the past two hundred years, the Meitei, living in the shadow of Brahmanic caste values, have acquired a great deal of caste consciousness in their habits and lifestyle. Like other caste groups in India, the Meitei, too, look upon their own caste as "the unit of ritual and social equality" and maintain their caste identity (Berre-

---

[13]The term Pangan is derived from Bangan or Bangal (Bengal).

man, 74:199) as an endogamous and commensal unit and also as a unit without any ritual prohibition of contact. The Brahman, a minority group, enjoys the highest ritual status as the remaining Meitei Kshatriya have an egalitarian relationship. A Brahman can have a hypergamic relationship with the Meitei by marrying a Meitei woman, though a Brahman husband maintains his ritual distance from his wife by not accepting cooked food and water from her.

There is no stratified caste system in a Meitei village. The Loi and Naga live apart in their own villages without any ritual or social tie and often with no economic obligation to the Meitei or the Brahman. The Meitei and the Brahman do not accept cooked food or water from the Loi or the Naga and maintain a social and ritual distance from them, so as to avoid any other contact. Although sometimes a Meitei looks upon other Indian caste groups as of low status, intermarriage is tolerated. There are some cases where low caste North Indians have become assimilated among the Meitei by marrying Meitei women. Scholars have cited cases of outsiders' gradual absorption into the mainstream of the community. (Hodson, 1908, reprinted 1975; Roy, 1974).

The absence of occupational caste (except for the Brahman) has helped the Meitei to develop a community life based on co-operative labour. Jobs considered fit only for the untouchables in India, e.g., cleaning of latrines and sewers and removal of animal carcasses, are performed by Meitei men themselves with the help of their fellow villagers. At present there are some North Indian barbers and cobblers in Nambol bazaar, but in the villages in the interior, the people are self-sufficient. There is no system of caste exploitation as found in the high-caste-dominated communities in India. The Loi and the Naga are considered outsiders to the Meitei Kshatriya community and, in fact, live independent of any caste obligation to the Meitei.

Orthodox elderly Meitei zealously guard their ritual purity by strict adherence to the rules of vegetarianism (with the addition of only fish) and commensality. I was often asked my caste identity before guests would accept tea from my kitchen.

3
Political Organization

In the past almost every sphere of Meitei society was under the strict supervision and control of the state. A rigidly structured social system defined a pattern of labour division between the sexes. While a rural man was directly under a formal political structure, a rural woman stayed outside of it, playing only an informal peripheral role.

Meitei society was governed by a highly organized administrative system existing from very ancient times. *Choitharol Kumbaba*, the royal chronicle, gives a list of more than forty-eight rulers, who ruled from the first century A.D. to the eighth century. The Meitei text *Loiyumba Silen* written in A.D. 1074 laid great stress on law and on a code of conduct for the people. The book describes how the state was divided into different revenue divisions, *panas*, to acquire free labour, *lallup*, from the subjects, and also provides a lengthy discussion on the particular occupations and codes of conduct of different families (Moirangthem, 1971: 52).

The history of Manipur is a revealing role of the people's love for independence. Their skilled martial ability enabled them to safeguard their freedom against repeated incursions by neighbouring states. In 1725, Garib Niwaz indulged in a series of attacks of his own against Burma, and defeated an army of 30,000, but had to retreat to defend his kingdom from the attack of another neighbouring state, Tripura, on the southwestern border. Soon after his death the Burmese army entered Manipur and conquered the throne. "From 1758 to 1826, within a period of sixty-eight years, Manipur was overrun and dominated by the Burmese force times without number." (Roy, 1973:40). During the last seven years of this period (1819-1826), the state remained occupied by the Burmese. A massive number of cattle and horses were lost. The Burmese army carried away and destroyed 300,000 persons (Roy, 1973). In Manipur, this period is referred to as *Chahi Tarek Khuntatpa* (seven years of catastrophe). At last, in 1825, Gambhir Singh, one of the exiled princes,

sought the support of the British government, and offered his own
levy of five hundred soldiers to fight against the common enemy.
The Anglo-Burmese War helped Manipur establish peace with
Burma after the treaty of Yandabo in 1826. "Finally when they
[Burmese] left the country, the number of adult male population in
the Valley did not exceed 3,000" (Roy, 1973: 72).

COLONIAL   CONTACT

The Anglo-Burmese War, entering the realms of history, Gambhir
Singh was King. He entered into an elaborate political treaty with
the British for trade and military alliance. In 1827, the British government appointed their first Political Agent, equivalent to an ambas-
sador, in Manipur. Later, during the period Chandrakirti, the relationship between the two governments became based on mutual
trust, and the king even sent his troops to suppress Indian revolu-
tionaries during the so-called Sepoy mutiny (1857) of India. After
the death of Chandrakirti, there was bitter conflict among the heirs
and as a result, in 1891, British sovereignty extended its tentacles
over the once independent state.

The British chose a six-year old boy, Churachand, from another
line of descent of the royal family for the throne, and appointed a
Political Agent and a Superintendent as joint regent. The most emi-
nent leader, Prince Tikendrajit, the third son of King Chandrakirti,
and the Commander-in-Chief (*senapati*) and Thangal Major, the
next important military official, were hanged at the royal polo
ground of Kangla. A colonial writer, B. C. Allen, describes the
event:

> In Raja's days a criminal sentenced to death was occasionally
> reprieved if a sufficient number of women appeared to intercede
> for him, and hoping that possibly the old custom might still prevail,
> the women had assembled in their thousands. As far as the eye
> could see the plain was white with women. (B. C. Allen, *Assam
> Gazetteers*, Vol. IX, Part II, quoted in Roy, 1973:133.)

When the foreign authority ignored this traditional plea, ". . . cries
and wailing of thousands of hearts probably heaved even the heart
of the mother earth" (Roy, *ibid*: 133). Other prominent leaders were
also exiled. The boy-king was sent to Mayo College in Ajmer for an
English education, and crowned at seventeen, maintained his alle-

giance to the British under continued supervision of British officers, and enjoyed a lengthy rule. The royal palace of Kangla and the Hindu temple of the royal family were shifted to a new site to make room for the British army cantonment.[14] In 1947, during the reign of his son Bodhachandra, India achieved independence. Bodhachandra agreed to come to terms with independent India and merged his state with the political entity of India. In 1972, with the Government of India abolishing the royal privy purse the King of Manipur, Crown Prince Okendra, ceased to function as the titular head of state.

THE STATE AND THE RURAL SOCIETY

A knowledge of the political structure of nineteenth century Manipur is important to our understanding of the traditional norms of sex roles among the Meitei. The entire Valley was under the strict supervision and control of the central state authority since the time of Gambhir Singh (1826), who modified and restructured the traditional form of government to bring every able-bodied male under the direct control of the state.

The country was divided into six *panas* or revenue divisions. Raja or *Ningthou* was the head, his sons holding the most important offices. The highest judicial authority was the Chirup court. There were 107 subdivisions of the *panas* to ensure proper service from the rural folk. The King's officials were engaged as intermediaries between the village officials and the central authority. The state had numerous institutions known as Loishangs (councils), all attached to the royal palace; each one in charge of a specific area of administration, e.g., revenue collection, religious matters, recruitment of free labour, etc.

Out of the hundreds of such Loishangs, I shall discuss some which directly affected the lives of a rural man to show how he was related to the Government legally, economically, socially, and ritually (Figure 2).

Lallup System

This was primarily a system which demanded that every able-bodied male from sixteen to sixty offer service to the state for ten

[14]The ground of Kangla was not only a matter of royal honour, it is also considered the centre of high ritual power and religious significance as described in the ancient Meitei scriptures.

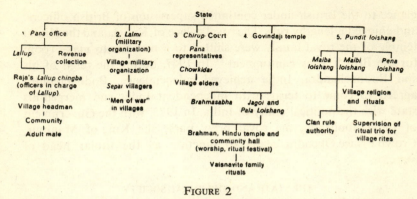

FIGURE 2

State and the Rural Man

days every thirty days. In return he received one *pari* (approximately three acres) of taxable land from the state in usufructuary right. The *panas*—revenue divisions—were organized to ensure the proper efficiency of Lallup. The headman of each village was responsible for the tax payable by each cultivator. The Brahmans, Meiteis, Muslims, were all equally liable for the performance of Lallup duty. The Lois and Nagas had the heavier and more menial duties assigned to them. Some officers of the Lallup belonged to the village while some belonged to the central body. *Lallup-chingba* ("Puller" of the Lallup) was an important official who worked between the state and villages.

The Lallup system was abolished in 1892 by the British administration. In place of Lallup, house tax and land rent were introduced. However, the house-tax was abolished in 1899-1900.

Lalmi

Lalmi consisted of men of war. This system adhered to the same rules as the Lallup. The central military organization was *Bijoy Garod*. This was controlled by a body of military personnel and a commander-in-chief (*senapati*). Villages were divided into *sepoy* (military) villages and civilian villages. Eight companies were settled in the military villages and were controlled by the village officers. But in case of an emergency—" . . .if five alarm guns were fired"—every able-bodied man had to present himself at the palace to receive orders from the King (Iboonghal Singh, 1963).

Chirup Court

The Chirup court was the chief court composed of twenty-five permanent members and about sixty to eighty ex-officio members. Both state and village officials held ex-officio status. One separate court was maintained only for women. This all-women court was known as *Paja*. The Paja comprised eleven members headed by the king's mother along with women members of the royal family.[15] This court dealt with matters like adultery, divorce, wife-beating, assault and other cases where women were involved. The Paja decided the form of punishment.

Other women were not included in any formal administrative body, but if people felt that any injustice was being done by the king or his officials, a group of women would go to the king to complain about it. Older women could also collectively approach the king if they felt any injustice in the exercise of male authority over women. (L. I. Singh, 1963:45). Women's strong collective protest against the death penalty of a criminal was often reason enough for the king to change the verdict (Roy, 1973:133). Under the traditional law, women and Brahmans were exempt from capital punishment.

In 1898, the British Government introduced a police force in the villages and one *chowkidar* (security officer) was appointed for about one hundred families. Old informants described the village administration of the earlier days as run by a chowkidar and his assistant, *nambor*. For further assistance, three villagers were selected among the elders, called *hanjaba*, *gopal hidang*, and *sanglakpa*, respectively. The *sanglakpa's* duty was to take care of the Lai Harouba festival.

Govindaji temple

Under the royal temple administration there were many Loishangs responsible for different duties. Three of these Loishangs were in direct contact with the rural population. These were: (*i*) *Brahma Sabha* (Council of Brahmans); (*ii*) *Jagoi Loishang* (Council of Dance); (*iii*) *Pala Loishang* (Council of Musicians). Of these, the Brahma Sabha has heretofore been the most significant. Headed by the king and a body of several learned Brahmans of high social rank, its duty was to take care of all Hindu religious matters. Today people often refer to the oppressive methods of Brahma Sabha, whereby a person

---

[15]Several legends are heard about the power of the Paja court in the past. King Choroirongha (1697-1709) was once even charged by it of adultery and was given token punishment by the stroke of a golden cane.

could be decreed an outcaste and sent to a Loi village, or an outcaste
could be admitted into the regular Meitei community by performing
shuddhi (purifying ceremony). The Brahma Sabha powers rose to
great heights during the reigns of Chandrakirti (1834-1844 and
1850-1886) and Churachand (1891-1941), and installed one or
more Brahmans in each village with a Hindu temple and *mandapa*
(community hall). The community was ordered to support these
financially. People were bound by several ritual obligations to these
Brahmans. Each family had to engage a Brahman for family rituals
and/or cooking for a feast, and were punished if they ignored the rule
of *chandan shenkhai*—wearing a Vaisnava mark on the forehead,
nose and throat, in public. The Brahma Sabha made various attempts
to control the customs of widow marriage and divorce. The custom
of *sati* was introduced in the royal family. However, when two
daughters-in-law of King Garib Niwaz became *sati*, he abolished the
custom. One male informant (85) said, "In our time we had to behave
according to the rules of Brahma Sabha. A Brahman was regarded
as a god. He gave orders according to Hindu scriptures. The
Brahmans were in charge of the *shuddhi* ceremony and could
offer the sacred thread to any one, and they were paid for this job by
the people. If a girl was kidnapped by a Naga, the Brahman could
perform the *shuddhi* ceremony for her acceptance back in her family.
But if the girl was kidnapped by a Muslim she had no chance to come
back. No Brahman would perform the ceremony for her. "Why
did they approve the case involving a Naga?" Because a Naga has
no caste or religion." Hodson (1908, reprinted 1975:95-96) remarks:

> . . . the long reign of Chandrakirti witnessed the consolidation of
> Hinduism which had lost much of its hold on the people during the
> sad times of the Burmese occupation. Gambhir Singh once ordered
> a Brahman who failed to take due and proper charge of a pet goose
> which was entrusted to his care, to eat the bird which had died of
> neglect, but in his son's time such an order was impossible.

Accordingly, the Brahma Sabha enforced the Hindu Vaisnavite
values of vegetarianism, the notions of purity, pollution, and caste
consciousness. Besides being a religious body, it worked as a powerful political authority exercising social control over the population.
    At present the power of the Brahma Sabha is defunct. Nonetheless,
the influence of Brahmans continues to linger. A *shuddhi* ceremony

was performed only a few years ago in Namgol. A local Brahman performed this ritual at a *mandapa* hall for a North Indian Teli of Bihar (oil-presser belonging to a low-caste group). The North Indian was the first non-Meitei to purchase a piece of land in the area. He adopted the sacred thread to achieve the status of a Kshatriya, receiving the clan name *Mayang langbam* (foreigner's family), and married a Meitei girl.

The Loishangs of Jagoi (dance) and Pala (music and songs) took care of ritual performances. Under the enthusiastic zeal of these Loishangs, Meitei ritual dance and music flourished into vibrant expression. Villages had their own groups for Jagoi and Pala and followed the rules and instructions of the central authority. They also joined the royal temple celebration with their own groups and organized year-round ritual activities involving dancing and singing at the *mandapa*. The performance adhered strictly to the repertoire and sequence as directed by the Loishangs.

Pundit Loishang

The Pundit Loishang was in charge of the organization of the traditional Lai-worship dating from ancient times. It was supervised by scholars well versed in ancient Meitei scriptures and ritual procedure. In spite of the overwhelming spread of Hinduism, Pundit Loishang remained a strong institution in Meitei society. The Loishang had three divisions: *Maiba Loishang, Maibi Loishang*, and *Pena Loishang*. It was a body of three ritual functionary groups responsible for the Lai religion and particularly for the annual Lai Harouba festival taking place in every village community. The three were in charge of the initiation of the female priestesses, and assigned them, along with *maibas* (the male scholars and priests) and *penakhongbas* (musicians playing a bowed instrument, *pena*) to different villages for officiating Lai Harouba. The Pundit Loishang was also responsible for the selection of *piba*, the head of the lineage in villages.

In 1972, the King withdrew all financial support from the Pundit Loishang, which then began to disintegrate. At present, the *maibas,* the *maibis*, and the *penakhonghas* are working hard to reorganize the Loishang and restore its importance. Many of them complain that they are losing the organizational integrity and it is going to be very hard to work without the protective umbrella of the Loishang. In 1978, the situation appeared to be improving. Some of the famous

pundits, *maibis*, and *penakhongbas* got together to work under the
headship of *Pundit Achouba* (chief pundit). In Nambol, all the villages
contracted the Loishang to engage ritual functionaries for their Lai
Harouba rituals.

RURAL ADMINISTRATION TODAY

The system of Panchayats was introduced to many villages in 1902
in place of the old administrative body. Its members were selected
from the village males. Until 1977, every village had a Panchayat
consisting of several members with one *pradhan* (head). The Panchayat
takes care of village administration e.g., handling of the budget,
government funding for village development (schools, roads, veteri-
nary care, etc.). A section of the Panchayat was the Naya Panchayat,
which dealt with the civil cases. If the cases could not be resolved
at the village level, they went to the Imphal court.

During my stay a major change in the Panchayat administration
came about. Several villages were grouped under one administrative
body. Both my sample villages were included in a five-village Panchayat. For the first time in the history of the area, a woman was
nominated to be a member of the body.

It was an interesting experience observing the election in my villages.
Radhagram had the largest number of voters and its candidate for
Pradhan (56) expected a cascade of votes in the election. The pre-
election meetings in his compound were always male affairs to the
complete exclusion of women, though the voters were of both sexes.
A few days before the election I found several groups of young *laishabis* (unmarried girls) conducting a door to door campaign for a very
young candidate (27) from an adjacent village. I gathered that the
college graduate had donated Rs. 250 to the girls two months before
for the *yaoshang* (spring festival) dance, and thus gained strong support from the potential female voters. I met a college educated girl(22)
from Thambalkhul, who said, "The old man gave feasts for about
thirty men at a time, but he never invited any women. He always
speaks to my father of the vote, but ignores us. He should know that
our votes will be counted too." Eventually the young candidate won
the election, although he had little support from his own village.
Some villagers commented, "He won because of the support of the
laishabis." There is also a shift towards younger educated candidates
in the elections of the surrounding villages of the area, but the candi-
dacy of a woman pradhan is very rare.

The preceding pages described how a rural society in Manipur was administered in the past and the changes more recent times have witnessed. It also illustrated the importance of the role of rural man in the hierarchical structure of political organization. Besides the institutions of Lallup and Lalmi there were other ways in which the king controlled the male population; he encouraged and patronized men of courage and of athletic ability to join various state fairs, and patronized athletic competitions which demanded high standards of martial skill, e.g., horse-polo, horse-racing, *thang-ta* (a war game of sword and spear), boatrace, *mukna* (wrestling). Every village had a Keirup—a tiger-hunting association. The king or a high official was invited to shoot the trapped tiger. Villagers were also encouraged to master the use of *langsoi*, an instrument for threatening and pacifying wild elephants and to bind their legs. Men showing merit in any of the skills were rewarded with high posts in administration and were married to daughters of the royal family.

Besides the repeated invasions from Burma, the Valley was also in continuous confrontation with the Naga tribes of the surrounding hills and other neighbouring states to the west and southwest. Thus every male was encouraged to be physically fit to respond to a possible royal order for an expedition or defensive action.

In the past, horse-polo contests were organized by the king and other high-ranking officers.[16] The British administrators took a great interest in the game and patronized it. However, the game is now rarely played.

The advent of colonial power rendered redundant the "men of war"—Lalmi. The absence of Lallup freed the village man from the strict control of the state. The gradual reduction of state patronage has also diminished the glamour and prestige of traditional athletic skills. *Thang-ta* and *mukna* can be seen on rare occasions. People express a passionate love for national soccer and hockey matches. Hindi movies demonstrating violent courage of heroes as boxers and wrestlers attract a large audience. The American movie *Kung Fu* became extremely popular. During my stay, Dara Singh's (a famous wrestler) visit attracted thousands of spectators. But most of the vigorous games of the past are no longer in vogue. The pressure of colonization has left a mark on the courageous

[16]Horse-polo is known to have originated among the Meitei. The British officers learned this game from the Meitei and later introduced it among other British army officers stationed in India.

Meitei male. Meitei historian Dr. Chandramani commented, "The
Meitei men in the past were men of courage and men of pride. Since
the British came to Manipur they have lost it. They wanted to work
as servants. They have lost their 'national character.' But our
women retained their character. They remained independent and
confident. Time has not changed this."[17]

WOMEN IN POLITICS

This potent comment lends us insight into the role of women in
the political sphere of society. The judicial system of the past
indicated the important role women played in the informal political
realm and to some extent in the formal structure of the women's
court. Scholars of Meitei society document the importance of the
collective opinion of market women in the affairs of the state. (Hodson, 1908, reprinted 1975; L.I. Singh, 1968; N. Tombi Singh, 1976;
S.Yambem, 1976). For example, in the beginning of this century the
king had to abandon his plan to introduce copper coins when the
women traders refused to accept them. In fact, the large market centres of Manipur run by women have a history of providing moral
consensus on the political problems of the state. The Meitei historian
S. Yambem puts it, "Apart from the economic activities the market
is also an important venue of social and political interaction. It was
this aspect of Khwarimbond bazaar which played a crucial role in
the outbreak of the *nupi-lan*."

Nupi-lan, women's war, is an important feature of Meitei society.
There have been a series of organized protests by women against the
colonial administrative policies at different times during this century,
all of which were led by market women. The first *nupi-lan* during
colonial rule occurred in 1904, when the residence of the British Political Agent was burnt down by some anti-government people. In
retaliation, Major Maxwell, the Political Agent, ordered a corvee of
free labour from the people to rebuild the house. Women gathered
by the thousands and agitated against the Government decision.
The unrest went so far that the crowd had to be dispersed by force,
and the government withdrew its order. In 1925, there was another
widespread agitation by women against the government imposition
of a water tax.

In 1939, tradeswomen again organized a massive demonstration

---

[17]Personal communication, November 9, 1977.

against the official policy of exporting rice. Thousands of women from all over the Valley gathered in the capital to protest Government approval of unlimited export of rice outside Manipur by Marwari merchants. At that time Manipur was on the verge of a famine. Women boycotted Khwarimbond bazaar, the main market at Imphal. After failing in their repeated pleas to the Administration, the women demonstrators confronted the Durbar in session. S.Yambem (1976: 325-26) gives an account of the event:

Women demonstrators who had gathered around the office began shouting slogans. "Stop the export of rice immediately." "Stop the export of rice mills," etc. The members of the Durbar fled through the back-door. But Sharpe, the President of the Durbar, was immediately surrounded by the women and had to face them alone... They went along with him to the telegraph office and confined him, the Civil Surgeon and other officers there. They refused to allow the President of the Durbar and other officers to leave the telegraph office until the receipt of necessary orders from the Maharaja. They also prevented the Commandant of the 4th Assam Rifles...women shouted "*Vande Mataram*" and "*Manipur Mata ki Jai*"... became more militant and aggressive. The situation became so dangerous that the sentry on the steps of the office sounded his bugle and troops charged in to clear the ground.

In spite of the attempts of the army to disperse the crowds of women, the officers were confined there until midnight. Twenty-one women were wounded seriously and many had minor injuries. Four of the leaders were later convicted of disturbance of peace. "The women possessed a high degree of consciousness... some women even lay down in front of the lorries loaded with rice and ready to move out." (*Ibid*: 329.) An order banning the export of rice was promptly issued. Women then demanded that all rice mills run by the Marwaris be closed down and their electricity cut off. About 10,000 women marched at night to stop the largest mill in Manipur. Once the women succeeded in controlling the economic catastrophe, several male leaders appeared on the scene and continued to pursue their other grievances against the Government. Their demands were now geared towards the change in the Durbar and other administrative policies. Women boycotted the market for more than one and a half years and convinced the State that their support stood behind the male leaders.

The movement for constitutional reform started in 1938. *Nupi-lan* accelerated this and eventually helped to widen the reform movement.

Apart from important events like these *nupi-lans*, there have been several other collective movements during the past few decades. Several elderly women at Khwarimbond bazaar talked about other twenty-four hour sit-down strikes in the sixties against the Government policy of increasing the rent on market plots. In 1975, women in several urban localities organized protests against liquor sale, drinking being a major social vice which had affected the lives of a large number of Meitei males. Mature women organized themselves into groups of "night patrollers" and guarded their neighbourhoods against any man consuming liquor and risking addiction to excessive drinking. Soon the political leaders were involved. During my stay I observed an eight-week-long sit-in strike at Laxmi bazaar of five hundred traders in Imphal. This was an expression of opposition plans to build an "urban bank" within the market. Women shouted slogans and displayed posters saying "Laxmi bazaar belongs to the Meitei women," and "Get out from Laxmi bazaar, do not disturb the Meitei women." Women expressed their objection thus: "The urban bank will have a lot of men working there. Many of them will be *mayangs*. The atmosphere of the bazaar will be changed. We will have no freedom." Excited and angry women held daily meetings and discussed their plans. About fifty women took turns at an all-night vigil and did not allow the construction workers to continue their work. Women yelled at them continuously until they left the spot. The women took their petitions to the Government ministers and eventually succeeded in stopping the construction of the building.

During my stay another incident occurred in a village two miles from my study area. Here a large group of women stood against a village youth club. The club house had a bad reputation for gambling and drinking and attracted many young men of the locality. The women of the village market urged the owner of the building to close down the club house. He refused. One evening a large number of mature women went over to the club and demolished the thatch-roofed building. When the police arrived at the scene, the women said that they did it out of desperation to save their own sons and grandsons. The villagers supported the women and there were no arrests.

The *nupi-lan* of 1939 protected some important leaders from among the women. The choice of leadership is made spontaneously.

The traders at Laxmi bazaar said, "Normally a woman with courage and good speaking power would come forward and lead the others." This was confirmed by the older women of Khwarimbond bazaar who got involved in a prolonged strike in the sixties. Apparently, a collective spirit rather than a single individual is the main force behind the women's upheavals.

Many educated Meitei men recall the event of *nupi-lan* as an expression of revolt against colonial oppression and the corruption of the monarchy. December 13 has been declared *Nupi Shingi Numit* (women's day). Several plays on *nupi-lan* have become popular on the Meitei stage. The leftist wing of the political party looks upon *nupi-lan* as "an expression of Meitei culture, a moral support to arouse Meitei consciousness as opposed to a Hindu identity" (*Resistance*, 1973: 5-10). A few years ago one of the important leaders of *nupi-lan* made a wish on her death-bed that her body be covered with a red cloth before cremation to express her allegiance to Marxism.

4
Economic Context

In a Meitei proverb it is said,"A man who does not go to Loishang, and a woman who does not go to the market, both are worthless" (O.Bhogendra Singh, 1976:524). In another, "The fruit of knowledge is from fathers and grandfathers: the reserved wealth is from mothers and grandmothers " (*Ibid*: 486). Both these proverbs underline a basic concept of division of labour between the sexes.

The subsistence base in Manipur Valley is agriculture. Next to agriculture, weaving is the most important economic activity. Whereas agricultural activities are open to both sexes, weaving is entirely in the hands of women. Women are also in full charge of the marketing of both agricultural and industrial products, which provide cash income for the family.

AGRICULTURE

Land has great importance in the life of the villager. In Radhagram and Thambalkhul there is no family without a piece of land for a home and a kitchen garden. But people recognize the term *lau* (land) only in relation to the paddy field. In the past the system of Lallup made tenure of land a basically male prerogative, and at present, too, land is strongly associated with male inheritance and right,[18] unless the land is purchased by a woman with her own income or is given to her as a gift.

Agriculture is a family enterprise in Meitei villages. Sons may share the harvest with their parents, though they may not share the same hearth. All members of the family contribute their labour; even children below the age of ten help in guarding the vegetable gardens from animals and birds. Rice cultivation relies heavily on

---

[18]The Indian system of Dayabhaga is followed which recommends a division of property among the sons and mothers. However, among the Meitei, unmarried, divorced, and widowed daughters and sisters have a right of residence in their natal home.

women's labour; in my study area almost all women below fifty years of age (unless they are owners of permanent shops) engage in some work in the rice fields. Some older women work in the field in the morning hours and come to the bazaar in the late afternoon. While women's labour is mostly performed in teams, called *khulong*, men work individually. During the harvest both males and females work together. Married women living in the same compound take their turn at domestic chores, work in groups on their family field, and put in extra hours for wage labour. Unmarried women usually devote more time to weaving, though they also work in their family field and sometimes also for some wage labour. In both villages, women engage in more wage labour than men because more boys than girls are in school,[19] and also because there is less work for men than women in the field.

Both men and women work as hired labour, women usually outnumbering men. When a member of the family earns cash by working extra hours in wage labour (outside the family field), the income is considered personal. Men earn Rs. 5 a day on an average, while women earn Rs. 3 a day. Men's labour is referred to as "hard job" (ploughing, threshing), and women's labour is called "soft job" (transplanting, weeding, winnowing), though both men and women engage in carrying heavy loads of paddy. There is a taboo against women using the plough.[20] The women's team, *khulong*, is institutionalized in Meitei tradition. Women of various age groups join *khulong* for their own field or as hired labour.[21]

Agricultural Cycle

There is only one crop a year and its season is from the middle of May to early December.

[19]In both villages, women's capacity for cash income has a negative influence on women's education. Young girls after the age of thirteen or fourteen often give up school to engage in full time weaving. Some mothers told me, "They can earn a lot more money by weaving than by working with a high school diploma."

[20]One young girl (24) of Thambalkhul said to me, "When my mother (divorced with a daughter) did not find a man to plough the land, I took up the plough and did the work. People warned me that our crops would fail. When that did not happen and we had a normal harvest, people still felt that it was not a good idea."

[21]Women work and sing songs together from a repertoire of *Khulong Ishei* (songs for *khulong*). The landlord pays for a songleader to assist them. Women often demand money from the white clad well dressed men who walk by the field. If they refuse, the women retaliate with mudballs.

The work schedule of the sexes is given below:

Phase I: May-June and early July: In a year of good monsoons, ploughing starts in early May. Farmers like to plough early to have some sun on the earth. If a family has two acres of paddyfield, two bullocks and one plough, one able-bodied man must plough from 5.00 a.m. till noon for four to five days to prepare the land. After successive ploughing, men level and furrow the land. Sowing the seeds in nurseries is done by men some time in February or March. The seedlings are sprinkled with water and are often guarded by children. After three or four leaves have unfurled, transplanting begins. Now the women's *khulong* works from 5.00 a.m. till noon, and after attending to their domestic chores, they go back to the field again to work from 3.00 p.m. to 7.00 p.m. Many older women work in the morning and go to the bazaar in the afternoon.

Phase II: August-September-October : Weeding is done by both men and women. Usually men work from 5.00 a.m. to 10.00 a.m. and women prepare meals, finish domestic chores, and leave home in the early afternoon. There is no specific pattern for working hours, which accommodate to necessity.

Phase III: November-December: The early variety of rice, *kumbifou*, is harvested now. Harvesting continues from 9.00 a.m. to dusk. This rice is used for the Hindu festival, Govardhan puja. During November-December, the prune time, *fouren* is harvested by most farmers. Threshing is done by men on huge mats spread on the field. Women collect paddy into bundles. Men beat the paddy (*foubi haya*) with sticks (*chairong*). Women do the final threshing (*chairong*) and winnowing (*humai*). At work time women distribute refreshments to all workers. Both men and women collect paddy in baskets and bags. Bullock carts or trucks carry the paddy home which is then stored in the family granary, *kei*.

Phase IV: Once the paddy is stored, male responsibility ceases. Women pound and husk paddy with *chakri* (grinding tool) and *sumbal* (pounding tool) for home consumption. The husk is saved for fuel. Surplus paddy is sold wholesale to female agents or retailed in the daily market. It is usual to have an older woman in charge of the sale.

In market gardening there are different responsibilities for the sexes. Ploughing is done by men. Young women join men in the preparation of the soil by crumbling earth-clods finely. Planting is usually done by older men and women. Watering is the responsibility of younger girls and boys while weeding is done by the old of both sexes. Here again marketing of the produce is the responsibility of older women.

In Thambalkhul, most of the families have a plot for market gardening. In season, every day eight or nine mini-buses carry loads of vegetables to the capital, Imphal, sixteen kms. to the northeast, and to Churachandpur, another town about twenty kms. to the southwest. Every afternoon streams of women from this and surrounding villages walk about two to three miles to Nambol bazaar with basketloads of vegetables. Paddy, rice and vegetables are the only cash crops in my area. The income from cash crops is usually considered the family fund and although it is handled by an older woman, younger women are also deemed quite competent to handle money transactions, and there are no rigid rules about the prerogative of one sex over the other in such matters.

WEAVING INDUSTRY

Weaving is a very conspicuous economic activity in Nambol area. This is a year-round pursuit for almost all younger women. In the agricultural season women often complain of "double work," i.e., cultivation added to their regular economic and domestic activities.

I found Radhagram the most involved in weaving among all the villages of the area. Here, women have progressed a great deal with the introduction of the fly-shuttle. However, Thambalkhul is more typical. There, women use both modern and old methods and have been unable to replace the old tools with more sophisticated types.

In Radhagram every household has one or more fly-shuttles in the

FIGURE 3

Shangoi : A Multipurpose Shed for a Meitei Home

shangoi,[22] and in case of too many fly-shuttles the *mangol*[23] area is used. Next to the fly-shuttle one can find the older types of weaving shuttle (*iyong*), spinning wheel (*taren-masa*), and bobbins (*langchak*), all used by women of the family. Some families have large wheels used for arranging thread on a roller for the looms.

The progress in weaving in Radhagram is rather recent. Informants in Nambol Awang often referred to Radhagram as a backward village in the past, with women in petty trading without any plots in the bazaar. The flourishing weaving industry has often contributed to the immense improvement of the village economy.

Credit for the success of Radhagram goes to a woman, known as Wankhai Ningol (daughter of Wankhai) of Wankhai *leikai* in Imphal, famous for its fine skill in weaving. About fifteen years ago this Wankhai woman was married to a man of this village. She brought her fly-shuttle with her as dowry. When she wove fine *inafis* (large shawls used by Meitei women) with a famous *moirangfi* design (a traditional temple motif), the women of the village were attracted by her skill, hers being a more sophisticated technique than theirs. The women learned the use of new tools from her. More and more women bought fly-shuttles and started to weave much finer clothes. The Wankhai woman died a few years ago, but she is remembered as a *lairembi* (goddess) by the women of her husband's village. Gradually the villagers recognized the monetary advantage of the new tool and every household bought at least one fly-shuttle. (A fly-shuttle costs Rs. 450.) Two women work on one machine. Often a girl receives her loom along with her dowry. When a girl from another village is married into this village, her first challenge is to learn how to handle a fly-shuttle. In Thambalkhul, as well as in other surrounding villages, women weave regularly but cannot produce in abundance for lack of more sophisticated tools.

OTHER ECONOMIC ACTIVITIES

In addition to agriculture and weaving, men and women in my sample villages have several other occupations as shown in Table 1. All occupations are caste-neutral except for that of a Brahman priest. Carpentry, masonry, mat-weaving, and smithing are considered to be solely male occupations and they are usually handed down

---

[22]*Shangoi* is a detached shed, with three sides closed, found in every Meitei compound. This is used as a multi-purpose room for domestic, economic, and recreational activities of both sexes.

[23]*Mangol* is the front porch of a Meitei house, used as a parlour.

patrilineally. In Nambol area, during the rainy season, fishing is done by large teams of women called *Eapal Lokpa* in the flooded rice fields. In other months women engage in fishing with large square nets in the village ponds and canals.[24]

TABLE 1 NON-AGRICULTURAL OCCUPATIONS OF THE SEXES

Occupation	Male	Female
1. Carpentry	Yes	Sometimes helps in finishing the product and selling it
2. House-building	Yes	Helps in painting and plastering
3. Smithing[25]	Yes	Helps in finishing and selling
4. Mat and basket making	Yes	Helps in selling
5. Fishing	No[26]	Yes; also weaves and sells the fishing net
6. Weaving	No	Yes; also sells
7. Embroidery	No	Yes; also sells
8. Rice pounding	No	Yes; also sells
9. Scripture reading	Yes; male only	No
10. Brahman priest	Yes; male only	No
11. Dance and music teacher	Yes	Yes
12. Bookkeeping	Yes; male only	No
13. *Maiba* (medicine man)	Yes; male only	No
14. *Maibi* (midwife)	No	Yes; female only
15. *Maibi* (ritual diviner)	No[27]	Yes; female only
16. Hotel-keeping (snacks and tea)	No	Yes; female only

Note: There are eight male and five female school teachers and twenty-four male and seven female office workers in Thambalkhul. In addition to their part-time occupations, both sexes engage in part-time agriculture and, in addition, females engage in part-time weaving.

[24] Ch. Buddhi Singh's (1972:42) study of the fishing communities of Thanga in Lake Loktak area (approximately fourteen kms. from my area) shows a strict division of labour between the sexes. Thanga men use more sophisticated tools than women, and have much greater fishing rights. Women are also ritually prohibited to enter some of the important fishing areas. The method of fishing restricted to them, called *eel chingba*, provides supplementary income to the families.

[25] There is no iron or gold smith in Thambalkhul. People depend on the artisans of Radhagram or Nambol.

[26] Although in fishing villages both sexes engage in fishing, in my sample villages, only women engage in small-scale fishing.

[27] The role of a *maibi* (diviner and priestess) is sometimes taken by a transvestite male. However, in my sample villages, all the *maibis* are females.

Men engage in cultivation for six months of the year and in the dry season many of them are not economically active. However, in addition to agricultural work, women engage in year-round economic activities, e.g., weaving, trading, and rice pounding. Radhagram is rather unusual in this respect; here men are adept at the fine skill of mat-weaving which provides year-round jobs even for old and disabled men, but such a balance of male-female occupation is rare in other villages. In Thambalkhul, during the non-agricultural season, older men and some of the younger ones engage in market gardening. Some also go outside the area, even up to Assam, to seek jobs.

Men and women with specialized occupations such as *maiba* (medicine man and diviner), *maibi* (ritual priestess), *maibi* (midwife), carpenter, and housebuilder have clientele from outside areas. Villagers also seek help from non-resident specialists in outside areas. A small number of men and women travel to Imphal for work.

Families as Economic Teams

In the two villages, I found a pattern of seven main categories of households which gave me an insight into the interdependence of the sexes and, particularly, the autonomous role of women in the economic sphere.

The seven basic types of families as economic teams are:

1. Widow with young children living on her own.
2. Divorced woman with older children. Older sons step into father's authority. Father is obliged to leave the family compound.
3. Husband/wife/children as a family team.
4. Divorced woman living in her parents' compound and maintaining herself and children on her own.
5. Widowed or divorced woman living with a widowed or divorced daughter as a mother-daughter team.
6. Polygynous family: man living with two or more wives in different sleeping quarters with common or separate kitchens in the same compound.
7. Second wife (living as a "single woman") and children as the earning team; husband, an occasional visitor, sometimes contributes partial expenses.

ECONOMIC ACTIVITIES OF WOMEN OF DIFFERENT AGE GROUPS

Meitei women employ different terms for different stages of the life cycle. Each of these also signifies a different economic aspect of life. These are:

1. *Macha nupi* (little woman): prepubescent or early adolescent girl.
2. *Laishabi* (who moves like flowers): unmarried maiden.
3. *Mou* (non-virgin or wife): married female.
4. *Hanubi* (matronly or old woman): older female.

Macha nupis learn weaving from the age of nine or ten from their elders, and soon after they begin weaving simple *khudei* (men's loin-cloth) and towels. By the age of twelve or thirteen they are capable of weaving *khudei matek* (shawls with temple designs for women's everyday use). In both villages, girls of this age group go to primary schools and weave after school hours. They earn about Rs. 35 to 40 a month each on an average. Two girls work on one loom under the supervision of an elderly relative. On many occasions I came across girls who refrained from going to school to work on their looms because their mothers or grandmothers were expecting agents very soon and orders had to be supplied on time. The money earned by these girls is kept by the mothers or grandmothers as savings to be used for their clothing, books and future dowry.

Laishabis are the most active weavers. There is a sudden drop in school attendance after a girl reaches the age of fifteen or sixteen. Those who are still students work hard at weaving and domestic chores after their school hours. The motivation of earning runs high among them. A full-time weaver earns from Rs. 175 to 300 a month according to the quality of the product. Some weavers possessing extraordinary skill of *engineer-fi*[28] with *munga* yarn (natural gold-coloured silk) earn about Rs. 500 to 600 a month. Their number is, however, very small. The *laishabi's* earning is also meant for her own personal use; a portion is saved for her dowry.

Several people maintain that they do not use the earnings of their daughters unless it really becomes a necessity. I have found some households where older unmarried girls (late twenties to early thirties) provide for their sibling's education from their own earnings. It is not unusual to find widowed or divorced mothers with daughters helping each other financially. However, it is considered unethical to deprive a girl of her earnings, as these should eventually be accumulated in her dowry.

[28]*Engineer-fi* means the expensive *inafi* that can be afforded only by the rich engineers.

Young *laishobis* are bashful in the presence of strangers, but they can turn into shrewd businesswomen during monetary transactions. They are very alert about cost of production and profits from their merchandise. Once I wanted to order a saree (six yards of material with a forty-five inch width) from two girls. The girls (15 and 17) wove *inafi* forty-five inches wide, but much shorter than a saree. They quickly calculated the cost and said that they could do the weaving if I ordered two sarees of the same design. One girl explained, "Each saree will consume thread for two and a half *inafis*. Our load of thread on a loom is meant for ten *inafis*. But if we weave one saree we will be left with thread of one-half *inafi* after we finish up the entire load. That thread will be wasted." Later I realized that they wove sarees for me only out of politeness. It is easier for them to sell an entire load of ten *inafis* to a wholesale agent. They are reluctant to go into retail sale. They prefer to work hard with larger loads and dispose of them all at once.

When *laishabis* get married, they take up the greater burdens of *mous* which become more onerous once they start having children. However, child care is seldom done by the mother. There are usually several households in a Meitei compound. One often comes across old women suckling babies at their dry breasts and younger girls playing with babies tied on their backs. Cooking is the main duty performed by a *mou*, and rice pounding is her responsibility,[29] although usually other members of the family help with this. Some earn extra money by pounding rice for others. *Mous* have much less time to weave and they are thus slower in supplying their orders. Wholesale traders prefer working with *laishabis* to *mous*, in spite of the expertise the latter exhibit. In the agricultural season more *mous* get involved in wage labour, outside their family fields. Women living in the same compound take turns in doing each other's domestic chores. When asked how they spend their earnings, a majority of them answered, "Oh, for the children, sometimes for social obligations." "Did you invest any money in jewellery?" "Yes, I like to make a pair of long gold earrings." "Do you share your earnings with your husband?" Most of the marrieds said, "Yes, we give to each other when it is necessary."

As the burden of child rearing diminishes and children grow older, a matronly *mou* gets more free time and achieves more freedom of

[29]It takes about one-and-a-half hours to cook a complete meal over firewood and paddy husk. Women cook two meals a day.

movement. This is the moment of remarkable change in her social and economic life. From then on she will no longer spend time in weaving or cooking or pounding rice, but instead in trading and in a managerial position, handling the family finances. A *hanubi* has many avenues of economic activities to choose from: she can be a wholesale trader for the produce of her family and neighbourhood and sell in the market (Nambol or others); she may travel to other villages to buy wholesale and sell in the market; she may stay within the village and work as an intermediary between the outside agents and the village weavers; she may open a "hotel" (tea snacks, cigaretters, tobacco/betel leaf) in the market or in front of her home. Once I remarked to one of my informants, "So the opening of a snack-shop at the doorfront of her home is the last economic resort for *hanubi*." She said, "No, come inside our house and look. My old mother started her life as a weaver and agricultural labourer. She also made money by pounding rice. Then she started trading at Nambol bazaar. When her health did not permit this, she opened a snack-shop in front of our house. Last year, even this job became too strenuous for her because of a back pain. So she sold her shop to her sister-in-law and opened a grocery at our *sangoi*. She stores only kerosene oil and potatoes (under her cot)". A very old woman may remain at home and wind thread on loom bobbins or unwind *munga* yarn from the cocoon and be paid by other weavers.

It is usually between the ages of forty and sixty that *hanubis* appear to be most efficient and active. Some women start going to the bazaar earlier, and some work up to the age of seventy or even eighty if they have a shorter walk to the market. The *hanubis* comprise the largest membership in credit associations and co-operative savings societies.

The weavers supply a considerable amount of clothes to their families, e.g., *inafi*, *khudei*, mosquito net, bedspreads. At present mill-made clothes are imported from outside, but women still weave some clothes for the family members though they are not always the sole suppliers.

CREDIT ASSOCIATION, CO-OPERATIVE SAVINGS SOCIETIES, AND WOMEN

An interesting aspect of the village economic system is the *marup* (friendship association), a type of co-operative credit and savings organization.

In Thambalkhul, I came across five major *marups* with membership from both sexes.

Two of them are called *luhungba marups* (marriage *marups*). In the first one there are thirty members with a membership fee of Rs. 20; if the son or daughter of one of the members gets married, every other member pays him or her Rs. 20, altogether Rs. 580 on the occasion. The members come from five other surrounding villages, besides Thambalkhul. The other with forty members and a fee of Rs. 10, is also a multi-village *marup*.

There is a *marup* called *singel marup* to cover funeral costs. This is a one hundred member *marup* with a membership fee of Rs. 5. In case of a death in the family of a member, each person will offer Rs. 5, altogether Rs. 495. This is a multi-village *marnp*. The *singel marup* is traditionally a male *marup*, but divorcees or widows without a male head of the family may also join.[30] The membership is compulsory for the families of Thambalkhul. Other villages can join at their own wish. There also exists a separate *singel marup* exclusively for the residents of Thambalkhul for one hundred members. The members pay Rs. 5 each time death visits a fellow member's family.

Another *marup*, *cheng marup*, is a rice *marup* of forty members. Every member pays Rs. 2 and one kg of rice at the wedding of a child of a member. The collection amounts to Rs. 80 and forty kgs. of rice.

In addition, there are *marups* of different types, for example, *korfu marup* with twelve members with Rs. 10 membership fee for each turn. Within a certain period each member receives a *korfu* (large brass cooking pot). *Balti marup* is for receiving a brass bucket. There are also bicycle *marup*, roofing *marup*, wooden cabinet *marup*, and gold necklace *marup*.

Apart from the *marups* for both sexes, there are several all-women *marups*. In Thambalkhol, women have a *cheng marup* for women only, with 105 members. The contribution is Re. 1 and one kg of rice. The members give names of persons (e.g., parents, mothers-in-law), known as *thouni*, on whose death the association will utilise the collection. In Radhagram, in one of the three *leikais*, each lineage has a woman leader, under whom other women work as a team. They

---

[30]Every *leikai* of a village or town has a *singlup* group. This is an ancient custom which requires every household to send one male member to attend the cremation in case of a death of a *leikai* member. Each household also pays a small sum of money for the purpose of firewood for cremation. *Singel marup* is formed in addition to the traditional *singlup* system. While *singlup* exists as a male institution, the *singel marup* includes both sexes.

have also formed *marups* with names of the lineage. The *marups*, are known as *chaklau marup* (*chak*=food, *lau*=land). I found three such in Radhagram.

In the first *chaklau marup*, the members work in their family field or perform wage labour for the family in the morning shift, working in the afternoon shift as wage labour to collect money for their association. Seventeen members contribute Rs. 40 collectively for a half-day's work. If the landowner cannot pay, women charge interest on the amount and collect this later, added to the original amount. In 1978, within two months of the agricultural season, the association had collected Rs. 500. In the past three years the association has collected Rs. 3,000. The money is lent to the members and at higher interest to non-members. An absent member must find a replacement for her work; if not, she has to pay a fine of Rs. 2. Every year on the last day of December the association organizes a feast. The average age of women is forty-three years.

In the second and third *chaklau marup* there is a practice of accepting paddy instead of money in return for the work of the members. The paddy is stocked and sold in the rainy season when the price is high. In case a landlord fails to pay, women follow the custom of *potmari* by snatching away some objects from his house as compensation. In 1978, the association had Rs. 6,000 in its fund. This money is lent only to members, at low interest. The association also manages an annual feast for the women in March.

The association introduced a system of *haitha potha*, to serve refreshments to the women during their working hours, the landowner paying Rs. 10 daily towards the expense.

Apart from the agricultural activities, this association organizes the annual *Bhagvat* (Hindu religious text) reading session for ten days and invites the village men to attend.

Although all of these *marup* members are mature adults, the younger girls of the village also form *marups* for their own benefit. One such is the *luhungba* (marriage) *marup* to ensure a large sum of money for themselves when they get married. The *laishabis* (unmarried women) of Thambalkhul have a fifty member *luhungba marup* to which they contribute from their own earnings.

There are several other *marups* for both sexes and *marups* for women only. Older women attending bazaars tend to join the *marups* which are formed exclusively by the traders. Several women from Radhagram and Thambalkhul joined such *marups* in Nambol bazaar.

The membership of a bazaar *marup* usually covers a multi-village network embracing women from a much wider geographic area. An average bazaar trader joins two to three *marups* according to her economic ability. Each group of traders specializing in one kind of merchandise (e.g., fish, trinkets, rice, etc.) has one *marup* for its members. The nature of contribution varies a great deal; it can be on a daily, weekly, bi-weekly, or monthly basis. Most traders are illiterate, so they engage a male bookkeeper who charges Rs. 5 whenever a collection goes to a member.

Traders often borrow money from a *marup* to expand their business. The bazaar *marups* also engage in various socio-religious activities, e.g., religious text reading and *nupi-pala* (women's group singing for religious festivals).

The *marup* system is pervasive among women traders. In Nambol bazaar, all plot owners joined more than one *marup*. In Imphal, Khwarimbond and Laxmi bazaars, almost all the plot owners belonged to more than one *marup*. Each member receives a lump sum when her turn comes, often decided by lottery. However, the *marup* will give special consideration to a member in case of an emergency. Members usually receive money on a monthly, quarterly, or annual basis. *Marups* for larger amounts of money may cover periods of three to four years.

NAMBOL BAZAAR: WOMEN IN THE PUBLIC DOMAIN

The rural economic system offers various alternatives in occupation for women in the villages. As a Meitei woman does not lead a secluded life, she has ample opportunity to move about within or outside her village, although young women seldom leave their village area in economic pursuit (except for some professional singers in *nupi-pala* groups). The bazaar is considered to be a place for mature women, for which women must wait. If for any reason a younger woman is forced to start a trade in the bazaar, she feels embarrassed to be there. One such woman said, "My husband died and I started my trade in the bazaar. I felt very out of place among the older women. Later I became used to it."

Nambol bazaar is one of the major market centres in the Valley. Traders come from about twenty-five villages in the surrounding area. An average of 1,360 traders came daily in July 1978, a busy time in the agricultural season when many prefer to work in the rice fields. One could expect more traders in the non-agricultural season. There are 820 permanent plots under a huge shed. Other traders sit in five to six rows on both sides of the road. Nambol's administrative body has planned to expand the area of the plots. Although the traders do not have permanent roadside spaces, there is general consensus on the allocation of the spots. Newcomers must depend on old-timers to procure a spot for trading. There are sixty permanent shops—grocers, drug stores, tea stalls, tailoring shops, restaurants—run by Meitei men and women and North Indian men. These surround the bazaar shed on three sides and extend on to the two sides of the road.

The bazaar attracts traders from distant places like Churachandpur, Moirang, Bishenpur, and the capital, Imphal, for wholesale trading, for it is situated on Tidim Road, a national highway running from northeast to southeast in the Valley, connecting several important urban centres with Imphal, the capital, in the northeast. This facilitates regular public transportation for the traders who commute daily from a distance.

Second World War and the Expansion of the Bazaar

At the turn of the century, the present Nambol bazaar was just a small roadside bazaar on the banks of the Nambol River. Tidim Road was constructed after the British came to Manipur and this probably prompted the expansion of the bazaar. As it was still a dirt road, it would become very muddy during the rainy season. At that time the Nambol River was navigable and women traders could travel to the Lake Loktak area by boat or on foot by the narrow road alongside the river. During World War II, known as Japan *lan* in Manipur (1942-45), Nambol became an arena of combat between the British-American and Japanese armies. A British-American battalion camped on the Khoriphoba temple hill at Nambol and the Japanese army camped only a half mile away behind another hill. For these few years the quiet rural life was in turmoil. The capital, Imphal, was bombed by the Japanese on May 10, 1942, and hundreds of refugees fled to the Nambol area to take shelter with their relatives. When Nambol became the epicentre of tension, many fled back to the capital. The bazaar had to observe curfew from dusk to dawn. All religious festivals were banned in the evening. One village man said, "We heard gun battles all the time. Tanks were rolling down the street. . . as adolescent boys we learned a great deal about modern machinery."

During the war the Tidim Road was paved. After the war, some of the disbanded military trucks were used for commercial transportation. Gradually, there was an increase in public transportation. Bus service was introduced between Nambol and Imphal. The residents of the area took advantage of modern transportation for traversing the Valley, from the far north-eastern to the far south-western regions. In 1955, Tidim Road was tarred. Apart from state and private transport from Imphal to Churachandpur, today Nambol has its own half-hourly mini-bus service from Nambol to Imphal and back between 5.30 a.m. and 7.00 p.m. every day.

The construction of Tidim Road in prewar days instigated the expansion of the Nambol bazaar. The aftermath of World War II witnessed rapid growth, accelerated as it was by the improved and modern transportation facilities.

Over the past thirty years, the agrarian communities around the area have developed a symbiotic relationship with the Nambol bazaar. The presence of a few shops and residences of North Indians on either side of Tidim Road imparts an urban feel to the rural society.

One block down into the interior away from this hubbub of motor-cars, public buses and the crowd on the Tidim Road, the dirt roads lead to the tranquil life of the rural communities. The influx of the urban traders buying rural produce and the increasing number of local traders travelling to distant market centres have created a complex business and social world, with a touch of sophistication which may be described as the "rural cosmopolitanism" (O. Lewis, 1955: 163) of Meitei women. Old traders often talk about the immense change they have witnessed in their lives. They say, "In our youth we had to walk miles to reach a big market. Now women can go to any place they want. They can carry heavy loads by bus. In our time we had to be content with small roadside bazaars." Many women talked about how they carried rice on their heads and walked with it eight miles to reach the Kwakeithel bazaar on the outskirts of the capital. Now it takes only twenty minutes. In the past women of Radhagram were petty traders in fish and vegetables and very few of them had permanent plots at Nambol bazaar. The plots were allocated to relatively established traders many years ago and were usually handed down from mothers to daughters. At present there are several established women traders in Radhagram, although they do not own any permanent plots in the bazaar. A large number of them engage in trading woven products in urban centres; some travel to urban centres to trade in fish, vegetables, and mats.

Women in Nambol area have taken full advantage of the modernization of transport facilities. They have an economic network covering almost the entire Valley. I even found some traders who travel up to Cachar, Silchar, Lakhimpur and other towns in the neighbouring state, Assam. Women travel in groups and while staying at their usual urban hotels, carry on business transactions with the North Indian merchants. One such trader (44) told me, "We know many women across the Valley. We stay informed of each other's travels, so we can all meet together sometimes in common hotels where we know the owners. Often we return together.[31] If the *mayang* men come to bother us we shout in Hindi "*Halla mat karo*" (stop making noise).

Daily Scene at the Bazaar

Although a number of women from Radhagram and Thambalkhul deal directly with urban agents visiting the village and a number of traders sell their village produce to Imphal, Churachandpur, and Moirang, the majority of traders prefer to work in Nambol bazaar. Wholesale traders from distant areas bring their commodities to Nambol bazaar to be sold to both Imphal and Nambol traders.

Busloads of women carry earthenware, dried fish, vegetables, mushrooms, spices, oil—almost everything needed in village life. Residents in my villages buy almost everything they need for their daily lives from Nambol bazaar. They visit Imphal bazaars for delicacies or to buy superior quality imported clothing, utensils, and food not found in the local market.

The bazaar is totally a woman's world. Male plot owners are non-existent and male customers are rare. It is hard even to find a male porter to carry loads for the traders.[32] The traders range between the ages of thirty-five and seventy. A striking aspect is the absence of children. Rarely does one see a young trader with a baby on her back. The women are very well groomed. Almost all come in clean clothes,

---

[31]Long before the progress in modern transportation the Valley women had the reputation of travelling to faraway places for trading. The fish traders from Lake Waithou area (approximately sixteen kms. from Imphal on the east) travelling back and forth to the capital walked so fast that they became known as *Waithougi Sogol* (Horses of Waithou).

[32]I found only two male coolies; they belonged to a hill village of the Kabui Nagas.

shining hair brushed back into a bun with tiny fresh flowers tucked around it, *chandan* marks on their forehead and nose. Richer traders display long hanging earrings of 24-karat gold; others wear gold-plated imitation jewelry. In the midst of hectic business transactions, women exchange flowers and gossip, giggle and sing and excude an aura of relaxation.

In the morning the bazaar is empty; only the permanent stalls are open. Women enter the scene at about 2.00 p.m. The wholesale traders are the first to arrive and prefer to return to their own market by the earlier buses. Traders from distant villages leave before dark. After dark the bazaar is lit with hundreds of tiny kerosene lamps. Women of the nearby villages stay until 9.00 p.m.

The evening scene at the bazaar reminded me of the evening bazaar of the Nupe and other evening bazaars of West Africa.[33] However, there is an important distinction, as there is no tradition of prostitution in Meitei society. So, one does not come across "walk about" women or "red light districts" common in several African market centres (Pellow, 1977; Little, 1973). Several old male informants told me that they first encountered prostitution in Cachar, in the neighbouring state of Assam and in Calcutta and were shocked by it.[34]

A majority of traders inherited the plots from mothers or from some relatives. Some inherited from their mothers-in-law. Some traders declared that their daughters were attending school and, since they would not be interested in trading anymore, they would give their plots to other relatives. The stall owners have usufructuary right on the plots and pay a nominal annual rent for their use. Occasionally a new member is added. During my stay a trinket trader (35) started her trade. She was recommended by a friend who was a fellow trader. The new trader had to pay Rs 30 to the joint fund of twelve trinket sellers of the bazaar. The members organized a feast to welcome the newcomer. In the clothing section a new member has to pay Rs. 60 to the co-operative fund. A part of that is spent on feasting for the new member.

The permanent bazaar shed is divided into several rows, each selling a different merchandise. There are different rows for rice, paddy, earthenware, dairy products, fish, cloth, tobacco and other articles.

[33] I spent about three years in Nigeria between 1961 and 1966.
[34] I also gathered that in the War years there were no "war-babies" among the Meitei.

A great majority of the women trade with a small amount of capital. Out of eleven trinket sellers, five received plots from their mothers, and one received from her grandmother. One old woman (75) had been trading for the past forty-five years. She said, "I do not make much money any more. Maybe Rs. 5 to 6 a day. But I still come. If I stay at home I shall be bored to death." Another old woman (65) said, "I took care of my family with my trade I still do." "How did you learn the secrets of the trade?" One said, "Mother knew the trade. She took me to Imphal and taught me what to buy from where for my business." Another said, "I was thinking of going for a trade. My friend asked me to try this one. She had five years of experience in trinket-trading. She taught me the trade and even had me settled on a permanent plot."

The tobacco traders bring home-pounded tobacco and home-made sweets. In one row of seven traders, five had received plots from their mothers. One eighty-year-old woman said, "I was here before anyone else was even born. My mother was here, her mother was here and so was her mother." Another dairy trader also voiced the same sentiment.

One day I was surprised to see two men sitting at the cloth section. I was told that one of the men has no children and was driven by loneliness to help the women in bookkeeping. The other man was only filling in temporarily for his wife who was ill and at home.

It is considered rather improper for a man to attend the bazaar trade. During my stay one man from a nearby village came to the bazaar with a basketload of vegetables from his garden. Women in the bazaar started to tease him, "Why don't you change into *fanek* and wear a wig?" "What kind of man are you?" "Did you have a fight with your wife?" The man was so embarrassed that he left his basket in the bazaar and fled.[35] An old neighbour took care of his produce. Apparently the man's wife had left him only a few days before and he was desperate to sell the vegetables. The women neighbours at last promised to help him sell the produce. Some Meitei males have permanent shops. These came into vogue only after the North Indian men started to open shops, and are family enterprises. In all shops run by Meitei males, one can observe the female members

[35]In the fishing communities of Thanga, when men try to fish by *nupleen*, fishing tools used by women only, they are ridiculed by people for their improper behaviour. (Ch. Buddhi Singh, 1972 : 206).

of the family conducting business transactions. In contrast, North Indian shops are run by males only.

I inquired about how the traders gathered their initial capital to start a business. There were different responses. Some invested their own savings (earned by weaving and wage labour), some received financial support from their husbands, some borrowed money from a *marup* or from women money lenders on a short term basis.[36]

In urban centres, the women traders are challenged not by the Meitei males, but by a number of North Indian traders with much larger capital, who came to Manipur after British colonization. Their presence is pervasive in the big stores of the main urban bazaars. Nevertheless, alongside, a vast number of women traders are to be found in the bazaar shed sitting on their own plots. Although there are a considerable number of medium-sized shops which are run by women, the distribution of the larger stock of imported goods is under the control of the North Indian traders. However, women still have control over the local agricultural produce and the weaving industry. Contact with the North Indian traders created an external market beyond their families and localities for the goods produced by women. Older methods of weaving were much slower and produced a limited amount of material for the local clientele. Commercial contact with North Indian traders opened a wider market for the woven products of Manipur in the rest of India.

In the urban centres women entrepreneurs engage younger weavers and advance them money or thread to acquire a larger stock. Lesser entrepreneurs act as agents in the Nambol area to lend money or supply thread to the young weavers. Many women have to depend on North Indian traders for imported cotton yarn, for which women weavers often crowd North Indian shops in Imphal bazaar. The Government offers a very limited supply, but that doesn't meet the demand.

In the past, Meitei women spun their own yarn and dyed it with natural dyes, a practice which is now rare because of the ready-made

---

[36]In Khwarimbond bazaar, Imphal, a large group of fish traders come empty-handed to the bazaar daily. Women money lenders lend money to them at twenty percent interest per day. The women take the money early in the morning and travel to Moirang (39 kms. from Imphal) to buy fish at wholesale prices. They sell them retail at Imphal bazaar and return the borrowed money in the evening, keeping the profit. They make about Rs. 350 to 400 a month. I did not come across such high rates of interest in the Nambol area.

supply of imported yarn, which is creating a dependency on outside traders. However, the supply is steady and thus the turnover is large.

A Meitei proverb says, "Husband brings firewood, wife brings all other goodies." This study shows that the husband's contribution of rice and fuel are also greatly dependent on the woman's labour. Comments of Meitei males often reveal both admiration for and ambivalence towards the economic contribution of their women. One college professor in my study area says, "Our women contribute fifty to seventy-five percent of the family income. Women work all year round, but men are idle six months of the year; they gamble and waste money during this period." He added, "Look, my mother always helps my father (a carpenter) in his work, but he never helps her." A politician in Imphal says, "My mother became a widow when we were young children, and she brought us up through her own toil." The headmaster of the high school at Radhagram said, "Women contribute at least fifty percent of the family income." Another Nambol professor said, "Yes, our women are very efficient, still they have a moral bond to their husbands. They regard their husbands as gods." An infirm farmer (dependent on four daughters and a wife) in my area patted the head of his ten-year-old boy and said, "I am lucky to have a son." "Don't you feel happy that you have such daughters?" "Yes, they are very hard working, they earn well and take care of me. But you know, women are stupid, they have no courage to go out at night. My son will go to school and bring status to my family." One of his daughters is an undergraduate student in Nambol College. One Meitei professor at the university in Imphal mentioned serveral times, "Do not feel deceived by the economic role of the Meitie women. In reality they have a much inferior status than men."

5
Social Organization

The Meitei use two terms of significance rather frequently in their social introductions among themselves: *yumnak*, the name of the *sagei* (lineage), and *yek*, the name of the *salei* (clan).

A Meitei name starts with *yumnak*, followed by a personal name and ends with "Singh", a title the Meitei adopted on their conversion to Hinduism, which denotes the Kshatriya status in Hindu caste hierarchy. The Brahmans, originally from North India, were given different *yumnaks* to serve as their family names. A Brahman's name starts with a *yumnak*, followed by a personal name, and ends with "Sharma". The last indicates his caste status as a Brahman. Women's names (both Meitei and Brahman) start with *yumnak* followed by personal names, and end with the term "Devi."

When a Meitei is referred to someone, his *yumnak* gets a special emphasis in any letter of introduction. The next question is, what is his *yek*? The *yumnaks* are subgroups of seven *yeks* or clans: *Ningthouja, Khuman, Luwang, Angem, Moirang, Khabangmaba,* and *Chenglei*, each divided into many *yumnaks*.[37]

Meitei society has rigid rules about *yek*-exogamy. Men and women belonging to the same clan are *namungba*, which means taboo against marriage. In the past a Meitei (both man and woman) was ostracized for in-clan marriage and was sent to a Loi village in the west, called Haujaupan. For other breaches of exogamic rules, e.g., for marrying a mother's sister or her children, the offender was sent to the Yathibi group of Loi.

[37]In Radhagram, out of 256 households there are thirty-seven *yumnaks* of different *sageis* (lineages) with seven of Brahmans, and three of RK. In Thambalkhul, out of sixty-six households, four are R K, one Brahman, and others belong to eleven *yumnaks* of the Meitei Kshatriya. A woman is also referred to by her maiden name alongwith her husbands' family name, i.e, Laishram Ningol Saibam Satyabhama Devi, the Satyabhama who is Laishram's daughter and Saibam's wife.

Nowadays, these rules have become rather relaxed. One informant phrased it thus: "Pundit Loishang has become too relaxed. Suppose a *khuman* wants to marry another *khuman*. He has to offer some money to Pundit Loishang and receive a certificate which says that he is not just a *khuman*, but a *Mayarbak* or *Maraibak khuman*, meaning that he is a *khuman* from a foreign land." A Brahman male can marry a Meitei female in a hypergamic relationship. Johnstone (1896: 8-9) refers to a custom of "reverse hypergamy" by which a Meitei woman could marry a low caste man and adopt him into her own caste. Dunn's report also discusses a custom ". . . by which a man of low caste marrying a woman of high caste (Meitei) is adopted into her tribe, and the children are considered as full-blooded members of their mother's caste" (Dunn, 1886, reprinted 1975:14). In recent years the incident of a low caste Teli becoming a Meitei Kshat-

Front view   Side view

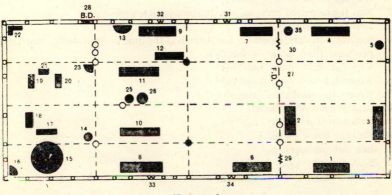

FIGURE 4

Traditional Plan of a Meitei Home (Key on page 60)

riya and marrying a Meitei woman (discussed earlier) supports this information. In this case the man was not adopted into his wife's lineage or clan; he was given a special lineage name (foreigner's family) and was accepted as a member of a Meitei clan.

THE STRUCTURE OF A MEITEI HOME

A traditional Meitei home is in a sense a microcosm of the familial and social stratification that is to be found in the culture. Figure 4 indicates the convention of seating, sleeping, and dining arrangements according to a person's sex and rank in the family and social hierarchy. The entire plan is based on a rigid structure with a strong emphasis on patrilineal values and the preponderance of male status.[38]

The house faces the east and is built on an oblong structure under one roof, with different sections. On the eastern side there is a large porch, *mangol*, which is used as a parlour. Across the compound there is a long shed, *shangoi*, with a roof and walls on three sides. The *shangoi* is like a multipurpose room used by all residents in a compound for a variety of domestic activities of both sexes. It faces west and must be at least thirty feet from the edge of the *mangol* of a home. In between the *shangoi* and the house there is the *tulsibong* (Vaisnavite altar). All household work is done in the *shangoi*, the *mangol*, and in the courtyard. These areas are open to outsiders.

KEY TO FIGURE 4
TRADITIONAL PLAN OF A MEITEI HOME

1. Seat for house owner (*phamel*)
2. Seat for respected persons, e.g. Brahmans, RK's (*phaktom*)
3. Seat for outsiders
4. Seat for outsiders, especially for women at the time of *nupi haiba* (marriage proposal from groom's family)
5. Exit for dead body (*naktha*)
6. Room for the sons (*lukhumka*)
7. Room for daughters (*ningolka*)
8. Master bedroom (*phamel*)
9. Bedroom for other children
10. Seat for house owner
11. Seat for outsiders
12. Seat for physician (*maiba*)
13. House deity, female (*leimarel*)

[38]The texts on architectural plans of the houses, *yumsarol*, are nine in number, which offer detailed instruction on house building.

14. Pot for cooking rice (*chengphu*)
15. Granary for paddy (*kot*)
16. House deity, male (*sanamahi*)
17. Dining seat for father
18. Dining seat for sons
19. Dining seat for mother
20. Dining seat for daughter-in-law
21. Dining seat for children
22. Cooking place (*chakhum*)
23. Feeding place for cats and servants (*houdong chakthapham*)
24. Earthen pot for water (*khonghampul*)
25. Spot for ritual offering (*phungalairoo*)
26. Hearth (*phunga*)
27. Front door (*mamangthong*)
28. Back door (*maningthong*)
29-34. Windows
35. Place for the physician to prepare the medicine

The *mangol* is the most important area of the house for around it the social life of the family revolves. There are different areas with seats assigned to persons according to their sex and social position. The southern side of the porch is for *phamel* (No. 1 in the diagram), the seat of the male head of the family. A mat is placed there exclusively for him. On the western back left is *phaktom* (No. 2), meant for men of high rank, e.g., R Ks, Brahmans, or high ranking Meiteis. The eastern side right is the seat for the outsider (No.3). The northern side is *mangsok* (No. 4) meant for women guests especially for *nupihaiba*, when women from a prospective groom's family come to negotiate a marriage proposal. Normally women guests are received at the *shangoi*, where women of the family keep busy with weaving or housework. On the northeastern side is *naktha*, used to take a dead body out of the house. No one is allowed to enter or exit in between the poles at that corner. At the middle of the porch is *mamangthong* (No. 27), a huge door used as an entrance.

As we enter the house through the front door, we may see *lukhumka* (No. 6), the room for the eldest son on the southern side and *ningolka* (No. 7), the room for the daughters on the northern side. Behind Nos. 6 and 7 in the interior there is a fireplace known as *phunga* (No. 26). In the past this fire was never extinguished. At present this is lighted only on ritual occasions. Next to the fireplace is a hole, called *phungalairoo* (No. 25). This is an auspicious spot on the western part of the hearth. Food cooked for *sagei apokpa* ritual (traditional worship for family ancestors by the males of the family) is offered here, and small savings (coins) buried beneath: people offer food here before their meals. This place is also held in high importance during all family rituals. People sit on both sides of the hearth, the family head on the south (No. 10) and outsiders (No. 11) on the north. *Phamel* (No. 8) is the master bedroom. The *phamjao*, the bed of the head of the family, is placed in such a way that his navel is in line with the *phunga*. No. 12 is the seat for *maiba*, the medicine man, in case of illness in the family. Behind this is an area known as *mangsok* (No. 9). This is reserved as children's sleeping quarters. Next is another line of poles. Behind this is the place for earthen cooking ware, *chengpu* (No. 14). No. 15 is *kot*, a small storage area. On the northwest corner is *chakhumka* (No. 22), the kitchen. The dining hall is in the middle with a separate seat for the head of the family and with the eldest son on the southern side (Nos. 18 and 17). No. 19 is for the wife, No. 20 for the daughter-in-law (if any), and No. 21 for daughters and children. No. 23 is *houdong chakthapham*, the dining area for cats and servants.[39] No. 24 is *khonghaampul*, a place for storage of water in an earthen pot. On the northwestern corner of the front porch (No. 5) is the cooking area for the visiting *mabia* medicine man and *shaman*. Nos. 29 through 34 indicate windows. The southwestern corner (No. 16) is regarded as the place for the house deity *sanamahi* and a spot at the northern side is meant for a female deity, *sanamahi*'s mother, *Ima Leimaren*. Both places are kept clean; there are no altars. Devout Meiteis offer flowers and food at these spots daily. The corners also have high ritual importance during family ceremonies.

The house plan has to adhere to detailed rules of location regarding the positioning of the different units in a compound. The laying of the corner-stone is associated with a ritual, *Jatra Hunba*, with a Brahman priest officiating in the name of the male head of the family.

Most homes in my area follow the traditional house plan with some modern alterations. The Brahman homes have an additional huge structure called *mandapa* and a temple. A *mandapa* is a hall for community rituals and feasts. This is constructed with large wooden poles; massive wooden beams support the enormous tin roof; the

---

[39]It is very rare to have a servant in a Meitei family. The absence of a rigid caste stratification allowed the Meitei to be self-sufficient. Their pattern of life reveals a society based on democratic relationships with the people depending on each other for mutual help and cooperation. In urban areas some families engage servants; during a family feast the servants sit along with their masters.

floor is cemented. The small temples, made of bricks, house the images of the Hindu deities, Radha and Krishna.

FAMILY: SOCIAL IDEOLOGY OF MALE SUPERIORITY

The Meitei are patrilineal and both patrilocal and virilocal. The eldest son of a *yumnak* (lineage name) holds the status of *piba*. A *piba*'s role is very important in family rituals. If the village temple belongs to a *sagei* (lineage), then the *piba* of that *sagei* and his wife play a prominent part in the annual Lai Harouba.[40] The Pundit Loishang scrutinizes the eligibility of the position of a *piba* according to the prescribed rules. If a man marries a divorcee or a widow, he is disqualified for the position. Similarly, a son of a widow or a divorcee and his family line are not entitled to the position of *piba* in the future.

The importance of a male child is constantly expressed in everyday conversation. Women say, "You get a lot of harsh words for not having a son, " or "Husbands take another wife, if the first wife cannot bear a son."

The midwife can expect a much larger remuneration if she delivers a male child. If the first-born is a girl, the midwife can expect a good fee, but she must not ask anything if the second and third are also females.

Parents without a son usually have an adopted son-in-law, *yaonginba*. He assumes the male responsibility in cultivation and other labour, but does not have any legal or ritual rights.

A child is born in his/her father's residence. A son's importance can be observed during family rituals, e.g., funeral rites of the parents, *shraddha*, annual ancestor worship, and the feast of *pitritarpan* (dedication to the forefathers). In all of these rites a daughter does not feature unless she is the only child. However, a daughter is obliged to offer *potpang*, a large sum of money for her parents' rites.[41]

In the event of a calamity or family emergency, a very important ritual is performed, the worship of Sagei Apokpa (Meitei ancestral deity). The ritual is performed at midnight. The male members of the

---

[40]There are two kinds of village temples in Manipur; *sagei* temple (temple for a particular lineage) and *khulong* temple (temple belonging to the village).

[41]The Meitei have two forms of gift giving: *poyeng* and *potpang*. *Poyeng* is given to the wider circle of friends and relatives, while *potpang* is a relatively large sum of money for very close relatives or friends. The *poyeng* can be of the order of Rs. 5, but the *potpang* is for buying rather expensive items.

family and the *piba* perform this in deep secrecy to the strict exclusion of females. Women are not allowed to eat the ritual fruits offered to the deity. One *maiba* (shaman) said, "If the women were allowed to eat these fruits, they would become too strong. That would destroy the *sagei*".[42] In my study villages, many families perform this ritual annually, but one informant in Nambol said, "I have witnessed it only once in my childhood. It is rather rare nowadays."

In spite of the tenets prescribed by *dayabhaga*, Meitei custom makes special provision for widowed, divorced and unmarried daughters by giving them a right of residence in their parents' home. Women inherit their mother's property and have rights on their own dowry, which is to be returned after a divorce. Stridhan (women's wealth) is composed of a woman's inherited wealth, her dowry, and her own savings.

Married sons build their own sleeping quarters and kitchen in their father's compound within a few years of their marriage. The youngest son lives with the parents. Daughters marry and leave their natal homes.[43]

A typical rural family compound consists of two or three small houses with separate kitchens. The elderly parents live in the main house with unmarried daughters and sons or, if all the children are married, with the youngest son and his family. In the past, when a young man got married, his friends would offer free labour to build his sleeping quarters, the young man merely supplying the raw materials. Today a young married couple usually share the main house and use a room for sleeping accommodation, waiting a few years to build their separate sleeping quarters and hearth. However, if a man can afford it, he builds his home in a new compound and leaves his father's household.

People marry both inside and outside their villages following the

[42]Male ambivalence towards the female is also found in some of their social behaviour. A man in no case may touch a woman's *fanek* (sarong-like cloth) even if it is clean and folded. Since it might have been worn during menstruation, there is a possibility of pollution. The term for vagina in Meitei is *thung*. This is often used as an abusive and derogatory word. This might also indicate an aversion to female sexuality.

[43]The rule of ultimogeniture is also a common feature in the neighbouring state of Burma. This is often found among people who used to have an abundance of land where older sons could get out of their village and move further to acquire new land for cultivation.

rules of clan exogamy. Parents do not like their daughters to be married in a distant place. "It should be within walking distance, not more than two or three miles." One father says, "In case she is not treated well, she should be able to come back. Her parents may not be able to help her if she is married too far away." There are a large number of marriages between Radhagram and Thambalkhul. In fact, most of the marriages occur within a village or with one of the adjacent villages.

KINSHIP

Living within a small social radius, people maintain a close link with their affinal and consanguinal kin groups. Even in cases of broken marriages I found that the affinal kins do not sever the contact, especially where there are children left behind by the mother (either with her in-laws or with her own mother). In a village, people broadly identify as relatives others belonging to a common lineage and clan.

Children learn to address elders by lumping them in the context of a generation. Any male in the father's generation would be *khura/ipa* and a female in the mother's generation would be *ine/indomcha*. Father's sisters are called *ine*, whereas mother's sisters are called *indomcha*.

Sex is specified in each term. Sometimes the sex of the ego is important, e.g., a man addresses his brother's wife as *iteimma*, whereas a woman calls her *inamma*.

All terms are extended to fictive kins, i.e., father's friends, mother's friends, etc. Terms vary according to the age, generational rank, and the sex of the ego and the sex of the kinsman.

Outside the kin group the most respectable way to address a woman is *iche* or sister, but for an elder woman it should be *ima* (mother) or *ine* (aunt). For a young man it is *tada* (brother); for an older man, *ipa* (father) or *khura* (uncle).

Younger women are addressed affectionately as *ibeyamma* by the elders. If the woman is very young, she is addressed as *meimma* by her kin and by outsiders.

Kin groups are bound by social obligations of *poyeng* and *potpang*, during the life cycle ceremonies of each other's families. When a baby is born, the woman's natal family sends special gifts through a procession of women carrying bamboo baskets and *firups* with clothing, food, jewelry, and other items, called *poyengba*. The woman's brother does a special role during the *shastipuja* ceremony, the ritual on the sixth day after a child's birth, throwing arrows in different directions from the ritual arena to protect the baby from evil eyes. A woman's maternal uncle is responsible for making her wedding bed for the bridal chamber.

A son-in-law and sister's husband have special obligations during any rite or feast in his in-law's family. They are expected to help the Brahman cook, in washing the lentils, cutting the vegetables, and cleaning the utensils. They are also responsible for cleaning up the waste left after a feast. A son-in-law or a sister's husband who neglects this duty is criticized for his irresponsible behaviour.

Once married, the woman does not spend nights in her parents' home unless there is an emergency. Her children are born in her husband's compound, her mother helping in delivery.

Although a family maintains close contact with married daughters, through calendrical rituals and feasts, it is considered rather improper for them to visit her too frequently or to interfere in her family affairs. However, in case of conflict, the two families often confront each other, especially after a divorce, when the woman's family demands repayment of her dowry.

As most of the marriages in my area occur in a limited social setting, people live in a world of kin groups with a continual process of reciprocity in all social obligations.

MARRIAGE CUSTOMS AND ROMANCE

The Meitei are a very romantic people. Most marriages are based on romantic love. "Only the ugly ones go through an arranged marriage" was a comment of one informant. Ancient Meitei literature and ballads are full of love stories. There are nine legends of the divine couple incarnated at different times (Joychandra, n.d.). The most well-known among them is that of the Khamba-Thoibi couple, who lived in the twelfth century. The story describes the faithful love of the courageous noble hero Khamba and the beautiful and intelligent princess Thoibi. The ballads describe the dazzlingly beautiful Thoibi thwarted by her father in her choice of a husband. After suffering exile, then reuniting through marriage, the couple lose their lives in tragic death (N. Tombi Singh, 1976). The ballads represent a vast repertoire of romantic verses with exquisite literary imagination. The ancient stories offer glorious descriptions of young men and women in love, their faithfulness and the ultimate tragedy.

Another ancient text is *Numban Pombi Luwaoba*. This describes a husband's confrontation with the god of death to win back the life of his dead wife. After his wife's death, Numban Pombi Luwaoba vowed not to perform the funeral rite so that the chance of his wife's coming back to life would remain. The god of death sent his emissaries to fight him. Numban Pombi defeated them and was at last granted his wife's life. (K. Singh Moirangthem, 1971: 43).[44]

Panthoibi Khongun (Footsteps of Panthoibi) is an important ancient text depicting romantic love of the divine couple, goddess Panthoibi and god Nongpokningthou (regarded as the divine mother and father of creation). The legend depicts the goddess Panthoibi born as a girl in the western hills and Nongpokningthou as the King of the eastern hills. They met while Panthoibi was busy in terrace cultivation and fell in love. But Panthoibi's parents gave her to another man, Khaba. Panthoibi appeared in fearful images to Khaba, but he did not recognize her as the goddess incarnate. Panthoibi always thought of her true love and there came a time when the lovers could not bear the pain of separation any longer. They left their homes in search of one another, meeting near Kangla and doing *chenba* (the traditional custom of elopement to be discussed later). Khaba followed the footsteps of Panthoibi and gradually he recognized her identity as the goddess, and started to worship her. Nongpokningthou and Panthoibi lived as man and wife at Numaijing hill to the east of the Valley.

Penakhongbas, the professional musicians of the bowed instrument, *pena*, and singers have presented these stories with fine theatrical skill to people through the ages.

Women's *khulong ishei* (songs for the team of women at rice cultivation) are full of the emotion of romantic love. Tradition thus encourages men and women to relate to each other emotionally before marriage. A physical relationship, however, is not sanctioned. The public display of affection between the sexes is regarded as being in very bad taste.

Romance in the Past

In the past, it was usual for boys and girls to meet in groups. Young people played a *cowrie* game called *likkol* at a family *shagnoi*

---

[44]This is opposite of the famous Indian legend of Savitri and Satyavana. When Savitri's husband died she took a vow to confront the god of death and retrieve the life of her husband. Her devotion crowned her with success. There is also a popular Bengali folk legend of Behula and Lakhinder. Behula confronted the god of death when her husband died. She pleased the god of death by her skillful dancing and won back her husband's life.

or *mangol* during special ceremonies, e.g., festivals of Krishna's birthday, Radha's birthday and such others. One old woman said, "On these days in the month of July, the fields were full of water. We used to go out in small boats and spend all day eating lilies. In the evening we played *likkol* together. We also collected rice and vegetables from our homes and had picnics together." If a boy and girl happened to fall in love, the *likkol* game served as a communication for them. The boy might say, as he played his *cowries*, "My mother's daughter-in-law, keep these with you." The girl might play her *cowries* and say, "I have kept them, my mother's son-in-law," or "Lover, keep these with you ..."

"Young men came to talk to us in the evening. They sat on the *mangol* and talked to us in the presence of other members of the family. Our parents always knew who they were and what was their behaviour."

Among the urban elite, marriages were sometimes arranged, but even there, the sentiments of the prospective couple were important.

In the rural areas, as the old women recall, the boys were offered smoking pipes at the family *mangol* as an expression of fondness from the girls' side. A sixty-year-old woman said, "When I was twelve I joined *sinaifam kabi*.[45] The boys came to sit at the family *shangoi* while the girls wove. Sometimes they brought fruits to share. Sometimes they helped in spinning." Some women spoke about their group theatrical performances at festival times. "After singing and playing late into the night we used to sleep in the open *shangoi*, boys on one side, girls on the other. Grown ups supervised us and served fruits and sweets. We never got into trouble with a pregnancy." (An insinuating remark aimed at the modern girls.)

Some women talked about the *Kang* game at the community *mandapa*,[46] played by both the married and the unmarried of both sexes.

[45]This was a custom whereby a team of girls worked under the supervision of an elderly female. The group would move from one house to another in turn, learning weaving.

[46]An ancient game of skill with seven people on each side of the *shangoi* each throwing *kangs* (lacquered disks) to the opposite line. The game requires a specially-made floor and special measurement of the area.

The *kang* games are traditional meeting places for the sexes. The ballads of Khmaba-Thoibi describes Thoibi's romantic encounter with Khamba during a *kang* game.

An ancient Meitei song says, "Where is my beloved? Is she combing her beautiful hair in her father's home or is she sitting between two village brothers in a *kang* game?"

Old people remarked that the most delightful time of their youth was at the Thabal Chombi dance festival in springtime. During the spring full moon, *laishabis* (unmarried maidens) and *pakhangs* (bachelors) assembled together and danced all night until dawn. During Thabal Chombi the young people were allowed to hold each other's hands, forbidden at other times. Brothers helped their sisters decorate the dancing ground with leaves and flowers. They hired *dholak* drummers and petromax lights with donations collected by the *laishabis*. While dancing, young men from other villages or those who did not have a sister in the group joined in. A brother had to seek a group apart from his sisters.

Old women often express real enthusiasm in talking about the romances of their youth. Women in their seventies and eighties giggle and with a twinkle in their eyes and with evident nostalgia discuss their romances. Women often referred to some happy old couples who were still deeply in love.

Romance at Present

Modernization has brought some changes. The romantic boatrides and lily-eating outings are things of the past. Boys do not come to a girl's house for their daily meetings. Movie houses, walks to school and college, or the village corners have replaced the former rendezvous.

Likkol is still a popular game during festival periods. I found eight such occasions when girls play this game with young boys. The first five and the eighth are played at the family *shangoi* and the other two are played at *Bamon mandapa* where worships are performed. The young people play all night until dawn, brothers helping in organizing but not joining in. Adults supervise but do not interfere.

Thabal Chombi (dancing in moonlight) is extremely popular and instils romantic notions into the minds of the young people. In my study villages, *laishabis* work extra hours during the transplanting season to collect money for Thabal Chombi. Of more recent date, instead of a dholak drum, the girls hire loudspeakers and play movie records. A song-leader helps the chorus of young dancers:

"Today, let us all, bachelors and maidens,
hold each other's hand
on our selected ground.
Let us dance Thabal Chombi
All refrain, 'Let us dance Thabal Chombi'."

If the money permits, they hire a band party to play Meitei traditional songs. Brothers, as in the past, help but do not join.

In the spring of 1978 in Thambalkhul of sixty-six families, the *laishabis* organized two dances, each attended by about two hundred men and women. One girl said, "We are all free toinght, all free." They hired four sets of public address systems, two band parties and several petromaxes, and each group spent a little over Rs. 500 for the festivals. The money came from the *laishabis*' earnings and from a collection from the village elders. Some of the boyfriends of the girls donated money to please the girls. Some young marrieds also joined in the dancing. One pregnant woman (33) said, "I join Thabal Chombi every year, but this year I am in such advanced stage, I am too shy to dance." She is a daughter of this village. I am told that, in other years when she danced, her husband did not join because his sisters were in the dance.

During the past thirty years, there has been a boom in school education in the Valley. At present, the most important communication is thus through letter-writing. In a society where public exhibition of emotion is forbidden, letter-writing becomes an important channel of self-expression and communication. Friends guard the privacy and secrecy of the couple with utmost care. One advocate of the civil court at Imphal said, "When a girl's parents try to prove a *chenba* (traditional custom of elopement) to be kidnapping, the boy's family usually produces huge bundles of letters. Most of the letters are full of emotion . . . the girls are too shy to sign their real names, they might write Moniradha for Radhamoni." In romances of mature people, I gathered, friends helped in sending messages and letter-writing.

In Meitei society, there is ample opportunity for meeting members of the opposite sex. There is no strict separation of the sexes in everyday life. One notices segregated seating arrangements during rituals and community feasts, but men and women sit together on several festive occasions. In July, during the eleven days of the Rathajatra festival, men and women clap and dance with light steps singing *khubak ishei* (clapping song). Men and women work side by side. They travel together in crowded buses in which, unlike some parts of India, seats are not reserved for women.[47] Men and women interact

---

[47]Some Meitei women students who went to study in Calcutta said that they did not understand the significance of "ladies seat", and often stood among crowds of men and were manhandled by middle-aged men. One said, "We were so shocked by this behaviour. A Meitei man would never do such a thing."

freely while travelling. When they fall in love, their relationship often leads to chenba, a public announcement of their desire to be married.

Marriage Customs

There are several types of marriages recognized in Meitei society. These are: (1) *Chenba*, (2) *Luhungba* and *Chelhong*, (3) *Loukhotpa*, (4) *Kainakatpa*, and (5) *Nambothaba*. The custom of *Nambothaba* is non-existent at present.

Chenba

This is the traditional elopement of two lovers. When a young man and a woman decide to marry, they can leave their parents' home without the knowledge of elders. However, a *chenba* must follow certain rules which are approved by the society.

There are two auspicious days, Monday and Wednesday, for *chenba*. The boy informs the girl beforehand and sets his plans. The girl sneaks out of the house in the evening or just goes out pretending to visit a girl friend in the neighbourhood, and meets the boy at a selected spot. The boy arrives with a group of friends, in this time and age often in a jeep, though in some cases the boys come out on their bicycles. In one case the boy's group came on foot and the girl ran through a paddy field to meet them. Most of the girls who did *chenba* said they were very nervous about the plans and in many cases their plans failed because of their elders' suspicion. *Chenba* needs well-planned preparation from the boy's side; his group must be strong and courageous so that in the event of a sudden confrontation with the girl's family they may not get beaten up. (There have been cases like this in my area.) After elopement, the boy's group goes to a family known to the boy's family (usually mother's sister or mother's friend's home). This family is obliged to give shelter to the couple and notify the boy's family about the incident, and it is inappropriate for the family to refuse shelter to the couple. The hostess is in charge of the well-being of the girl, as the couple is not supposed to sleep together.[48]

When a girl does not return home before dinnertime (Meitei women and men seldom go out in the evening), her family becomes alarmed. The girl's close friends are immediately summoned and

---

[48] I have heard different stories about this system. Some people complained that modern couples do not care about such prohibition and they are just too eager to have sexual pleasure. Some said it depends very much on the girl's attitude.

cross-examined. They can identify the boy but they seldom have any knowledge of the name of the host or the location of his house. If the girl's family does not approve of this boy, they spend the night in real anxiety.

The next morning the boy's father and two other elderly men should go to the girl's father. This custom is known as *haidokpa*. The boy's father is supposed to apologize for the boy's behaviour and request for the arrangement of a wedding ceremony. A sanskritized ceremony with an officiating Brahman priest is called *luhungba*, but such a ceremony performed after a *chenba* is called *chelhong*.

If the girl's family objects to the match, her father demands the girl's return immediately. Both parents confront each other's relatives, and friends intervene and try to bring them to some understanding. In a *chenba*, the girl's father and her elder brothers are genuinely shocked. The mother and the sisters often have some prior knowledge of the girl's relationship with the boy. The girl's father demands *machinhangba*, which involves interrogation of the girl by married female relatives. A group of matronly women led by the girl's mother visit the girl in the house where she has taken shelter to find out whether the girl was lured into the situation or even kidnapped. When the group of well-dressed women appear in the host's house, another dramatic scene ensues. If the girl's family disapproves of the boy, they attempt pressurising the girl. In one instance, the young man was listening to the interrogation of his girl friend from the adjoining room and felt so helpless that he started to cry. The girl's aunt saw him and yelled, "Look, he is not even a man. He behaves like a child. How can he be your husband?" The young man happened to be an engineer! In such a situation, the boy's family often intervenes and pleads on his behalf. It is considered a disgrace if a girl rejects a groom after *chenba*. Usually, after *machinhangba*, the girl's family takes the girl with them and arranges a wedding date. Some girls are afraid to return immediately and return only on the day of the wedding. If the girl's family cannot afford an expensive wedding like *luhungba* (the Hindu ceremony), they arrange a traditional wedding. If the girl's family is reluctant to go through the ceremony, sometimes the boy's family can arrange it. However, no wedding is complete until the girl's family arranges the *loukhotpa* ritual, which legitimizes the union. *Luhungba* after a *chenba*, i.e., *chelhong*, is not regarded as a proper custom by orthodox villagers. After *chenba* a girl is not considered a virgin or a *laishabi* and in *luhungba* the girl is supposed to be a virgin. However, if a man and a woman simply continue to live together after a *chenba*, they are also recognized as husband and wife, though *chenba* alone is not considered an elegant way to establish a marital relationship. On my asking "What is the difference between a mistress and a wife acquired by *chenba*?" one informant expressed it thus: "There is a basic difference here. In *chenba* the two people make a public proclamation of their desire to be united and it is supported by a group of people and families. *Chenba* is socially approved, but living with a man, casually, without any social recognition is considered very improper and anti-social."

Luhungba

This is the most respected form of marriage ritual. The central part of the ritual is exactly the same as that in the upper caste Hindu marriages seen in other parts of India. The most important part of the ritual is *sampradana*, offering the virgin bride (*kanyadana*) as a gift to the groom who is called *vara*, the honoured one. The bride's father, the groom, and the Brahman priest are the principal participants in the ritual. The bride has a very passive role to play. The rest of the ritual follows Meitei traditional custom and is marked by the prominence of female participation.

The wedding procedure is elaborate and sometimes covers a period of several months. There are different phases prior to the ritual of *luhungba* beginning with a formal proposal by a group of women on behalf of the bridegroom's family, followed by negotiations between the two families, horoscope matching, fixing of a wedding date by an astrologer, and the actual betrothal, the ritual of *heijenpot*. The wedding procession from the groom's home with gifts for the bride is headed by an "ideal woman" (one who has never been widowed or divorced and has a first-born living male child). The bridegroom and his party are first received by the bride's mother, the bridegroom prostrating himself before her (*mayamokpa*). During the wedding ceremony the bridegroom's mother assumes importance. She sits in the front row of the women's section and the groom must face her from his wedding seat. She is offered a *maiknaiba fanek*[49] by the

[49]*Maiknaiba fanek*, a sarong-like skirt, is the traditional formal attire of Meitei women. The material is woven on loin-loom in fine cotton or silk into a thick and smooth texture with their stripes in different colours. The borders are embroidered with extremely fine design. For formal occasions women wear the *fanek* across the bust (over a blouse, if modern). Modern women wear the *fanek* at waist-

bride's family. After the *sampradana* ritual the bride's best friend, a *laishabi* (sometimes a Brahman woman) ties the couple's hands together (the girl's left hand is placed over the right hand of the boy) and a tray with coconut is placed on them. The bride's mother is the first person to give blessings to the couple and this is followed by other women and men guests, who offer money on the tray, which is then taken to the groom's mother. She places the tray on her lap and covers it with her shawl (*kujabawa*). When the bride arrives at her in-laws' home, her mother-in-law embraces her first. The bride changes her own *fanek* for her mother-in-law's.

During the two-and-a-half hour wedding ceremony in the bride's house, *sankirtana*, the Vaisnavite singing session by professional parties takes an important part.[50] Apart from *sankirtana* there is invariably a band party playing traditional tunes in between the *sankirtana* sessions.[51] *Luhungba* is complete only after a feast, *mangani chakoba*, given by the bride's family to the groom's family, after the five day wedding.

In most of the *luhungbas* I have observed in my area, the girl's dowry consisted of several large bell-metal and brass utensils, two beds, one glass-door cupboard, a loom and several other articles, and clothing. A bride is also given some gold jewelry. This dowry is often purchased with the money earned by the girl herself. In my study area, a few of the poorer families demanded brideprice from the groom's family. The amount ranges from Rs. 800 to 5,000. A large part of the money is spent on the wedding. However, one man from Thambalkhul said, "When you accept brideprice for your daughter,

---

line. Finely woven thin shawls, *inafis*, are used on top. Every person must wear the *chandan* mark on forehead and nose and a tiny bouquet of fresh flowers in the hair. Gold or gold-plated earrings, necklaces and hairpins are popular. Very few wear bangles.

[50] The elder males of both parties occasionally enter the arena to prostrate themselves in front of the altar and the *sankirtana* players, to offer *dakshina* of money and cloth. Dakshina is a custom of offering to a person as an expression of respect and Vaisnavite humility. The giver bows to the person regardless of the person's age, sex or social status.

[51] Band parties are now an inevitable part of Meitei culture. Band music was introduced into Manipur in the early colonial period, and has established itself with immense popularity. The members wear western-style theatrical costumes. Although foreign instruments are used, the musicians and drummers play in a very creative way with innovative performances of drumming.

she turns into a slave of her husband's family. She is never free from her obligation and cannot return even if they treat her badly."

Luhungba is not only the most prestigious form of marriage, it is also the most expensive. Very few couples in my area had *luhungba*, the most common form there being *chenba* followed by *loukhotpa*.

Loukhotpa

After a *chenba*, the girl may return to her family or wait until her parents arrange the ceremony. It is common for angry parents to wait until their daughter gives birth to a baby. In one case in my area, the couple waited ten years and had three children before they had *loukhotpa*. This couple had a *yektinnaba* (in-clan union) and the girl's father refused to arrange *loukhotpa*. After the father's death, the brothers arranged the ceremony. The children of the couple were barred from the ceremony.

A *loukhotpa* starts with loud reading from the *Bhagvata Purana*, an important Vaisnava text, with an assembly of guests of both sexes. The dowry is much smaller than that given in an average *luhungba*. A group of women from the husband's house arrives with several baskets of fruit, clothing, and large trays of offerings to the house deities. Food is distributed among the guests. A large tray called *athenpot* is taken inside and food is offered to the family deities. In the meantime the couple arrives. In one case I found the women yelling, "*Nupa di hanure*," teasing, "the groom is too old". This was a *loukhotpa* after ten years of marriage. The couple bow to the ancestral deities and the elders. The husband sits on the *mangol* accompanied by his friends. The wife is supposed to have her evening meal at her parents' home. This simple ceremony legitimizes the marriage. In orthodox families, the mother-in-law does not allow the daughter-in-law to cook in the family kitchen unless her parents perform *loukhotpa* after a *chenba*.

Kainakatpa

Sometimes mature couples (divorced or widowed) have a *chenba* but are too embarrassed to go through *loukhotpa*. They invite a group of elderly men and women from the neighbourhood to a gathering at the *tulsibong* (altar with a basil plant) and request that they be accepted as man and wife. They exchange *kanthis* (tulsi-bead necklaces) or flower garlands and bow at the altar and then to the elders. The couple enter the house and bow to the family deities.

This form of wedding is known as *kainakatpa*.

The custom of cohabitation after *chenba, loukhotpa* or *kainakatpa* without an officiating Brahman priest was scorned by the Brahma Sabha. The penalty for such marriages, especially *chenba* and *kainakatpa*, was the loss of the right to obtain a royal office. (Hodson, 1908, reprinted 1975: 115). Nonetheless, marriages outside Brahmanic rules remained popular in rural areas.

In Nambol and, according to my rural informants, in other areas of the Valley as well, about 90 percent of all marriages start with a *chenba*. In pre-war days, there was another custom called *nambothaba*. A young *pakhang* (bachelor) would come to a girl's house with a huge bundle consisting of various articles, e.g., clothing, firewood, an iron machete, a kit for *chandan* and mirror, and ask for the girl's hand. If the girl and her family did not grant his appeal, he would refuse to leave the premises. One informant said, "Sometimes the boy was severely beaten and was chased out by the girl's brothers. Sometimes the boy was stubborn and would not leave the place and even lie there wounded. If he survived all verbal and physical abuses, the village elders would ask the family to accept him." If a boy was overly keen on marrying a girl and the girl refused to respond, the boy might threaten her, "I shall do *nambothaba*." An informant (male) added, "It is not an easy thing to go through all this humiliation. After all, society respects the love of the boy." There have been no cases of *nambothaba* in this area since World War II. I have met one woman of seventy-five whose husband married her through *nambothaba*. She said, "I was the only child, so he came and became *yaoningba* (adopted son-in-law)."

Conflicts in Chenba

In the past, after a *chenba*, in the case of a disagreement between the two families, the Naya Panchayat would adjudicate to resolve the conflict. It still does in some cases. After *Yaoshang's Thabal Chombi* dance festivals, there is always a large increase in the number of *chenba* cases. In Thambalkhul with sixty-six households, there were six *chenba* cases during *Thabal Chombi* dance sessions in the spring of 1978. The social attitude towards *chenba* has undergone a change in recent times. In the past, the parents were aware of a boy's where a bouts. More recently, the parents are shocked at having to deal with an unknown family. Some outraged parents approach the police to have the couple arrested, and sue the boy on kidnapping charges. If the kidnapping motive is proved, the boy may have to serve time in prison under section 366 of the Indian Penal Code. The civil court in Imphal is kept busy with hundreds of *chenba* cases from all over the Valley.

The confusion arises because of the prevailing custom of *thaba*, abduction for marriage, found among the Meitei. Very often the boy's family tries to establish a *thaba* case as a *chenba*. On the other hand, an unwilling girl's family would like to prove a real *chenba* case as a *thaba*. If the girl is a minor, the boy may face possible criminal charges. A woman gynaecologist at Imphal said, "I am called to examine the girl to determine her age and to say if she is a virgo intacta. However, the ruptured hymen may not be a proof of loss of virginity. So we just say whether the hymen is ruptured or not." During *Thabal Chombi* sessions, she had to examine twenty girls in one month. They came from all over the state. Otherwise, she has an average of five cases a month. If a girl refuses the examination, the court returns the girl to the parents, because her adulthood (18) has not been established. An advocate at Imphal civil court said, "There are some real kidnapping cases and even rape after kidnapping. But the girls are too ashamed to admit a rape in front of the court. They are also afraid to face society after everything... Unless a girl comes from a rich and influential family, she may not have the courage to refuse the man ... I have seen six *thaba* cases where in each case the girl refused to accept the man. The girls' families had high status and they later married without any problem. Otherwise, a *laishabi* is not considered a *laishabi* after a *chenba* or *thaba* and she has no hope of getting a *pakhang* (bachelor) as her husband. Only once-married men would like to marry her." He added, "Sometimes an outspoken girl can also lose the sympathy of the jury... Some pretty girls flirt with several boys and one of the boys, a pig-headed type, may try to do *thaba* to win her over."

Although a large number of *chenba/thaba* cases come to the court, very few await judgement for resolving the conflict. One informant said, "We Meiteis are like pumpkin creepers, entangled with relatives from all over. You can always find a friend or a relative among the opponent group." The friends and relatives also put pressure on the girl's family and try to get the matter reconciled out of court." Sometimes it is really difficult to determine whether the girl went of her own will and changed her mind under pressure from her family, or whether the girl was kidnapped and changed her mind under pressure from the boy's family or from a sense of shame.

During my stay in May 1978, a violent abduction took place in Nambol area. A Brahman girl of twenty was dragged out of a minibus by a boy of twenty-five and a group of his friends who were armed and held the other passengers and the driver at gunpoint. The girl's mother who had accompanied her screamed and cried for help in vain.

The girl's family reported the kidnapping to the police. The boy was from a rich family living in a village four miles from Nambol. They searched for them unsuccessfully—some say the police were bribed by the boy's family. Eventually, the couple was discovered and during *machinghangba* (interrogation) the girl told her family that she had come on her own. This outraged them for it was an insult to all their endeavours, and they tried to no avail to change her mind. At this, they cut off their relationship with her. Two weeks later, however, a relative of the girl received Rs. 3000 from the boy's relatives and arranged a grand *luhungba* ceremony at the *mandapa* in the girl's village. The couple arrived for the wedding and were married by a Brahman priest. The male relative acted as the girl's father; her family did not join the festivities. Amidst the din of the band I saw the groom walking with a group of men and women as honoured person behind the *dolai* (carriage) of the bride. I was surprised and asked a villager, "How can they approve of such an ill-made match?" He answered, "The girl has agreed, and is happy. Why should anyone else disapprove now?" After speaking to several people there, I realized that a boy who commits *thaba* is not really considered a low individual to be despised. In this case the girl knew the boy for some time, but was not eager to accept him as her boyfriend. The boy lost his patience and kidnapping was his solution. It may not be the right thing to do, but it is not considered the worst. One man said, "When a man kidnaps a girl, he does it not to rape her, but to have her as his lawful wife." Some people show sympathy for a rejected lover who commits *thaba* out of desperation.

Eight months after this case in Nambol, I received a letter from my assistant: "Five months after the marriage the girl has left her husband. She came to her parents and they have accepted her back without comment."

I heard of six more cases of *thaba* in Nambol area, which occurred in the past five years. In three cases the girls refused to accept the men as their husbands. In two cases the girls married the men, but divorced them after some time. In one instance the girl remained married because her very poor family had accepted bride-price from the man's family. However, parental support can often provide a girl with the courage to refuse in a *thaba* situation. In Thambalkhul I met a soft-spoken school teacher (26) working on her loom after teaching hours. Her younger sister later told me the following story:

Two years earlier, a village farmer kidnapped her and took her to a faraway village. The boy's family sent three men for *haidokpa* but the girl's father refused to communicate with them. He demanded to see the girl at once. The boy was illiterate while the girl was a college graduate. The boy's family could not find them until they returned three days later and the girl's family came for *machingh ingba*. Her cousins and her sisters accompanied the married women, although it is unusual for unmarried girls to do so; both sisters of the girl were educated and persistent about seeing the girl. The sister said, "When we entered the room, we saw the man lying on the bed and my sister lying by him. I immediately realized she was no longer a virgin. We spoke in English so that the illiterate man could not understand us. I said, 'Be honest and tell us the truth.' 'I am not a *lai-shabi* any more,' she replied. 'I have become a *mou*. So I have decided to accept him as my husband.' They left to explain the situation to the girl's mother who was outraged, entered the room, and began to beat the girl, saying, "Did I send you to college to become a slave to an illiterate farmer?" The members of the boy's family stopped her. The other women failed to persuade the girl to return with them. The girl kept telling them she was ashamed to go back. The boy's family had told her that once a *chenba* had occurred, there was no returning with honour, and had app ied much pressure. Bitter, her father and uncle—both illiterate farmers—could not sleep all night knowing she had been taken by force. Two days later the father went to the boy's house very early in the morning and called out for the girl. Before anyone could stop her, she ran out to meet him. He took hold of her and dragged her out of the compound. The boy's family tried to pull her back, but the girl did not want to leave her father. He brought her home and told her, "You can stay as a single woman forever, but you musn't take this brute for your husband." The boy's parents ventured to negotiate and settle the matter, but the girl found enough courage to yell at them to get out. The boy is still single. He spread gossip that the girl changed her mind after she had agreed to and carried out the *chenba*. The sister said, "People talk about her, and that makes her so reserved."

I found in most situations girls are too confused to do anything. The friends of a girl yell and report the incident to her family. In a number of cases the boy's friends plead with the girl to accept him as her husband. Sometimes the elders of a boy's family are overcome with the anxiety that their son may be charged with kidnapping and they plead with the girl. In one such case, the old father of the boy prostrated himself in front of the girl asking her to forgive his son and accept him as her husband. The girl said, "I was so embarrassed when such an old man acted like that, I had to say 'Yes'." Later, when the girl was returned to her father's home for the arrangement of a proper wedding, she changed her mind. When the old father came to plead again, the girl was busy weaving. She chased after the man with her *taren* (a long, flat stick used for weaving), saying, "If you come again I will kill you. You are as bad as your son."

The victim of a *thaba* is always a *laishabi*. Married women do not worry about being kidnapped. But occasionally a married man may do *thaba* to get a new wife.

While an average Meitei girl may look forward to having a *chenba* with her boyfriend, fear of becoming a victim to *thaba* lingers in her mind. In the daytime girls travel freely in public, but in the evening, it is almost a forbidden freedom. Girls are seldom found alone. They group together in work, play and travel. In the daytime the girls bicycle around the village roads and bazaar, but they refuse to participate in anything after dark. It is considered improper and unsafe for girls to go out in the dark even though the well-lit bazaar might be crowded with mature women.

Polygyny

Polygyny is an accepted custom among the Meitei. Colonial writers like Dunn (1886, reprinted 1975), Hodson (1908, reprinted 1975), Grimwood (1891) mention a wide acceptance of polygyny among the royal clan and the urban elite but find it a rarity in rural areas.

At present some Meitei male writers strongly support the custom. L.I. Singh (1963) supports polygyny, but describes a woman's later marriage as concubinage. N. Tombi Singh (1975:168) describes the ideal of a first wife: "... She wanted to be a good wife ... took all sufferings to herself ... She never raised a finger against her husband. Naturally as the time passed she became the supreme authority. The younger wives were frequently divorced and reunited. Kalachand (husband) did not have much faith in them in later years. He took only Lalita (first wife) into his confidence and gave her all the powers for domestic administration."

This male fantasy of a happy polygynous marriage is far from reality in Meitei society. At the turn of the century, Hodson remarked on the frequent tension and unhappiness in polygynous homes. Today, polygyny is most prevalent in urban areas, and one can seldom find the model of an ideal first wife. A young lady, a government employee, reeled off a list of forty educated polygynous men. The list included names of political office bearers, the principal of a college, engineers, Brahman pundits and so on. A male college professor remarked about an engineer, "He is a clever man with a great sense of discipline. He bought seven radios for seven wives." I gathered that the engineer now has thirty-five children. In the capital, women sometimes refer to another woman as so-and-so's second wife. Recently one M.B.B.S. doctor became the second wife of a politician. In most polygynous marriages, the wives live separately in different homes. If the first wife has grown-up children, especially sons, she has every chance of staying in the husband's home and the younger wives either live with their parents or in their own houses. The husband then becomes an occasional visitor in the second wife's home.

When men with children take new wives, disruption of the family is a common occurrence. The fathers often drift away from their children. The case of Sanahambi portrays an urban family in this situation.

Sanahambi is a college educated woman in her mid-fifties. Her husband was a foreign trained engineer. She had a *chenba* followed by a *luhungba* about twenty years ago, and had two sons. The couple was happy till the woman came to know of her husband's interest in an uneducated young girl from a poor family. The engineer did not want to leave his wife so he had the girl stay at her own parents' home. The wife was a modern woman, educated outside of Manipur, and she refused to accept the arrangement. When she found that the young girl was pregnant, she asked her husband to leave. She told me the only reason she could manage this was their house had been built on her land inherited from her mother. "Our two sons are with me," she said, "when I am gone they will have the house."

"I know you will marry soon," said her husband, "and the boys will be deprived of everything."

"Even though the girl was pregnant," Sanahambi told me, "he had no intention of marrying her. He didn't even have a *chenba* with her. He was so desperate to have this clear that he hired a man to be a surrogate father at the ritual of *shastipuja* to be performed six days after the birth of a child. The ritual is considered essential for the identification of the baby's *yek* and *yumnak*. I realized his plans of exploiting both the girl and myself and told him I could not live with him. When he understood I meant it and there was no hope for us to be together, he went away to live with the girl. She eventually had several children with him. He introduces her to people as his wife, but people still gossip about their anti-social behaviour (cohabitation without even a *chenba*)."

The engineer had wanted both the sons of his first wife, but every time he took them away they would sneak back to their mother. I asked her why she did not consider remarriage. "My only interest," she replied "is to bring up my boys. They have lost their father to that woman. I don't want them to feel they have lost me too."

When I asked whether she found people sympathetic, she told me, "Only some women, who have real feelings about me. Most of my husband's male friends turned against me. In the beginning they said I was too stubborn, I should accept the girl into my house. They found no fault with his behaviour because he was willing to keep the girl in a separate house. Eventually they spread a lot of gossip about me to prove that I was an unworthy wife... My sons have grown up to be nicely educated young men. When I visit Khwaribond bazaar the *imas* (mother, address for an older woman) come to praise me. 'You have done the right thing,' they tell me. 'People will love you because you have proved yourself to be a good mother.' It makes me feel really satisfied. I started in a government job after my separation. I was hurt badly by my husband, but now I am reaping rich rewards from my life."

Another woman (35) said, "I did not want to leave my home. But he hadn't room enough to keep two wives. He just made a partition inside our bedroom. At night I could hear all the noises. It was too humiliating. So I left with my two kids." A trader (37) in Laxmi bazaar said, "I refused to have sex with him after he slept with the other woman. I left him. He came for reconciliation many times and then he started to come on the pretext of seeing our daughter (10). I said, 'If you come again I shall cut off your penis.' Now he sees her in the school." An educated first wife said:

My husband is fifty and a high official in the government. I am an M.A. and I used to teach in school. My husband had a *chenba* with a young teacher; she has a B.A. I will not allow her in my house. I have four children after I had a love marriage and a proper *luhungba*."
"Why did you not go to court?" I asked.
"What will I gain by going to court? He lives here and visits her. I will not engage in sex with him now, and I have no respect for him. I told him that it is *my* house and if that woman comes here I will murder her. My in-laws support me in this."

Most women express a deep feeling of hurt and loss of honour when their husbands take other wives. After some years of marriage, when the husband does a *chenba*, the household experiences a terrible storm expressed in verbal abuse, shouting and crying. Frequently, the women diviners are kept busy with a large clientele of frustrated wives. Women with grown-up children are strong within the family and they seldom allow another woman in the house. Here are some responses of second wives:

"He brought me to this home, but his mother and the first wife did not allow me to enter the main house. My husband built a small hut at one corner of the compound. I had two children, but was still treated as an outsider." Eventually the woman left her husband and took special training to become a police constable.
A school teacher living separately said, "It was the greatest mistake of my life. I have two kids, still I have no right in my husband's house. He lives there, my mother-in-law refuses to baby-sit my children. I feel helpless."

Men give several reasons for taking a second wife. "She (first wife) is a very dominating wife"; "She has no male child"; "She is barren"; "She neglects me."
However one young man (32) spoke of his own misery in a polygynous marriage. He keeps his second wife in her parents' house.

He said, "I am living in a hell. Both of my wives work and have good earnings. Neither cares about me. My children, by either wife, are too distant from me. I feel so insecure. It was a great mistake to involve myself in two marriages." My informant commented, "He must really be miserable. Meitei men are usually too proud to talk this way."

But a retired government officer (60) spoke to me of his happy polygynous family. "I have four wives. Two live in my own house (the downstairs floor is for the first, the upstairs is for the second). The women were attracted to me because of my social position, I am an S.D.C. officer and I accepted them. I follow a rule of living one month at a time with each woman. All of my wives earn good money by trading. I provide for my twelve children's clothing and education. In my house I rest in my first wife's room. She is the cleverest of all and gets the maximum money for her children."

A Meitei proverb expresses women's prejudice against second wives: "Why should I be a second wife? I do not even want to be grass in a compound where a second wife lives." (Bhogendra, 1976: 597). In the market gossip, in daily conversation at the shangoi, the role of a second wife is rather ambivalent. A woman who decides to be a second wife is often held in suspicion by first wives. Older women who chose to be second wives in their early years often blame their misjudgement. Some are embarrassed to even talk about it, if the subject is brought up in the company of women. Popular notion dictates that the first wife is always good, and the other always evil, a *hinchhabi* (witch). In my study area, almost all second wives come from different villages which are frequently far from the husband's village. It is rather rare for a woman of the same village to become a second wife, for fear of lack of support from the fellow women.

Three women traded some gossip with me: An ex-*pradhan* of a village (48) took a second wife. His first had borne a son, and she agreed to have the other woman in her compound on the condition that she cook in another kitchen. The woman had a son a year after she moved in. Since the first wife had been a daughter of the village she married in, all the women neighbours there were her friends and relatives, and they made every effort to make the second wife, who was from another village, feel miserable and unwelcome. Eventually she left with her baby.

The three women told me this story with zealous enthusiasm. One of them said, "Look. If all the women around you treat you badly and make no place for you, what can your husband do to make you welcome? She (the second wife) was unhappy here anyway. . . It serves her right!'' They told me that they chased out the second wife of another man in very much the same way. Throughout the whole conversation the first wife of the ex-*pradhan* was silent. I asked her why she did not consider leaving her husband after all that he had done. ''I have a sixteen-year-old son,'' she said. ''He goes to school here. I could not leave him . . . Things are all right now; we have peace at home.''

The romantic ballads of Khamba-Thoibi and other legends of Langol (incarnation of the divine couple) express the concept of monogamous love with no room for a third person. Women's most common reason for leaving the husband after he takes another woman is, ''I had no peace of mind''. Older wives seek solace in their grown up children, especially sons. Younger women search for renewed comfort from another husband, and are left with little choice other than becoming a second wife of another man.

In rural areas polygyny is the exception rather than the rule. Even in urban centres a large number of second wives lead households of their own without any male head. These women pursue their own profession or trade. Husbands contribute some money (sometimes none) for the children. The second wife as a ''single woman'' has an independent life style and is not under the direct authority of the husband. The husband, as would an occasional boy friend or lover, visits without making too much demand on her time. In the capital, several professional women, e.g., doctors, *sankirtana* singers, Vaisnavite dancers, chose to be second wives though some of them were *laishabis* (unmarried maidens) and could have become first wives. In rural areas most of the second wives have established trades. Some of them end up with a husband living uxorilocally, because the husband's first wife and her sons refuse to allow him to live there with his new wife. In many cases a woman becomes the second wife without a ceremony, and merely cohabits after a *chenba*. A woman who becomes a mistress without a *chenba* is called *oktabi* (lustful) or *kasubi* (prostitute).[52]

I met Ibeyamma, whose case can give some insight into the lives of other single women like her.

---

[52]*Kasubi* is an imported Hindi word. There is no Meitei term for prostitute.

Ibeyamma Devi (30) is a Brahman woman. She had wanted to marry a Meitei boy she knew but her parents forced her into marrying another Brahman. "I couldn't look at his face," she said, "he was kind to me but I still hated him." After two years she left her husband to *chenba* with her former lover, who had, in the meantime, already married two other women. Since her parents disapproved of this *chenba*, Ibeyamma had no *loukhotpa*. Her second husband built her a small house where she now lives alone and he visits her often. I asked if he gave her any money for personal expenses. She giggled and answered, "How can he? He earns only Rs. 350 a month [as an office employee]. His first wife is a nice woman. But the second is really like a *hinchhabi*, demanding money from him all the time. He brings fish or gifts for me whenever he finds some extra money. He's so nice! Sometimes he'll cook for me too."

Ibeyamma is a skilled *munga inafi* weaver. She makes about Rs. 450 a month and says she is happy with her marital arrangement. In her small house she keeps her loom in the *mangol* and keeps the one room well decorated and clean. She is very good friends with another divorced Meitei woman who, like her, is a skilled weaver. The two women are so close that they often share the same rice plate in spite of Ibeyamma's belonging to the Brahman caste. The divorced friend left her husband when he took a second wife. She came to her parents' home with three of her children. Her father gave her a room but later she constructed for herself a separate room and kitchen in the same compound as her brother. When her mother died her father married a widow and moved away to his wife's house.

Ibeyamma has no children and so she is bringing up one of her brother's sons. About her friend she said, "We are so close that some of our other friends tease us by saying we are like an *anichappa* [couple]." Ibeyamma's friend is now taking care of her brother's three children and his wife. The brother, a carpenter, left home nine years ago to go to Cachhar and never returned. She said, "We think he has taken a second wife there. This wife is not very clever in earning. She takes care of the six children, her three and my three, and cooks, and I work hard to make money for all of us."

The three women appear to be very sweet and tender with each other. They frequently make fun of each other, women who became second wives, although Ibeyamma is a third wife. I asked why she had not minded becoming one. "I would have been the first wife," she said, "but our luck kept us apart. What can I do?!"

The consensus of bazaar women on matters important to them exerts a strong pressure against women's anti-social behaviour. The gossip constantly going its round helps sustain a standard of proper behaviour.[53]

The Meitei show a generally tolerant attitude towards deviant behaviour, e.g., homosexuality, lesbianism, etc. About a woman with a bad reputation, one old man (80) said, "If a woman behaves like a *kasubi*, people will hate her, but they will not make her an outcast or denounce her forever. If she improves her nature, people will forgive her past." A woman with an illegitimate pregnancy may develop a sense of shame after becoming an object of gossip, but her child will not face any social stigma provided a surrogate father can officiate during *shastipuja* and give him a lineage and clan identification. In some cases the child becomes known as the "son of such-and-such" (mother's name). There was a famous *sankirtana* singer during Maharaj Churachand's reign who became known by his mother's name.[54]

An eighty-five-year-old midwife in my study area provided a picture of harsh reality for women facing unwanted pregnancy. She said, "I have done it [abortion] on thousands of divorcees, widows and unmarrieds. I received Rs. 30 to 40 for each one." Although children are so valuable in this society, the large number of abortions (perhaps somewhat exaggerated by the midwife) is indicative of the stigma attached to women's lax morality.

Khainaba or *Divorce*

The social scene associated with polygyny changes in the rural area. Most marriages split up after the husband marries another

---

[53]In the past, until 1696, the Paja court (women's court) awarded the most severe punishment *khungoinaba* for the gravest offences (e.g., murder and abortion) to women criminals by exposing them at the market centres. The chronicles describe how a woman should be ordered to stand with shaven head and half-naked, with only a tiny loin cloth, and how in this state of humiliation made to walk through the women's market centres. (Hodson 1908, reprinted 1975 : 88; Johnstone 1896 : 138).

[54]The singer's biological father came from an RK family who refused to accept the mother. When the singer achieved a high social status for the excellence of his performance, the King arranged a special ceremony to offer him the clan and family name of Ningthouja of the RK's.

woman.[55] An old proverb expresses the dilemma of divorce and successive remarriages of women. "How can one know the permanent shed of a cow and the *yumnak* (lineage name) of a woman?" (Bhogendra, 1976 : 761). In Radhagram, of 256 households, there are only three polygynous families. The common mode of married life is based on a monogamous union, although both sexes may marry a number of times in their lifetime. *Khainaba* means separation of the couple. Very few women take any legal procedure for *khainaba*; instead, they just abandon the husbands' homes. If a woman has older sons, she may team up with them and manage to "push out" the husband from the family compound, as happened in the following case:

Harimati Devi, a fifty-five-year-old divorced woman with grown up sons, lives in her family house with the youngest of them. He has a wife, a son and daughter, and two infant children. His occupation is carpentry and matmaking. Her older son, also a carpenter and mat maker, lives with his family in the same compound but in a separate home. There are also two other houses belonging to Harimati's brother-in-law's sons. All four families share a very large *shangoi* stretching across the courtyard facing all the houses. Harimati works as an intermediary between the nearby village weavers and agents outside the neighbourhood. She prefers to work in her own village because of her two baby grandchildren who need to be cared for when their mother is busy weaving. When I arrived at her house she was nursing her two-year-old grandson. Her daughter-in-law had the other baby bound to her back, and she was working with her partner on a flyshuttle. "My daughter-in-law came from Ishok village, a fishing community. When she came she knew only how to catch and dry fish and how to weave a fishing net. But she is a clever girl, and learned to weave in a short time. Now she earns for our food," she said. Harimati spoke rather theatrically. A group of women and children gathered in the compound and laughed at her speech.

"My husband married a second woman," she said, "a widow—six or seven years ago. When he brought that wife to live here my sons

---

[55]Ch. Buddhi Singh's study of the fishing communities of Thanga (1972) shows that the common mode of marriage is based on monogamous union. He indicates a high percentage of separation because of the husband's second marriage.

'pushed' both of them out. Now he lives as a *yaongingba*[56] at his second wife's house." This statement seemed to amuse her listeners greatly. Her husband was also a carpenter. The sons were quite well established in the profession themselves, so they stood up for their mother against him.

The life stories of Ngambi, Nayansakhi, Laxmipriya and Chamusana show varied experiences in the lives of women after a divorce.

Ngambi Devi (56) is a divorced woman living in her parent's compound. She was born and married in the same village. Her first husband was a cultivator who died after she had a son. Remaining in her in-laws' home, she remarried. Her son by her first marriage was taken care of by her first husband's family. Her second husband was a hired labourer. When he took another wife (a divorced, successful trader), Ngambi returned to her deceased parents' home to live with her brothers, who built her a small room of her own with a separate kitchen. At this point her first son came to live with her. Ngambi was a weaver in her youth and had begun trade in vegetables before her separation with her second husband. She continued this trade at her father's house. Her son now works as a hired labourer during the agricultural season.

Nayansakhi Devi (65), a divorcee, said that her first husband had been a man from a neighbouring village, who died when her daughter was only two years old. She came back to her parents' home. Her father gave her a share of land, a room and a separate kitchen. This made her brothers very angry and they tried in vain to "push her out." Two years later she remarried and her daughter was brought up by her parents. After she had another daughter by her second husband, he married another woman, at which time Nayansakhi divorced him and came again to her father for shelter. The husband supplied money to feed their daughter until the girl died. She now has a betel shop in front of her father's house and earns Rs. 250 a month from it. Her first daughter has also become a divorcee and is living with her. She maintains herself and her son with a separate income from trading vegetables and has a separate kitchen. The woman has been taking care of her old father since her mother's death. "My brothers are very jealous of me," she said.

---

[56] *Yaongingba* is a term for an incoming son-in-law. The woman used the term in a derogatory way, because here the man is living in his wife's home (not in his father-in-law's home), as an adopted (i.e. incoming) husband.

Laxmipriya Devi (38), a woman from Thambalkhul, goes to Churachandpur (twenty-five kms. by bus) to sell vegetables from her home village. She also buys certain articles, e.g., firewood and vegetables, at Churachandpur and sells them at Nambol bazaar. She earns about Rs. 10 a day, and owns no land.

This woman returned to her parents after four years of her first marriage, remarried five years later, and then returned again after two years. Since then she had been living with her mother. She had a separate house and a kitchen in the family compound, but then her mother died and she took in her orphaned niece and nephew, who had been living with her mother. The niece (17) earns about Rs. 175 by weaving. The little boy goes to school. The woman borrowed money at five percent interest from a bazaar women's *marup* (credit association) to buy a loom for her niece.

Chamusana Devi (50) is a trader involved in the buying of woven products from the surrounding villages for sale to outside traders. She lives with her divorced daughter (29) along with three more younger children. The daughter is a very fine weaver and earns on an average Rs. 375 a month, and offers instruction in weaving as well. About fifteen years ago, Chamusana's husband left his family for a new wife. Five years later, he came back and after Chamusana gave birth to a son, he left her again and went to live with his second wife. Chamusana's daughter married a man from Imphal and then discovered he had two other wives. She returned to her mother three months after the wedding. Now, the mother and daughter live together and uphold the family finances.

Khainaba *Rule*

In the past, if a man or a woman wanted *khainaba*, he or she approached the village *chowkidar*. With the help of the village *hanjaba* and other elders, the *chowkidar* tried to bring about a reconciliation. If a woman wanted *khainaba* to marry another man, her second husband had to pay *nupimamal* (price of a woman) of Rs. 50 to the first husband. If the husband demanded *khainaba* where the wife was not at fault, the wife could take all movable property with her "except his loin cloth." After a *khainaba* the wife's family could demand the return of her original dowry. According to the rules, the woman should leave all her children behind except the suckling child.

At present, Naya Panchayat, a branch of the village Panchayat, takes care of *khainaba* cases. The custom of payment of nupimamal is not in vogue any longer. A woman is eligible to take all of her *stridhan,* her own earnings and her dowry, with her. A village man said, "If a husband finds his wife committing adultery, he may force the man to marry his wife. This is the most honourable way to get rid of an unfaithful wife." I did not find any such cases in my area. A majority of *khainaba* cases arise from the husband's taking a new wife, though I encountered some cases where the wives were attracted to other men and decided to leave their husbands. When a husband takes a second wife, in an urban family, the conflict continues for a extended period. But in my rural area, the first wife simply refuses to accept the situation and leaves for her parents' home. The *khainaba* wife's parents send a group of young men to the husband's house with a truck to bring back the dowry. Though the law permits the man to retain custody of children, that is seldom done. In a majority of the cases, the children live with the mother, and if the mother remarries they live with the mother's mother. Traditional custom lays down that a divorcee or a widow cannot adopt a child without the husband's consent. Several divorcees adopt children of their natal families in an informal arrangement without paying attention to the legal customs.

In my study area, one out of three first marriages ends in divorce and it is common for a woman to remarry after a divorce. But in her remarriage, she may not have much choice other than becoming a second or third wife of a man, unless she finds a widower. A Meitei proverb says, "It is better to have dried fish than to marry a woman who was married before."

A *khainaba* woman cannot expect to marry a bachelor. It is considered almost unethical for a *mou* to marry a *pakhang* (bachelor). Women with older children seldom remarry.

Although the Pandit Loishang condemns widow marriage for a *piba,* the lineage head, I found little prejudice against it. One old man (85) of Nambol said, "In my youth the Brahmans warned us against marrying widows. They said if one married a widow, his ancestors would live in hell. Very few people followed their advice." In my area several young widows were helped even by their in-laws in their remarriage. The in-laws took care of the young children the widows left behind. Popular sentiment favours a close relationship between the children and their mother even when she is remarried and lives away from them. Older women are often reunited with grown up sons and daughters. At the time of a marriage, the presence of the groom's mother is of high importance in the *kujabawa* ritual. Remarried mothers are called back to take part in this. My informant told me of a touching event in an urban family:

Premavati was twenty when she left her husband, who was a drunkard and had beaten her often. She gave her four-year-old son to her husband's elder brother's wife, saying, "I have no means with which to bring him up. I trust you and I know you will bring him up as your own child." She then returned to her parents, who were very poor. She worked hard, training to be a midwife and nurse, and eventually became the second wife of another man. This husband lives separately with his first wife and children, though he visits her often.

Premavati's son grew up to be an educated young man. His father remarried, but he was brought up by his aunt as his mother had wished. She had hardly been in touch with him because she was too afraid to come into contact with her brutal ex-husband. When the boy planned marriage, he demanded the presence of his real mother at the wedding, for the *kujabawa* ritual. His father protested vehemently: "She left you an orphan and never kept in touch. I will not allow her in the house after she has done this to you." His relatives, however, persuaded his father to change his mind. They said, "You cannot deny the fact that she gave birth to him." So Premavati came to the wedding and sat with tears rolling down her cheeks, her eyes fixed on her son throughout the entire ceremony. The women around her were so moved by this that they all cried along with her. After the wedding she blessed the couple and left.

"I met her two months after the wedding," my informant added. "Premavati looked very happy. She told me, 'My son sometimes comes to me and gives me rides in his new jeep. He is such a fine boy.' "

Life Cycle of Meitei Women

The four different terms used for the four phases of a woman's life have both economic and social significance. In the economic context, I have already noted the significance of these stages of life in relation to different options available to women for earning an income or being usefully employed. These options depend on and vary according to their social roles.

Macha Nupi (Little Woman). Up to the age of four, there is very little difference in the socialization of children. Boys and girls who play together roam naked, with jingling ankle bangles, earrings and *chandan* marks on their foreheads. *Afaba angang* (good child) is the term used to praise children of both sexes. Around the age of four during *nahutpa* (ear-piercing ritual), the boys and girls are dressed differently, but they still play together, "like small calves", as a Meitei expression has it.

From the age of five, gender identification becomes prominent. The boys wear shorts and shirts (traditional dresses on special occasions). The girls wear tiny *faneks* with blouses. The two games common among the little girls are *chak thombi* (cooking) and *kaithel kabi* (trading in the bazaar). They also start playing with dolls in male and female dresses and sometimes represent three generations with the dolls, grandparents, parents and babies. They imitate marriage ceremonies. Girls move together in groups, sometimes two or three under one shawl. In a creche in Nambol (age group from five to seven) boys and girls always play separately. The girls huddle together and yell to defend themselves if any aggressive boy comes to attack one of them.

From the age of nine, the *macha nupis* start helping in housework along with older girls in cleaning utensils, washing clothes, pounding rice, and tending babies. Groups of young girls walk along the village paths to fetch drinking water. Little girls are seen following them with smaller pitchers and buckets in hand. A ten-year-old *macha nupi* may be responsible for domestic chores as well as for some help in the rice field.

In both Radhagram and Thambalkhul, the children of both sexes below puberty (6-12) are enrolled in school.

Laishabi (Who Moves Like a Flower Maiden). After puberty a girl is called a *laishabi* until her marriage. In pre-war days the *laishabis* wore *fanek* above their breast and also wore bangles to mark their transition from the stage of *macha nupi* to *laishabi*. Nowadays, a younger *laishabi* may dress with a blouse and *fanek* wrapped at the waist line. The more developed, older ones are expected to have a shawl (*inafi* or *khudei matek*) over the blouse. The *laishabis* keep their hair open with flowers tucked behind their ears or wrapped in single hairs.

A *laishabi* learns to follow strict rules during her menstrual period.

A menstruating woman must not touch a cooking vessel or water pitcher for five days. After five days she takes a bath and must wash her daily clothes and bed linen. Most *laishabis* refrain from housework at this period and spend time in weaving.[67]

The *laishabis* band together in both social and economic activities. In Radhagram and Thambalkhul the *laishabis* have formed several associations for economic and recreational activities. The *laishabis* are not only active in organizing Thabal Chombi dances in the spring, they are also the most enthusiastic and competent group in fund-raising for drama presentations by professional *shumang leela* groups from Imphal, polo games, *pena* recitals, etc. I have already mentioned their involvement in the village Panchayat election campaign.

Rarely is a domestic chore performed by one *laishabi* alone. The girls manage to work together in daily routine chores, e.g., fetching water, washing clothes. In addition to their school (if they are still enrolled in school) *laishabis* help their mothers with housework, e.g. wiping of the earthen floor, cooking, pounding rice.

In daily behaviour *laishabis* appear shy in front of elders. Older women, especially mothers, scrutinise their proper conduct. A mother may beat an older *laishabi* if she does not approve of her behaviour. But in case of a *chenba*, the disciplinarian mother may be a girl's closest advisor and confidante. This mother-daughter bond continues to work for the rest of their lives.

As a daughter and younger sister, a *laishabi* must obey the authority of the father and elder brothers. However, some social license in the behaviour of the *laishabi* may be observed during *yaosong*, the spring festival. During the five days of the festival, *laishabis* enjoy an atmosphere of "ritual rebellion". The young girls need not be bashful and gentle; instead, they approach menfolk (even strangers) rather aggressively, demanding money and often robbing them of wrist-watches and glasses if they refuse to pay them. Men appear to tolerate the domineering behaviour of the unmarried girls without expressing humiliation.

Laishabis help each other by exchanging messages and letters from boyfriends. They also guide each other in choosing a partner. Once a

---

[57]*Shumang leela* is a style of theatre originally brought in from Calcutta during the time of King Chandrakirti in the latter half of the nineteenth century. These are all-male theatre groups.

young man stopped my informant to complain against the friends of his girl friend. He was on his way to a shaman to seek help. He said, "I know she cares for me, but her girl friends always guard her against me. I have no chance to meet her alone."

Despite some economic independence and relative freedom outside her home, a *laishabi's* life is under strict control and is expected to meet the standard of conduct. She must be extremely careful about men and avoid meeting a boy friend alone. Any public display of affection might raise questions about her virginity. A notorious reputation may well spoil her chances to marry a bachelor. A Meitei proverb advises a woman to win a fight with a powerful man by her gentle, feminine ways, not by counter-violence: "A soft piece of bamboo can tie a bundle of strong firewood. A woman's sweet words can control a harsh man." The girls employ pleading and crying for self-defence and resort to rather oblique tactics to defy male domination, especially during *chenba* and *thaba*. I found an interesting case of a *laishabi* who was forced to marry a man she was not in love with:

A girl of sixteen was very much in love with a boy of twenty-two from a neighbouring village. The girl's family did not approve because he came from the same *yek* (clan) as she. They hurriedly arranged a marriage for her and received Rs. 3,000 as bridewealth. The girl cried for days in vain and I attended her wedding only to find the contrast of a gloomy face in a bright wedding dress.

Two weeks later my assistant hurried to me with the news: "She was such a well-behaved girl! No one would have thought she could be so violent. On her wedding night at her husband's home she kicked the man away when he came to her bed. 'You are a thief!' she cried. 'You bought me with money because my family is poor when you knew whom I really loved . . . ' The girl's boy friend came from the same village as her husband, and since her marriage he had gone away. The man pleaded with the girl but she yelled, 'I am afraid of my father and uncles, but I am not afraid of you. If you touch me, I shall kill you. I shall kill myself.' The boy's family was greatly embarrassed. All the neighbours knew what had happened and it was a real scandal. The girl's family was in trouble too, for they spent most of the bridewealth on dowry for the girl. They tried to convince her that she must accept her lawful husband. When they talk to her, she says nothing, she just cries. Eventually the girl returned home without consummation of her marriage."

I heard of an arranged marriage in Imphal where on her wedding night the bride (23) did not feel attracted to her husband. So she told him that she was menstruating and he would have to wait for five days. She said, "I was stalling for time. On the fifth day I took a bath and cooked delicious dinner with *ukabi* fish for the family. When my husband and other family members were busy enjoying the dinner, I ran about three miles to reach my parents' home. I refused to go back to my husband." The girl's in-laws were so offended that they returned her dowry "even the *ngarubaks*" (baskets for storing dried fish). Later the girl opened a betel stall and adopted her brother's son.

Mou (Wife or Once-Married Woman). The bonds of childhood change after a *laishabi* becomes a *mou*. Although most of the *laishabis* in my area married close to their natal homes, their life style changed after their marriage. Married daughters are not bound by any ritual obligation for ancestor worship and other rites to their natal home, unless the woman is an only child. But a married woman has to meet social obligations to her parents' home and must offer *potpang* to all family rituals. In Radhagram and Thambalkhul married women contribute to *marups*, with a view to saving for their parents' rites in the future. The husbands are often jealous of wives' friends of unmarried years. Married women tend to form friendships with other married women of the neighbourhood, though the old friendships do not fade. During the ritual of *Ningon Chakoba* in November, married daughters are invited to their natal home for sumptuous feasts and are offered gifts. *Ningon Chakoba* corresponds to the North Indian *Bhratridvitiya*, a ritual performed by sisters wishing good health to their brothers. On this day brothers are fed by their sisters, who greet them by putting dots on their forehead with several things, e.g., sandalwood paste, curd, lamp black from the wick of an oil lamp and morning dew collected from the grass. The brothers offer gifts to the sisters. In the past, the Meitei had observed this day as in the rest of North India. King Chandrakirti (1834-1844 and 1850-1886) ordered that the pattern of ritual be reversed and that it henceforth be Ningon Chakoba (daughters' feast) day.

In July, during *Rathajatra* festival, there is a special day for *Ningon*

Pali, for their daughters' obligation to join in a *nupi-pala* session. In Radhagram, all married daughters must visit the temple during the annual *Lai Harouba* festival. The villagers say, "This will bring prosperity in their own homes and families and bring children to them."

Thus, through the calendrical rituals and community feasts, old friends do continue to meet, but they have to find new friends in their husband's neighbourhood and team up with them for *khulong* (rice cultivation team), *eepal lokpa* (fishing team), *marup* (credit association), and other economic activities.

A newly married woman is affectionately called *mou anobi* (new wife). As a *mou anobi* or *mou,* a woman follows a certain code of behaviour within her family compound. She shows some sense of avoidance and respect towards her father-in-law and elder brother-in-law. She must not keep her hair down like a *laishabi,* but instead must put it in a bun. A Meitei woman does not wear any wedding mark to indicate her marital status. Nor does a *mou* have to cover her face or follow the rule of avoidance towards the other men of her husband's neighbourhood.

In my area, in most cases the bride is previously known to the husband's family. Even if the bride is a stranger, the *laishabis* and *mous* of the neighbourhood surround her with warmth and friendliness, and soon she finds a group of married women of her age group. A *mou anobi's* life is very much like that of a *laishabi* until she has a baby and has to prepare for a separate home and hearth. If she happens to be the wife of the youngest son, her role as an earner may create a special relationship between herself and her mother-in-law. When a mother-in-law and a daughter-in-law live together, there is mutual dependence. It is not at all unusual to see an old grandmother suckling her baby grandchild while the daughter-in-law is busy weaving. The old woman may well be responsible for selling the woven products. In the event of a son's second marriage, the old mother may not approve and the son may end up residing in his new wife's home.

Within a few years of her marriage, a *mou* starts a new household with her husband and young children. Now she has to take on the full responsibility of rice pounding and cooking, besides rearing the children, with little time left for weaving. Her labour is also needed in the family field. In fact most *mous* prefer to earn money and have a ready income by working extra hours in someone's rice field.

A young husband may wait a few years to assume the full responsibility of family head of a new household. Over the years of marriage, a husband's role gradually changes from that of a romantic lover to an authoritarian figure. The Meitei term for husband is *ipuroiba* (my lord) or *mapuroiba* (her lord).

I heard about a case in Radhagram, when an outraged husband chased a wife to beat her up. The wife's girl friends rushed and stood encircling her and said, "You have to touch us first before you touch her." They reported the brutality of the husband to the wife's family. The wife's family members came and took her back with them. After a few days, when the husband went to the wife's home (adjacent village) her male relatives threatened to beat him and told him not to come back. A brutal husband is also equally disliked by his community, though general opinion approves of a husband's dominating behaviour. In a Meitei home, husbands and wives sleep apart on two beds. The husband's bed is bigger and higher, called *phamjao*, and the wife's bed is smaller and lower, called *khuda*. One husband said, "My wife looks upon me as her god. She will bow to me if her foot touches mine." However, when I repeated these comments, some *mous* were amused. One said, "Yes, some lord he is! He sits there doing nothing and you just do *seva* (service to god)." In fact, this kind of remark about husbands is rather common among women. Men reminded me, often rather emphatically, of their roles as "lords" of their wives, but women never referred to their husbands as "lords." Whenever I brought up the subject, they giggled at the self-indulgent attitude of the men. Women would laugh and, caricaturing a prayer postur, say, "*seva koro, seva koro* (worship him, worship him)".

A Meitei family is based on the husband-wife economic team with mutual dependence and co-operation.[58] Marital conflict arises from suspicion of unfaithfulness on the part of one of the spouses. Confrontation between the couple comes in an indirect way. A woman's usual way of expressing discontent is to refrain from eating, even if she does the cooking for the family. A mother (30) of five children came to know of her husband's affair with another woman. She yelled at her twelve-year-old son, "When you grow up, you will marry two or three wives like some of those irresponsible men and your

---

[58]The mutual dependence of a couple is also found in the economy of the fishing communities of the Valley. Among the fishing communities in Lake Loktak area, a husband-wife fishing team is called *hiyeiba* (Ch. Buddhi Singh, 1972:205).

children will starve. Get out of my house. I do not want to have a son." The husband understood the situation and admitted his interest in the other woman. The wife came out in a violent rage, "If you bring another woman in this house I will kill her. I am not afraid of jail." The husband yelled back, "If you cannot be tolerant, you better get out of this house." She replied, "I have five children with two sons. This house belongs to me. You are the one who does not like this family. You get out." In this case the husband decided to give up the idea of another wife. However, when pleading, crying, yelling, or arguing does not work, a *mou's* last step is *mapanda chotpa* (going to my father's home). If a *mou* leaves her husband's household, this confirms her desire for *khainaba* (separation).

A husband sometimes exercises his authority by threatening his wife that he will take another wife if she does not obey him. Some *mous* said that when they wished to use contraceptives (after having four or five children), their husbands threatened then that they would marry again. A *mou* with sons has a strong hold on her husband's home and seldom leaves if the children are grown up.

In the case of a stable marriage, the husband and wife grow old together, with mutual dependence in social and economic spheres. Older husbands become less dominating and rather passive progressively. They engage in religious rites, attend religious sessions and scripture-reading in the community *mandapa*. Older *mous* as *hanubis*, in contrast, leave their compound for a much wider socio-spatial world and become most active.

Hanubi (Mature or Older Woman). As an older *mou* relieves herself of the domestic burden, she gradually expands her social and economic life. With the high rate of divorce (approximately thirty-three per cent in my data from Radhagram and Thambalkhul) some rural women do not really have a stronghold, a permanent base, until they reach this stage. A woman past the age of forty-five seldom considers remarriage. By this time she can settle down, according to her marital status as a wife, as a divorcee mother with her children, as a widow with her children, as a second wife in a polygynous household, as a second wife with a visiting husband, or in any other suitable role. This is the time of her life when she can don the managerial robe in the handling of the entire family finances.

As a mother, an older woman is emotionally closer to her children than her old husband, who has to adopt a rather restrained attitude in his authoritarian role in the family structure. A mother usually avoids physical punishment of her sons once they attain puberty, but she may continue disciplining her daughters long after this period. In case of a *chenba* of a son, a mother acts as the go-between between the father and the son. In the case of a daughter's *chenba*, the mother leads the women's group for interrogation during *machinhangba*.

I have already discussed how freedom of movement opens up new avenues of economic activities in a *hanubi's* life. This freedom also offers her various stimuli for socio-religious activities. In the market, the women team up for trading needs. Sometimes they travel in groups for several miles on foot or by bus. I have found some very old women who find it hard to be energetic in economic transactions but still continue to frequent the bazaar. A common excuse for these women (in their seventies or eighties) is, "If I sit at home I get headache and backache. I feel very lonely." The bazaar thus provides a social world for both younger and older *hanubis*. The *marup* is also an important institution for economic as well as social bonding. The *marup* members organize feasts, outdoor picnics, pilgrimages, scripture-reading sessions, *nupipala* groups, and other group activities. The *marups* at the bazaar provide an opportunity for making new contact for women. In the urban area, it is common for old mothers to open a tea stall in front of the house or trade in the market centres. One college professor gave me an insight into this aspect:

I was educated in Calcutta. When I came back to Manipur, I did not like my mother to go to bazaar and trade. I and my brother told her, "Look, you have two grown up sons. We will give you pocket money. You need not work." In a few month's time, there was no peace in the family. My wife was very unhappy. My mother was unhappy. She was bored and complaining about my wife. So we decided to build a small tea shop. She is now very happy, and enjoys meeting people in her stall. My children help her all the time. She takes my children to places in her leisure time. She has admitted my daughter to a famous *nupipala* group and escorts her to rehearsals regularly. My wife is very happy with the new arrangement.

Perhaps the professor had acquired a value typical of the North Indian upper caste culture. It did not work in the Meitei situation; the traditional mode of living offered an alternative life style for the aged mother.

Meitei women show an adaptability to different environments and to team up for social and economic survival. After moving out of her own village, the *mou anobi* (new bride) gradually finds an economic team (e.g., *marup, khulong* or *eepal lokpa* teams) and also moral backing from her age group in her husband's community (e.g., the case of wife-beating).

As the social horizon expands, a woman, as a *hanubi*, adapts herself to the larger world beyond the village boundary. Here, too, she is not alone, but invariably is a member of a group.

My meetings with several groups of women traders of *shumang leela*[59] associations in Imphal revealed some important aspects of women's interdependence. In one association, I met eleven performers of whom ten had had unhappy experiences in marriage. One woman said, "We needed something to forget our 'bad memories'. When we come to rehearse, we meet our friends and forget the agonies of life." Some who still live with their husbands said, "At first our husbands objected[60], but we were performing *langol* stories at the *lai* temple during *Lai Harouba*. It was meant for the *lai*. So they could not stop us. . .gradually people started to invite us and pay for it and we became very busy."

These women are all traders. Sometimes they travel far to perform and earn a little extra money. I went to watch one of the plays and found that a part of the audience consisted of the performers' children and relatives. Among the enthusiastic cheering crowd the husbands were conspicuously absent. One woman said, "Husbands feel really embarrassed to watch their wives dressed up and acting." Some of the children help a great deal in carrying the costumes and props. The women hired a male *shumang leela* director to direct the play. One older woman proudly told me, "My son takes me to places for rehearsals and performances on the back seat of his motor-bike."

In another association, I met Sanatambi Devi (43), a cloth trader, and a happily married woman. She said, "My husband hates the idea of my joining a *shumangleela* group. I keep his clothes clean and

[59]*Shumang leela* theatre presentation is originally an all-male performance. Recently women have started forming separate all-women theatre groups. At present there is a growing popularity for women's *leela*.

[60]Several of the women are first wives with grown up children. The second wives live in separate homes.

ironed; I cook good meals for him to keep him quiet. Once I come to the market, I am on my own from noon to 7.00 p.m. I always make time for rehearsals." The rehearsals are usually like a get-together. Women contribute money to have good refreshments and hot milk.

Women thus enjoy a social bond through recreational activities which ensure their emotional security. This was confirmed during my interview with the first group.

"Acting helps us recover from our mental depression," said one woman. "We help each other in bad times. If the husband treats one of us badly, we give advice." Another answered me, when I asked why she did not remarry for companionship, "You never know what kind of stepfather he is going to be. We forget our loneliness when we are with friends."

6
Religious Context

An observer in the Manipur Valley is often struck by the pervasive influence of Hindu Vaisnava culture. From my second floor apartment in Imphal, I could see the surrounding domes of numerous Vaisnava temples with huge corrugated tin-roofed *mandapas* attached to them. The quiet of the mornings and evenings would resonate with the sound of temple gongs and cymbals. The drumming of *poongs* and devotional singing at the community *mandapas* could often be heard late into the night. In my host village, Nambol Awang, there are four such temples with impressive *mandapas* attached to them, which remain busy throughout the year with socio-religious activities such as scripture reading, devotional singing sessions, ritual feasting, weddings, funeral ceremonies. Every Meitei home has a *tulsibong* (basil plant on an earthen mound) in the courtyard as a sign of adherence to the Vaisnava faith. All Meitei women, orthodox men and children wear *chandan* marks on their nose and forehead after the daily bath.

In spite of this, after a closer look at the culture, I came to realize that among the Meitei, their traditional pre-Hindu faith is not a forgotten story. In fact, Meitei religious life is marked by the co-existence of the traditional belief system and Vaisnavite Hindu faith.

Inside a Meitei home, there is usually no altar for Vaisnavite deities, but the most auspicious corners, the south-west and northeast, are dedicated to the ancient deities, Sanamahi and his mother, Ima Laimaren. The hearth is associated with the ancestral deity of lineage, Sagei Apokpa.

Vaisnava rituals and other Brahman-officiated family rituals are usually performed in the courtyard or *shangoi*. Very often these rituals are not complete without the propitiation of Meitei house deities.[60]

[60]Discussing a grave crisis in the life of the pious king Bhagyachandra, the Meitei writer N. Tombi Singh (1975: 5-6) depicts the true sentiment of a Meitei

VAISNAVITE FAITH IN MANIPUR

From the fifteenth century or even earlier, one can trace the influence of Puranic Hinduism in Meitei folklore, art, music, and life-cycle ceremonies. A more full-fledged effort at Sanskritization started about two hundred years ago during the reign of Garib Niwaz. The stories about that king, named Pamheiba, but better known under his adopted Hinduized name of Garib Niwaz (refuge of the poor), and about his Guru Shantidas, tell us of the violent and oppressive methods by which these two tried to replace the ancient faith with Vaisnavism.

The confrontation between the king and traditional Meitei scholars culminated in a bitter struggle. The king ordered all important religious texts written in the ancient Meitei script burned; but a few scholars fled with important scriptures and hid them in secrecy. The king prohibited the use of the Meitei script and replaced it with Bengali,[61] in deference to the language of the Vaisnava scripture he served.[62] He donned the "sacred thread" at the hands of his Guru and declared himself a Kshatriya. He also declared Vaisnavism to be the state religion and he ordered all his subjects to don the sacred thread and adopt the Vaisnava customs. Thus he did his utmost to change the people to a Hindu way of life, e.g., the practice of vegetarianism, wearing of the Vaisnava mark, the organizing of Vaisnavite ceremonies, etc. Hodson (1908, reprinted 1975:97) remarks: "The records distinctly show that up to the

---

religious mind: "The moment he heard of the ordeal, he gathered his moral strength and decided to face the event in full submission to Gobindajie...He remembered his ancestral deities one after another ... Pakhangba is the supreme deity and protector of the throne...the ruling clan of the Ningthoujas to whom Bhagyachandra belongs, traces its origin to Pakhangba who was a god-king ruling over the region about two thousand years ago...conversion to Hindu cult does not stand in the way of this worship. In the same manner the king worships the other ancestral deities. He remembered Sanamahi, the ruling deity of every Manipuri household ... They were very alive and real to him now."

[61]There was a belief that those who sing in the Meitei language would be transformed into owls hereafter in another birth if they die at night, and into cows if they die in the daytime, and would then fly in the Makoi-Nugel hill and be condemned to hell. (K. Singh Moirangthem, 1971:320).

[63]*Chaitanya Charitamrita*, written in Bengali by Krishnadas Kaviraj, a biography and an interpretation of Vaisnava philosophy as presented by Sree Chaitanya, the sixteenth century Vaisnava saint, and a vast repertoire of religious verses written during the fifteenth to eighteenth centuries, in Bengali, are considered the basic sources of Vaisnava theology.

formal introduction of Hinduism in the reign of Pamheiba (Garib Niwaz), the people buried their dead, ate meat, drank ardent spirits, and behaved just like the hill people of the present day."

During the reign of the grandson of Garib Niwaz, the pious king Bhagyachandra (Meitei name: Chingthongkhomba), Vaisnava culture provided an extremely rich and vibrant environment. Bhagyachandra did not allow oppressive methods to popularize the faith; instead, he created an aesthetic atmosphere for it assimilation. He collected the best musicians and dancers in the society and encouraged them to choreograph dances for Vaisnavite rituals. The ritual performances of the ancient Meitei religion were already a rich source for dance and music, and the fresh contact with North Indian music and Vaisnavite lyrics enriched the quality of this traditional music. Numerous dances were choreographed with traditional movements and a vast repertoire of ritual performances evolved. Inspired choreographers and composers were patronized by the kings, who took special pride in aesthetic enlightenment. The aesthetic devotional aspect of Vaisnavite rituals, presented in a grand manner, attracted the common people more readily as they already had a deep devotion to dance and music developed by their traditional religious ceremonies.

The Royal Temple of Sri Govindaji

A Meitei (N. Tombi Singh, 1975: 84) says, "Govindaji belonged to the community through the king...Govindaji cannot become a family deity; Govindaji is more than a deity. It is an institution." The Meitei kings thus created the institution of Govindaji as a "unifying force" among the people. Regular services were performed eight times a day. Visitors—noblemen and commoners—came in a constant flow. Different *pala* groups (male and female groups for devotional singing sessions) were assigned to take turns at the daily rituals. King Bhagyachandra formed a special *Loishang*, *Pala Loishang*, in 1776 with master musicians and dance teachers to supervise and administer the rules and regulations of the ritual performances. Newly composed or choreographed works had to be first approved by the *Loishang* before their presentation to the *mandapas*.

The immigrant Brahmans (the majority from Bengal) maintained a constant flow of knowledge of Vaisnava theology from Navadwip and Vrindavana, the two important centres of Vaisnavism. Sanskritization worked through a complex structure of royal administration and over a period of two hundred years it became embedded in the lives of the common people.

Each of the major Vaisnava ceremonies begins at the Govindaji temple and moves on to Bijoy Govinda temple, followed by hundreds of smaller temples all over the Valley. Since Govindaji became the royal deity, his institution had the highest status among rites and temples and in the socio-religious system. The festivals of Govindaji temple became marked with a royal grandeur and sophistication. At present the festivals are attended by the people from all over the Valley. Villagers who represent their *pala* groups in joining the festivals take special pride in their privilege. The temple administrative bodies, *Brahmasabha, Pala Loishang* and *Jagoi Loishang*, take care of the complex structure of hierarchy and formality in Vaisnava activity both in daily life and in the religious ceremonies. There are different categories of Vaisnava festivals: family, community, and state. Besides many calendrical rituals, there are rituals which are non-calendrical and non-cyclical, e.g., as when a family wants to offer prayers and thanks for having received some specific boon or blessing. These rituals could range from simple scripture reading or *sankirtana* sessions to rather expensive and elaborate dance rituals lasting for one or two days.

The dance rituals involve fees for the teachers, professional singers, and musicians, and feasting for the performers. Dancers are selected from the community. Although one family may sponsor and bear the major burden of expense, the rituals are supported by the entire community. Families sometimes travel to Imphal to worship at the royal temple and to take a vow to perform a special ritual. Regional and state festivals, on the other hand, follow calendrical cycles. In rural areas, these are organized by the community under the supervision of the Brahman priest at his residence *mandapa*. At the royal temple the festivals are organized by the temple committee.

VAISNAVA RELIGIOUS WORLD AND WOMEN

The royal family and the elite adopted the Vaisnava way of life, while common people emulated them as a respected reference group. Gradually, with time, the imported faith adapted itself to the ethnic religious environment and Meitei culture, and thus it became quite distinct in the world of pan-Indian culture. The distinction found its most profound expression in the public prominence of women in core religious rituals. Thus was introduced a feature unusual to the patriarchic nature of Brahmanic Hinduism. In most of the rituals both sexes participate together. In some, women have more prominence than men.

The major ritual performances in Vaisnavite ceremonies can be arranged under two categories: *Raslila*: There are two kinds of *Raslila*—*Goshtaras* and *Sankirtanaras*, both basically dance rituals. *Sankirtana*: These are religious singing sessions performed by both sexes and known respectively as *nupa-pala* (male *sankirtana*) and *nupi-pala* (female *sankirtana*).

Goshtaras is a term for a dance ritual which depicts the legend of Krishna's childhood days and his life with his cowherd (*gopa*) friends. The roles are taken by children of both sexes. However, a boy dancer must be below seven or eight years of age, although the girls may be older. I have seen fifteen-year-old girls performing as Krishna and *gopa* in male costume at Bijoy Govinda temple.

The *Goshtaras* rituals of my study villages followed the basic patterns that I found at Bijoy Govinda temple. The adult roles for Krishna's parents, relatives and enemies are taken by professional performers of both sexes. The singers, *sutradharis*, are female, but the musicians (in flute, *poong*-drum and conch shell) are male. A *Goshtaras* follows the prescribed repertoire laid down by the temple *loishang*. This is conducted and taught by an *ojha* (a professional teacher) of either sex, known as *rashdhari*.

Sankirtanaras, a dance ritual of the royal temple, is performed only by women. There are four types. One can watch the first three kinds of *ras* at the royal temple without any male dance participation. The images of the deities, Radha and Krishna, are placed at the centre of the ritual arena and women dance all night long, circling the images. The singers and musicians are of both sexes. The audience sits on four sides of the square arena in many rows and in galleries at the back, with special seats for the King and members of the immediate royal family. Men and women sometimes sit separately, sometimes together.

Dressed in brilliantly embroidered red skirts and bright green velvet jackets, their faces covered with fine transparent white veils and heavily adorned with gold and silver jewellery, the dancers glide and float in soft, gentle, flowery movements. Hundreds of lighted candles, incense, drumbeating, blowing of huge conch shells, music and songs create a mystical aura around the dancers, who number between thirty and forty at a time. The entire scene takes on an ethereal atmosphere, and the audience becomes ecstatic. Often the men break out in tears and women hum songs and move their palms in the flowery dance style, in devotional joy. *Raslila* performances follow in other temples after its celebration at the royal temple. In these *Raslilas*, Krishna's role is taken by a child, a boy or a girl. Here, too, the part is played by a boy, who has to be below seven or eight years of age. There is no restriction on the ages of women.

In Manipur, women's dancing in religious ceremonies, regarded as *thougal* (dedication), cuts across all social classes and age groups. I have found female dancers in *Raslila* ritual at the royal temple *mandapa* ranging from commoners to members of the royal family and from pre-teenagers to women in their sixties, all dressed in splendid costumes following designs laid down during the time of King Bhagyachandra.

The tradition of Vaisnavite dance ritual was set by King Bhagyachandra's daughter, Bimbabati (Meitei name Sija Lairobi, i.e., the princess who has dedicated herself to God), who took the central role of Radha, consort of the Hindu deity Lord Krishna, in the rituals at the royal temple. More recently Maharani Dhanamanjari Devi, the chief queen of Maharaja Churachand (1891-1941), led the women dancers at the royal *mandapa* with superb skill and devotion. At present one can observe two traditional *nupi-palas* (women's devotional singing), known as *Jalakeli* and *Raseswari*, annually performed by the princesses of two descent lines of the royal family. The performances at the royal temple *mandapa* are open to spectators mostly composed of common people who have come to accept the religious dancing as an expression of elegant elite culture. People followed the elite, and today, one can observe dance rituals and *nupi-pala* in all the community *mandapas* throughout the Valley. If they are able, people contribute large sums of money to the temple fund to enable their daughters to perform in the royal temple ceremonies. In rural areas, too, families of participants in dance rituals of the community *mandapa* take special pride in this honour.

Sankirtana

The art of *sankirtana* has developed into a religious institution over the past two hundred years with an overt dominance of male performers. A *sankirtana* can be divided into two sections, the *kirtana*, musical and vocal style, and the *cholam*, rhythmic style. There are two kinds of *cholam*, *pala cholam* and *poong cholam*. *Pala cholam* is a dance form performed by the participants during *sankirtana* with gentle and firm footwork and graceful movements of the body. *Poong cholam* is the dance of the male drummer.

The training of a *sankirtana* performer takes a number of years of rigorous practice under a Guru. Performers devote their lives to this. A *sankirtana* session follows rigid rules and regulations concerning the style of presentation, time and sequence of the programme, and other ritual formalities as laid down by the *Loishang* at Sri Govindaji temple. Under the umbrella of *Pala Loishang*, the performances are ranked in hierarchical order according to seniority and scale of excellence. A collective social patronage helped *sankirtana* develop into a vibrant and flourishing art. The performers live in a competitive world and audiences are discriminating in the selection of a performing group.

Although women's *sankirtana* sessions, *nupi-palas*, are quite popular, the exuberant demonstration of *sankirtana* is found only in *nupa-pala*, the male singing sessions. While *Raslila* dancing is performed by females, *sankirtana* singing has been a male prerogative, developing into a highly professional skill with a much larger economic premise. Women are not allowed to perform in the technique of male *sankirtana*, and are barred from entering the ritual arena during *sankirtana*, because the Brahmans regarded them as polluting agents. The dominant aspect of male *sankirtana* is reflected in the costume of the dancers. The male performers wear stark white *dhotis*, large imposing turbans with a touch of black on the top (sometimes red for particular groups), and the sacred thread showing on bare chests. Women wear plain-looking, faded pastel orange *pungo fanek* with white *inafi*, whether they are spectators or performers. During the Holi festival at Sri Govindaji temple, male *sankirtana* groups attend in the hundreds, representing different communities of the Valley, each carrying banners to indicate its status in the *Loishang*. Men come in spectacular colours—orange, bright saffron, shocking pink—in *dhoti*, turban, and kurta. Old men carry their grandsons who are in identical dress. When a grandfather does not have a grandson he dresses up his granddaughter in a male costume. Women also attend, in simple *pungo fanek*. In fact, in all Vaisnavite ceremonies, women wear *pungo fanek*, but men may attend in imposing formal attire. Over the past two decades, however, Meitei society has witnessed a significant change in socio-religious life. Five years ago, there were usually one or two women's groups at the royal temple found during the Holi festival. In 1978, I saw over thirty women's groups (some with over 150 members), who came carrying banners, singing and dancing in devotional joy. They were accompanied by male drummers. Some women's groups sat on the ritual ground and performed; some stood and danced ecstatically.

The present popularity of women's *sankirtana* can be attributed in part to the courage and zeal of a famous female *sankirtana* singer, Manimacha Devi (47).[63] She was the first professional woman to give up the plain-looking attire and wear the traditional attire, *maiknaiba*, with brilliant coloured stripes and heavy gold or gold-plated jewellery. She also rejected the use of tiny cymbals, *manjira*, and adopted the large *khartal* (large cymbal), till then used only by males. Manimacha Devi was gifted with a beautiful voice and a fine singing talent. She formed a *sankirtana* group of women and started to perform like male *sankirtana* singers. Instead of sitting on the ground in a passive position, she and her companions stood up, sang and danced in feminine ecstasy. This happened about twelve years ago. The Sangit Sabha, the council of the *sankirtana* singers, was offended by this action and sued her in court, condemning her act as sacrilegious and against Vaisnava ideology. She won the court battle and the Secretary of the Sabha was fined Rs. 500 twice by the court for disturbing her unusual performances, which attracted a large audience from all over the Valley. I found her so busy that she could barely find a free morning to meet me. Since Manimacha's victory, several other women's groups have taken up the male style *sankirtana* and perform professionally. The old pundits of the Sangit Sabha resent this new popularity of the women's groups and their success in the profession. Several leading female singers are afraid to follow Manimacha Devi, lest their male teachers become critical of them. Some of them, like another famous singer Yaiskul

---

[63] I gathered that a few years ago, some important *sankirtana* Gurus allowed a very rich woman of Bombay to play *poong* drum (played only by men) during a *sankirtana* session at Govindaji temple. The permission was given to her as a special favour. But after watching her perform in a male programme, some Meitei women demanded that they should be allowed to perform in some programmes. The Gurus could not raise objections to this any longer.

Gambhini Devi, have adopted a middle path. They stand up and shake a medium-sized cymbal but do not dance or act like the ecstatic male dancers.

The recent breakthrough by women has also created a relaxed attitude towards the participation of *nupi-pala* groups in the temple festivals and more and more groups are participating nowadays. Their members come from all strata of society. In one such group, *dhupa-pala*, I found the Queen Mother present, along with puffed-rice traders of the Khwarimbond bazaar. The majority of women singers are between thirty and sixty years of age. However, several younger singers may be found among professional groups attending family and community rituals.

The *nupi-pala* is popular in rural areas. Both *nupa* and *nupi-pala* groups are part of the socio-religious life of the rural people. I watched a *hali-pala* (springtime *sankirtana*) of a group of female traders of the Nambol bazaar. Fifteen women represented a forty-member *pala* association. The women came from several surrounding villages. They sang and danced with vigorous clapping and shaking of handkerchiefs. The male drummer danced with masculine energy along with them. Old men as spectators entered the ritual arena, bowing *sashtanga*[64] to them and offered *dakhshina*. Several of them cried loudly in devotional joy. Women spectators quietly wiped their tears with *inafi*. In another *ahoratro* (twenty-four-hour non-stop session of singing) at Nambol thirteen women from a reputed *pala* group called Radheshyam (formed thirty years ago) performed. Male spectators, especially the older ones, wept during the *sankirtana* session.

Important Vaisnava ceremonies follow the all-India Hindu calendar, e.g., *Doljatra* corresponding to the calendrical *Doljatra* or Holi, *Kangchingba Kanglen* corresponding to the eleven-day Hindu *Rathjatra* festival, *Janmastami* (Krishna's birthday) and several other celebrations. The community *mandapa* is busy throughout the year with ritual activities. Most of the rituals are attended by men, women and children.

---

[64]*Sashtanga*, a Sanskrit word, means bowing with eight parts of the body. This is a style of prostration, lying face down with two hands stretched forward. *Sashtanga* is considered an expression of Vaisnava humility, a surrender of the ego.

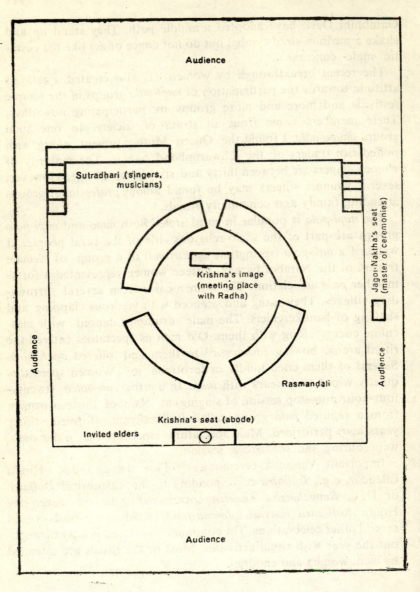

FIGURE 5 : Raslila Floor Plan

Raslila in Rural Areas

In rural areas common people organize *Raslila* in their community mandapa. In Nambol, by the middle of the year 1978, there

were already three *Raslilas* and one *Sansenba*[65] organized with a turnout of five to six hundred people from surrounding villages. One family organized a *Raslila* because the grandparents vowed it, if their ailing grandson recovered. For another, the vow was for an ailing granddaughter. In both *Raslilas*, the boy and the girl took the role of Krishna. Hundreds of men, women and children came to join *Raskhurumba* (to bow to *ras*). A well-defined floor plan for the ritual arena (Figure 5) and a dance and music repertoire are prescribed by the Sri Govindaji *Loishang*. This is very carefully followed in the *Raslila* performances of the village *mandapa*. After one all-night non-stop programme of dancing and singing, the ritual ended at 4.00 a.m. with a special programme, *Mangalarati*. Most children were wide awake all night and alerted the present anthropologist from her occasional dozing with teasing giggles. The participants worshipped the two children who took the central role of Krishna and his consort Radha. Smoke from a large incense-burner filled the area. Several sticks with cotton dipped in clarified butter were lighted in front of the child-couple. The audience became ecstatic. Many hummed the song and raised their hands above their heads in an expression of joy. After the programme ended, people collected *Rasdhuli*, the dust from the ritual arena.[66]

THE LAND OF THE LAIS: THE PRE-HINDU FAITH

In the midst of such an exuberant Vaisnava environment, the traditional system and belief maintains its strength and character in the people's lives. The ancient religious complex is outside the Vaisnava framework. Instead of the Brahman priests, the Meitei *maiba* (priest and diviner) and especially *maibi* (priestess and diviner) play highly important roles in officiating for Meitei *Lai* worship. These traditional ritual specialists are kept busy throughout the year conducting various ritual ceremonies. The *Pundit Loishang* (in charge of *Maiba Loishang*, *Maibi Loishang* and *Pena Loishang*) remained active and responsible for the indigenous reli-

---

[65] *Sansenba*: A dance theatre presented as a ritual depicting Krishna herding cattle with other cowherd playmates in his childhood. The Nambol *Sansenba* was performed for two nights with a large group of young boys and girls assisted and trained by professional singers, dance teachers and actors.

[66] *Rasdhuli* is considered an auspicious thing to keep at home. In case of a death, *Rasdhuli* is scattered on the ground and the dead body placed on it.

gion, side by side with the *Loishangs* of the Sri Govindaji temple. While Vaisnava culture received major attention from the royal administration, the ancient faith retained its place in the core religious conscience of the society. The pious kings resorted to *maibis* in the event of political calamities, and depended on their prophetic powers before commencing an expedition. A *maibi* or *maiba's* propitiatory rites were necessary to prevent any evil omen. Like Sri Govindaji, the high god of the Meitei faith remained absolutely important for the protection of society. The two faiths are seldom fused together. Sri Govindaji has no place in the Meitei *Lai* pantheon.

The ancient Meitei religion is based on a vast body of knowledge written in the archaic Meitei language. The original Meitei script, especially its archaic form, is read only by the pundits, who preserve their expertise in great secrecy. The other ritual functionaries, the *maibis*, are not literate people and they acquire spiritual knowledge through oral traditions from their Gurus. Yet they also work very closely with the pundits, who often verify their understanding of the tradition. Some of the *maibis* are well known for the depth of their knowledge of sacred literature. My interviews with some of the *maibis* and with a pundit introduced me to the basics of the creation myth, important to our understanding of the *Lai Harouba* ritual.

A Short Explanation of the Creation Myth

There is a supreme creator, an "impersonal absolute," and also an abstract power, known as Guru Atiya Sidaba. The texts explain two stages of the Guru's existence until the appearance of two identities, Sidaba (male) and Sidabi (female). The male Guru is described as the sky god and the female as the divine mother, Ima Laimaren, the earth goddess. Together, as husband and wife, they created the earth. Rajo Maibi (in *Langol*, 1977) says that, one day, Atingkok Sidaba Guru (our eternal, primal Guru) thought to himself, "I do not want to be alone." He breathed through his right nostril and planned to create an image of himself. Guru said, "I want to create you just like myself. But you have created layers of cloud. Hence, I shall name you 'The Creator of the Cloud'." From the left nostril of Guru came a female form. Guru said, "You two create living forms which should have resemblance to me."

The divine couple, the second male Guru and his consort Ima

Laimaren (Sidaba and Sidabi), had three sons. There is a minutely detailed account indicating how one of the sons, Sanamahi, followed Guru's order faithfully but how the youngest son, Pakhamba, obstructed the creation. After repeated efforts, Sanamahi succeeded in the creation of earth, fire, water, sky and air. Asiba (Sanamahi) asked the divine parents to come down and look at the earth. At Guru's request Ima came down. She pressed her feet on the newly-formed earth and performed the dance of *Leinetma-Jagoi* (dance of levelling the earth). She said to Guru, "Look at the creation of your son." Now Guru came down and danced together with his wife. Guru said, "We will take different names on the earth... Today is the birth of 'one day'. We spent this day happily. So I shall take the name, Noupok Apanba (*noupok*: one day; *apanba*: brightness). From now on I shall be 'incarnated' in seven male forms." Ima said, "I shall be known as Panthoibi. I shall be incarnated in seven female forms and be united with the seven males." (Rajo Maibi, 1977:6). But then the Guru asked Sanamahi to create living forms like himself; Sanamahi failed. He could create only a frog. He kept trying and in successive attempts he created a lizard, a monkey, and other animals until, at last, he created human beings. Sanamahi exclaimed "Hoi!" on each of his attempts. But each time he created a creature, Guru said, "This is not human. You try again." Ima Laimaren said, "You try to create humans after the image of your father." Sanamahi created sixty-one species and continued to create more and more.

Now these creations emanated from the womb of the "mother". When the mother was seven months pregnant, she asked Guru, "What will the creature of my womb look like?" Guru said, "Like myself." After ten months Guru said, "You come out of the womb and look at your creation...Come, your mother will nourish you with her milk." The baby was none else but Pakhamba, he who knew his father. The myth describes the birth of a baby from the body of the divine mother who finally looked exactly like the Guru. Along with the birth of the baby, the growth of culture started with the introduction of hoe cultivation, agriculture of paddy, drying of fish for preservation, cultivation of cotton, skill in spinning and weaving, use of fire, and so on: all the necessities for human survival appeared one after another. The myth has another episode: Guru once appeared in the form of a dead bull. He planned to find out who was the cleverer of the two sons. Sanamahi failed to recognize Guru in the form of the bull, but Pakhamba did so. Whereupon, Guru, said, "You make grass with my body hair. My four legs would be four *panas* (revenue divisions discussed in chapter 2). My brows will be two big mountains, Cheenga and Phisum...my eyes will be rivers...seven gods and seven goddesses will come to live in the four *panas*" (reference to seven clans. Rajo Maibi, 1977: 11-17). The myth deals extensively with the conflict and competition of the two brothers, Sanamahi and Pakhamba. When creation was complete, Guru asked his two sons to compete in a race around the world. He promised the throne to the winner. Sanamahi, the hard worker, set out to make his way around the world. Pakhamba, the youngest son, took secret advice from the mother, Ima Laimaren. He went around his father, the Guru, who is himself the symbol of the universe, for the world was created after his image. When Sanamahi returned he found Pakhamba on the throne. Sanamahi was furious and was about to challenge Pakhamba, but Pakhamba was immediately protected by seven *Lairembis* (female *Lais*), who encircled him. Sanamahi then said, "If your advisor is a male, I shall kill him; if it is a female, I shall marry her." Guru pacified Sanamahi by giving him the status of a household deity to be worshipped in every Meitei home. Sanamahi's mother, Ima Laimaren, also became another house deity along with her son.

Pakhamba is worshipped as the supreme ancestral deity of the royal clan, *Ningthouja*. Pakhamba is also the name of the earliest mentioned Meitei king in A.D. 33. The legend goes that he took the form of a snake by night and the form of a human by day. In an ancient text, *Pafal Lambaba*, I found 364 designs of Pakhamba motifs in pictorial representations. The divine snake is drawn in the form of various animals, e.g., tiger, lizard, dragon, fox, human, black cat, duck, antelope, cobra. Some are two or six-faced with the tongue lolling out. The Meitei Pundit Kulachandra explained some forms as evil and some as auspicious. As Pakhabma is the royal deity, and the members of the royal clan and their daughters do not kill any snakes, Pundit Kulachandra says, "Under the Kangla (former palace) grounds there are several tunnels criss-crossing like the coils of Pakhamba. There were different spots (e.g., place for royal court, place of execution, etc.) according to the coiling patterns of the tunnels."[67] An intricate snake symbol is used for

[67]Personal·communication, Spring 1978.

the royal flag. Pakhamba's coiling patterns are also of high ritual importance in the *Lai* worship ceremonies, especially in the dance rituals of *Lai Harouba*.

The myth describes seven planets marrying seven goddesses, who gave birth to seven sons, who eventually established the seven clans, the *salei/yek*, of the Meitei.

There is a vast literature and folklore based on the legends of *langol* (incarnation) of the divine couple in human form. The romantic ballads offer legends associated with different clans near Moirang, which is in fact the homeland of the Meitei ballad literature (Joychandra n.d.). The ballads are endowed with rich poetic descriptions and are sung and acted by traditional performers, *penakhongbas*. The *langol* themes, especially those of Khamba-Thoibi episode, are extremely popular and are presented in the dances of the *Lai Harouba* ceremony. It is said that Khamba and Thoibi, as a married couple, danced together in the famous temple of Thangjing of Moirang, eight hundred years ago.

The Religious Belief of a Common Person

A common Meitei shows little interest in the complex knowledge of this ancient scripture and is concerned even less with interpretations of the creation myth. People know of Sanamahi, Ima Laimaren, and Sagei ancestor Guru Apokpa; they are also aware of the royal ancestral deity, Pakhamba. But their immediate concern is with the *Lais: Umang Lais* (forest deities), *Soraren* (agricultural deity), and *Inum Lais* (house deities). The Meitei have 364 *Umang Lais* presiding over the four corners of the Valley. There is deep reverence for several important *Lais* guarding the Valley in different directions, who are remembered and honoured during the family rituals, different *Lai* worship ceremonies, and at the time of *Lai Harouba*. These *Lais* are: Thangjing at Moirang on the southwestern part, Kobru on the top of the mountain at the northwest, Marjing at the northeast, and Wangbren at Sugnu at the southeast. The four *Lais* are also credited with the creation of the four rivers, Thoubal, Iril, Imphal, and Nambol, which drain the Valley. Thangjing is known as the lord of the tiger hunters, Marjing as the lord of the cattle and polo game, Wangbren as the lord of the rivers and Kobru as the lord of all.

Another famous *Lai* is associated with the mountain Numaijing to the east. Under the influence of Hinduism, the pilgrimage to

Numaijing peak has become associated with the worship of the Hindu diety, Siva. The summit is also associated with the legend of the divine couple, Nongpokningthou and goddess Panthoibi. This legend is an important part of the ritual dance repertoire of *Lai Harouba*.

Heibowakching and Hiyanthang, two hillocks located in the southern outskirts of Imphal, are associated with the Guru and Ima Laimaren. With the advent of Hinduism and in accordance with the wish of the rulers, the identity of Hiyanthang Lairembi was changed to Kamakhya Devi, a Hindu goddess. A Brahman priest officiated at her worship and a part of the offering from the people's yearly pilgrimage was dedicated to the royal temple of Govindaji. But still the worship of Ima Laimaren and her son Sanamahi is carried on every Sunday in the premises outside the temple structure. Recently, the Sagei community, which originally owned the Lai temple, has started a movement to reinstate the ancient Lairembi and to change the identity of the temple deity back to Hiyanthang Lairembi. In 1978 I witnessed an elaborate *Lai Harouba* ceremony there to honour Hiyangthang Lairembi.

A body of literature and folklore sets all *Lais* in hierarchical order and likens them to a large family under one absolute creator. According to the pundits, the *Lais* are not real gods, but their emissaries. To a common man, each *Lai* is a most viable god, wielding omnipotent power. He looks upon all the *Lais* with great awe, fear and devotion. A rural man said to me, "We are very careful not to offend the Lais. If you are not very careful, you may face real danger. They have great power to protect you." "What about Govindaji?" "Yes, Govindaji is another *Lai* , a very big *Lai*, but he is a *Mayang Lai* (Hindu), not a Meitei one."

Each of the *Lai* temples has a constant pair of male and female deities, the *Lai* and the Lairembi, as husband and wife. The temple may be named after either the male or the female deity. Their images are made with a bronze mask fixed on cone-like structures made of bamboo (approximately three-and-a-half feet) and dressed beautifully in *dhoti*, *kurta*, shawl, and turban for the male, and *maiknaiba*, tiara-like crown, *inafi* and blouse for the female. Smaller temples are situated in large open courtyards with sheds for the audience on three facing sides. The shed on the right side of the temple is meant for males and the left for females. There is a porch in front of the altar room with the two sides reserved separately for the male and female devotees. The rural temples do not display any images of the *Lais* during the year; they bring them out only during *Lai Harouba*. The Lai-Mapu, the male temple keeper, takes care of all materials to be used for the image and brings them in bundles on the eve of *Lai Harouba*. It is then that the images are adorned with a fine sense of beauty by the *maibis*. These are dismantled immediately after the concluding ceremony and put away in bundles again. The larger and better known temples, like the Khoriphoba temple at Nambol Awang, display images all the year round.

In the past, there were no permanent *Lai* temples in the villages. Thatched-roof structures were built every year to be burned after a *Lai Harouba* ceremony. Today, *Lai* temples are constructed with bricks. These are smaller than the average Hindu temples built in the villages.

Belief in Witchcraft and Evil Spirits

People rely a great deal on the traditional *maiba* (priest) and *maibi* (priestess). There is another variety of specialist, also called *maiba*. They are not traditional priests, but act as shamans and curers. All these specialists help people combat witchcraft, or protect them from the infliction of harm by evil spirits.

The common people are consumed by the constant fear that harm may befall them from the two most popularly known female spirits, *hinchhabi* and *heloi*. *Hinchhabi* is believed to live inside some women who project their supernatural selves into the bodies of victims and cause illness, mental affliction, bad luck, and even death. Villagers say that a woman in whose body the *hinchhabi* resides may not even be aware of it. A *hinchhabi*'s daughter also becomes a *hinchhabi*. I was often asked to visit a village *maiba* because of a pain in my back. People said, "Some *hinchhabi* has put an evil eye on you." If a child cries all night in gripping pain, the family may suspect that a *hinchhabi* has touched the baby. Meitei folklore indeed describes *hinchhabis* as immortals who live by eating babies. An urban informant talked about a trader at Khwarimbond bazaar with the reputation of being a *hinchhabi*. She lives a normal life with her husband and children. But people avoid inviting her for a *shastipuja* ritual.

During my stay, I heard complaints about *hinchhabis* quite frequently. In Thambalkhul, a *maiba* explained *hinchhabi* as the most vicious of spirits. People believe that all kinds of illnesses, e.g., bladder stone, tongue cancer, and even difficult labour, are caused by a *hinchhabi*.

The *maiba* described *heloi* as the most powerful among the female spirits who cause disease. Women may get sick in their sexual organs and men become insane from the attacks of *heloi*. The highest rate of insanity attacks occurs in March and April during the period of Yaosong, the spring festival. Incidentally, this is the time of the *Thabal Chombi* dance participated in by both men and women.

Helois always appear as beautiful *laishabis* luring young men to the woods, only to turn them insane. In a preventive ritual, the *maiba* feeds the spirits with animal faeces and some specially prepared ritual food called *saramngaram*. While the *heloi* is a wandering spirit, a *hinchhabi* resides in the body of a woman. "Why do these spirits appear as women?" "Durga has seven daughters. Among the seven daughters one has an evil power. She is the *hinchhabi*. She has a fearful appearance."

Where a *hinchhabi* is at work, the *maiba* receives clients of both sexes from all strata of society. The spirits do not spare even the Brahman priests, so a village Brahman may have to seek the help of a *maiba* when confounded by such problems as are beyond the jurisdiction of Hindu gods.

Maibis and both kinds of *maibas* are known for their skill in *semjanba* (sorcery). They can apply their skill to diagnose a case of witchcraft and prescribe a cure for it. In both rural and urban areas, my informants mentioned the anxiety such problems cause. To illustrate, one morning an informant of mine appeared very excited. She said, "I found a lemon in my garden with three iron stick spierced in it. Someone is trying to cause harm to me and my two children." The informant happened to be a "first wife" living apart from her husband. She was convinced that the lemon had been placed in her garden by the second wife. She immediately summoned a *maibi*, who performed a rite to prevent possible harm.

In another case a female informant, a government officer, narrated her story thus:

I was ready for a promotion. But three of my colleagues were trying to have me fired from my position. One of them was a politician with a lot of influence. I felt helpless and went to a *maiba*. With the *maiba*'s instruction I went up a distant hilltop. There he took me to a small pond. He chanted *mantras* for a long time and then asked me to give the names of the three men. He wrote their names on three saltplates—indigenous solidified salt sold in flat plates—and immersed them in the water. One plate dissolved immediately. The second one vanished after a while, but the third one stayed half-melted for a long time and then dissolved...One of the three men came to my house that evening and apologized for his misdeed. Another one had an accident and was confined in a hospital. The third one fought hard against me for a long time but failed to do anything.

I have also witnessed a married woman performing a *semjanba* with the help of a *maibi* to obtain an easy divorce from her husband. Her husband was stubborn and kept threatening her that if she left him he would punish her.

RECENT TREND OF MEITEIIZATION: REJUVENATION OF THE ANCIENT FAITH

Over the past few decades, there has been a rise in the awareness of their Meitei identity among the people of the Valley. An anti-Brahman and anti-Hindu movement was active in the neighbouring district of Cachar way back in 1930 led by a Meitei named Naoria Phullo. Phullo established a political group called Apokpa Marup (association in the name of a Meitei ancestor deity) and confronted Maharaj Churachand and his associate Brahman pundits. After Phullo's death, his followers in the Valley initiated a movement called Sanamahi (named after a Meitei house deity) in 1945. The movement was geared to an extremist attempt towards the de-Sanskritization of Meitei culture and the revival of Meitei heritage. The movement strongly opposed the Meitei identity with the Kshatriya caste and denied any link with the Indo-Aryan heritage claimed by the early promoters of Hinduism. Now the central organization known as Meitei Phurup has branches (*marups*) scattered all over the Valley with popular support from the young people. However, the sentiment of the movement is indicative more of a political trend than a regeneration of religious belief.[68] In re-

[68]Several educated Meitei have denied calling the Sanamahi movement revivalist (Kabui, 1974:74). They believe that Manipur has been a culture of religious syncreticism where Brahmans worshipped Meitei deities and Meitei worshipped Sri Govindaji. The two religious systems always co-existed.

cent years politically motivated radical groups have voiced their anger and protest against Brahmanic oppression. Although political animus was often directed against the Government of India, the movement has created a consciousness of their heritage among the younger generation. Discussing the glory of pre-Vaisnava days, a radical newspaper (*Resistance*, June 14, 1977:8) writes:

> Along with the conversion of the Meiteis to Hinduism in the eighteenth century, the fanatic cohorts of the new faith attempted to destroy the martial spirit of the Meiteis in order to engage them in religious pursuits...The advent of more publicized, universally acclaimed fighting skills like Kung-fu (or Shaolin boxing) Karate, Judo, Jiu-Jitsu, etc. from the *Mongoloid caste* has made it all the more necessary to establish the identity and style of Sarit Sarat (a Meitei method of unarmed combat) and trace its racial ancestory. (Emphasis mine)

During the heyday of Hindu Vaisnavism there was a concerted effort to identify the Meitei with the Aryan heritage of North Indian culture. The legend of Chitrangada, the queen of Manipur and her marriage with Arjuna, the hero of the Hindu epic Mahabharata, was often referred to as the Aryan origin of the Meitei people. The new movement aims to unlearn this "Indo-Aryan" teaching and establish Meitei affinity with the Mongolian ancestry. Enthusiastic leaders are now keen to introduce the original Meitei script in school. There is a growing trend among the young educated to drop the Kshatriya title Singh at the end of their personal name; instead, they use their lineage identity.

The new consciousness of Meitei identity has also brought in its wake a great interest in ancient religious rituals. During my visit to the deserted royal temple in the palace ground in Kangla, I found a group of about forty people listening to ancient Meitei scriptures. Inside the altar room, instead of the Hindu deity Govindaji, Pakhamba was being worshipped. Back in 1951, a group called the Sanamahi cult, worshipped Meitei *Lais* at Numaijing instead of the Hindu deity Siva (Lightfoot, 1958). The new consciousness is also the reason behind the movement to reinstate the Meitei deity Hiyanthang Lairembi, who had to cede her place to a Hindu goddess in the past.

At present, different *leikais* are forming new administrative bodies to organize *Lai Harouba* festivals and build permanent brick temples for the community. An older *maibi* (60s) at the Khoriphoba *Lai Harouba* festival in Nambol said, "Nowadays, we attend more *Lai Haroubas* than we did twenty years ago. People are becoming real believers in *Lais*." There is also a trend towards young educated men replacing the older group on *Lai Harouba* committees. In Thambalkhul, in 1978, a committee was formed with elected members between the ages of twenty-five and forty-five years, including both married and unmarried men. Of the previous committee the membership was composed only of married men above the age of forty-five years, and as old as eighty years. While the majority of the members of the present committee are literate with the advent of modern education, the older members were all illiterate.

In urban areas, the growing interest in *Lai Harouba* has created a trend towards secularization. At *Lai Harouba* of Hiyanthang Lairembi, of Laiputhiba at Khurai or of Laikhurembi at Uripok, one experiences a carnival-type atmosphere that overwhelms the traditional ritual ceremonies. However, in the midst of the noise and secular entertainment, priestesses still dance to the gentle and haunting melodies played on the *pena*. They become possessed and deliver an oracle when the music stops, which people listen to with great attention.

The secularization of traditional ritual has gone so far that a group of original *maibis* were included in the grand Republic Day parade on January 26, 1978. The *maibis* performed a sacred dance, *Loiching Jagoi*, highly regarded for its esoteric value. I also witnessed a group of *maibis* performing *Loiching Jagoi* on the Imphal Dance Academy stage, in honour of a visiting high official from New Delhi.

The ancient fervour of the pre-Vaisnava faith is vibrant in rural society. One can still observe traditional ritual behaviour among the rural folk. Of the non-Vaisnava community festivals, I found three which enjoyed the most importance: (1) *Chairaoba*, the ritual of New Year's Day, (2) *Sarai-Khangba*, the three weekend-long rituals at the end of the Meitei year, and (3) the annual ceremony of *Lai Harouba*. While all of these rituals are important in rural life, *Lai Harouba* is the prime ritual, celebrated in a most spectacular and grand manner.

LAI HAROUBA FESTIVAL

Several Vaisnavite and non-Vaisnavite ceremonies present the religious culture of the Meitei as a community-oriented affair. Of all the ceremonies, *Lai Harouba* exemplifies the most exuberant and integrated community life and is celebrated entirely outside the Vaisnava framework.

In almost all villages of the Valley, *Lai Harouba* (in pleasure of *Lai*) is an annual festival performed locally for the benefit of the entire community. The fishing community of Thanga, an island in Lake Loktak, observes the festival for twenty days.[69] In both Radhagram and Thambalkhul villages, *Lai Harouba* was celebrated for five days in the month of March. During the months March through June, the villages around Nambol perform *Lai Harouba* one after another, often overlapping.[70] Of these ceremonies, the eleven-day grand festival at Khoriphoba temple of Nambol is the most important and attracts devotees from the largest region. Lord Khoriphoba is considered the guardian deity of eight villages surrounding a small hillock, but "Khoriphoba" is also referred to as *Lainingthou* (the King of the *Lais*), and *Lai* temples in several villages with lesser status outside the jurisdiction of Khoriphoba temple (including two of my villages) send offerings to Khoriphoba during *Lai Harouba*.

Temple Committee

Each temple has an all-male committee (*marup*) including a *Lai mapu* or *Lai selumba* (caretaker). The committee oversees the temple fund which comes from annual collection and from the sales of paddy grown on fields owned by the temple. In my villages, the main task of the committee is to organize *Lai Harouba* annually. Every family of the village contributes to the collection. The average expense for a five-day celebration is, in my villages, about Rs. 3,500. At Nambol, the committee, with representatives of eight villages, supervises a much larger fund. As in some other famous *Lai* temples, there is a weekend worship every Sunday morning at Khoriphoba

[69]I gathered that in some of the Lai communities as in Andro village in the east, *Lai Harouba* is performed for about a month. No outsider is allowed to observe this festival, but one could probably recognize there the original form of *Lai Harouba* as it was performed in ancient times.

[70]In some areas of the Valley, the festival is observed during the harvesting season. I observed one in November in Chaijing village.

temple. Pilgrims from all over the Valley attend the Sunday ritual with their offerings and listen to *Laipao*, the *maibi* delivering the oracle in a trance. The Sunday collection and the income from various paddy fields are contributed to the temple fund. The committee supervises the entire festival.

When the village committee decides on a particular period for a *Lai Harouba*, it has to contact the *Pundit Loishang* at the palace. The *Loishang* assigns the three ritual functionaries: *maibi, maiba,* and *penakhongba*. It is essential to have at least a trio for a *Lai Harouba* ceremony, but the number of *maibis* and *penakhongbas* vary according to the funds available to the committee. Each of the functionaries is paid a fee specified by the *Loishang*. The fee differs according to the status of the person in the hierarchy of the *Loishang* and also the reputation of the person in the professional field. If a village can afford it, it can request the principal *maibi* to bring assistants with her. Radhagram hired one *penakhongba*, one *maiba*, and five *maibis*. In Thambalkhul, there was one *penakhongba*, one *maiba*, and three *maibis*. In Khoriphoba *Harouba*, there was one *maiba*, two *penakhongbas* and six *maibis*, including one older *maibi* of a high professional status. The villages might have their own *maibis* who work as diviners or predictors, but for a *Lai Harouba*, the committee has to approach the *Loishang* for the supply of ritual functionaries, though it may request for a particular person. Six months of the year, the *maibis* and other ritual functionaries travel all over the Valley and up to Kachhar and Lakhimpur and Silchar in Assam and to Tripura, the neighbouring states. They travel from one place to another and spend the period in location. They are boarded and lodged by the committee.

The committee, *Khoriphoba Thougal Marup* (the Association for Khoriphoba Worship) sets a plan of events for the eleven-day period which falls around May 9 through May 19.

Among nine different *Lai Haroubas* (both urban and rural) I observed, I shall focus on three, two in my villages, and the third at Khoriphoba temple in my host village, Nambol Awang.[71]

The core of the ritual was the same in all the three *Lai Haroubas*, with some rituals especially dedicated to Lord Khoriphoba.

[71]In Manipur, there are three kinds of *Lai Harouba*: *Kanglei, Chakpa* and *Moirang*. There is sometimes a combination of *Chakpa* and *Kanglei*. In Nambol I witnessed only the *Kanglei Lai Harouba*.

In Nambol, people evinced excitement months before the event. One could sense the festive season at Nambol bazaar, which swelled with crowds of devotees buying fruit, flowers, and clothes made for offerings, and various herbal leaves meant especially for offering to Khoriphoba. During this period, there is an abundant supply of fruit and flowers at the bazaar. The temple is situated on a hillock on the northwestern side of the national highway, Tidim Road, only a quarter mile from the Nambol bazaar. Streams of visitors come in buses or on foot.

7
Lai Harouba: The Prime Meitei Ritual

In pre-Hindu days, *Lai Harouba* was the most important state-supervised ritual. With the advent of Hinduism, the attention of royalty turned to the grandeur of the Hinduized ceremonies; nonetheless, *Lai Harouba,* as the prime community festival remained important in people's lives.

The organizational framework of *Lai Harouba* is under male authority. But women have very important roles to play in ritual participation of *Lai Harouba.*

Kabok Chaiqa

Kabok Chaiba, according to a Meitei *maiba* and some *maibis,* is a twenty-four hour long *Lai Harouba*[72] performed annually in some temples of Lairembi. Although the ritual is family-based, it involves the entire community and even the premises of the royal palace and the King in person.

Kabok Chaiba (sprinkling of puffed rice/festival of puffed rice) of Sorangthen Lairembi at Senjamei Leikei, Imphal, is organized every year by the members of the Sorangthen lineage. The deity is regarded as the wife of the earlier ancestor, Pakhamba. The ritual is organized by the males of the family, but during the ritual, they must remain outside the large temple, while women of the family along with some women of the community go inside. Eleven *maibis,* two *maibas* and two *penakhangbas* participate in the ritual dance and music inside the room. The *piba,* the lineage head, is not allowed to join. Only the wives of the lineage and married daughters can participate in the ritual.

All day on March 3, 1978 women prepared puffed rice inside the temple. In the evening, the ritual functionaries joined them and

---

[72]A family-based *Lai Harouba* is rather rare. There are only four other places where this ritual is performed. The deities are all female, e.g., Ayang Lairembi (Panthoibi) and Loishangthem Lairembi.

started their performance. Along with some Meitei friends I reached the temple at 8.00 p.m., an hour after the ritual had started. As we proceeded towards the temple we could hear from a distance a *maibi's* oracle broadcast loudly over the public address system. The temple courtyard and the porch were crowded with about three hundred people. Men had to sit outside, while women were packed inside the room. The *maibi's* head was covered with a thin veil. She sat in front of the deity and rang the brass bell in her left hand, chanting all the while in the archaic Meitei language. Her body shook in frenzied motion; her voice choked with occasional loss of breath. Some men were taking notes of the *maibi's* oracle. The *maibi* predicted the events of the coming year for the Sorang-then family and the community. After about fifteen minutes, a *maiba* sprinkled some water with *tairen* leaves over the *maibi* and her shaking began to lessen in its intensity. The *maiba* standing behind her, placed his hands over , and pressed the navel of the *maibi*. He murmured some *mantra*. The shaking stopped. The *maibi* received her veil. Her eyes were red and her body perspired profusely. She walked over towards a group of *maibis* sitting in one corner of the room and leaned against one of them in sheer exhaustion. The trance behaviour, *Laipao* was very similar to what I had witnessed previously during the *Laipao* sessions at the weekend rituals of some *Lai* temples. After some more *Laipao* sessions, the *maibis* got up in a group and performed *Loiching Jagoi* (dance welcoming the *Lai*). Later, Ima Rajani *maibi* (79) explained the movements to me: "The rotating fingers of the two hands symbolize the Guru and the divine mother. They move anti-clock-wise because this is the way the world rotated during the creation...The turned-out ankles in stepping shows the stepping on the earth still soft immediately after the creation." The *maibis* started the dance by placing their palms below the navel in a triangular shape reaching the points of fingers to the sexual zone. Another *maibi* said, "This posture symbolizes the birth canal, the passage to the womb which creates the human body." The dance started with gentle and subtle body movements and steps and gradually developed into a vigorous motion. Several *maibis* went into a trance as the dance gained momentum (about four to five minutes after the gentle beginning), and the *maibi* covered the head and face of one of them. The others were pacified by the sprinkling of *tairen* water and by gentle pressure on the navel. As the *maibi* in trance shook vigorously, the micro-

A veteran trader poses happily with a novice.

Macha nupi after a *Nahutpa* ceremony.

A scene from *Luhungba*.

Ima, with a stick, tasting her fruits.

Ima Rajani Maibi in *Panthoibi Jagoi*.

Pot-traders during evening hours.

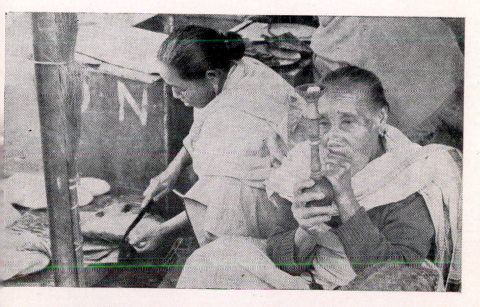

At the fish market *Ima* enjoys her hookah while her assistant dresses a fish.

Modern *Laishabis* (traditional hairstyle, right).

Ima embroiders a *Maiknaiba* border;
Machanupi, her granddaughter gives
company.

A Vaisnavite mythological play
at Nambol.

phones were brought near her. The *Laipao* lasted for about twenty minutes; predicting the future of the community she talked about children, illness, accident, and good fortune of the people, then for about six hours different *maibis* danced and took their turn in *Laipao* in a state of trance. The *penakhongbas* played music and sang. They danced with gentle steps along with the *maibi*'s dancing, but whenever the *Laipao* started they stopped and a silence fell over the crowds. After all the *maibis* had danced and been in a trance, an elderly Brahman woman said, "Now the ritual is over. We would like you to perform some dance and music." The room was darkened. The atmosphere changed. The *maibis* sang erotic songs from *Lai Harouba* repertoire. Women giggled. We left at 2.00 a.m. I was later told that the dance and music went on till daybreak.

Next day, the ritual started around 3.00 p.m. About forty women from the Sorangthen *sagei* carried baskets of puffed rice on their heads and proceeded in a procession towards the palace. The women wore brightly coloured *maiknaiba*, gold and gold-plated jewellery, flowers and expensive *inafis*, and were followed by two *maibas*, two *penakhongbas* and a group of *maibis*, as well as a band party playing traditional ritual music. The procession stopped at various spots on its way to the palace, a walk of about two miles, and each time the *maibis* performed a ritual dance on the street. They walked through national highways, among motor cars and cycles, and pedestrian passers-by.

On arriving at the palace the party sat down to rest. The *piba*'s wife distributed betel leaf and *biri* to all. A *maibi* led a small group of women, carrying offering baskets to the palace deity, Pakhamba, to Yumjao Lairembi (goddess of the house), and Guru Nong-Shaba (a male *Lai*), respectively. The next offering went to the Maharaja (King) and Rajamata (King's mother) and the last one to Pundit Achouba, the head of Pundit *Loishang*.

As the King has not held official status since 1972, he did not appear during the ceremony. Instead, an empty chair was placed on a carpet in the front veranda of the palace. The baskets were placed there. Then the *maibis* performed several dances, enacting different pieces of the creation myth. They performed *Loiching Jagoi*, the dance of hoe cultivation, the dance of cotton growing, spinning, weaving, etc., in a mood of joyous celebration. *Penakhongbas* and the band party accompanied them. I was told that had the Maharaja been present, the *maibis* would have performed a special dance, *Laisen Jagoi* (dance of creation) and entered a state of trance to deliver the oracle pertaining to the future of the kingdom. In the past, the king relied a great deal on such predictions. Women in the procession sat down on the palace steps and the lawn to relax while they watched the performance. After an hour of dancing, the party went towards the huts of the Pundit *Loishang*. The *maibis* now danced *Panthoiba Jagoi* (dance dedicated to the divine mother) in front of Pundit Achouba, a very old Pundit, head of the *Loishang* Pundits. An older *maibi* said, "Some years we perform *Kukthuk Jagoi*, forming a snake design to show Pakhamba coiled into a resting position." With this dance, the ritual was over.

Lai Harouba OF THE COMMUNITY

The original source prescribing the procedure for the *Lai Harouba* ritual is unfound an ancient Meitei text, *Laithak Laikharol*, written in the archaic script. In a modern Meitei text, Pundit Kulachandra, who is a *maiba* for *Lai Harouba*, explains the expression as *Lai Hoi Lauba*, meaning "rejoice for the God." The term *Lai Harouba* is derived from this:

> The day Asiba (Sanamahi) completed the creation of earth, he became confused. The Guru opened his mouth and showed the image of his creation. Asiba then exclaimed, *"Lai Hoi Lauba."* *Lai Harouba* is the imitation of this. . . .In *Lai Harouba* people ask for prosperity of the earth. We believe that if this ritual is not done properly, there will be destruction of our land. (Kulachandra, 1963:2)

I shall describe the rituals in the sequence I observed them in Radhagram and Thambalkhul in March 1978, and at Khoriphoba temple in May, 1978. The ritual period at both villages was five days, but at Khoriphoba it lasted for eleven days. As the basic rituals and the core programme were the same in all three places, I shall not mention the names of the temples separately. However, I shall discuss the additional rituals observed at Khoriphoba temple as well as how they were practised in the smaller temples of the villages.

Laifi Shetpa

Lai Harouba began with *Laifi Shetpa* (clothing of the *Lais*). This ritual was observed in both villages as there are no permanent images in their temples. In the afternoon the *Lai mapu* brought some bundles and the *maibis* dressed the *Lais* with bronze masks. The villagers came with large baskets and trays with offerings of paddy, rice, fruits, and clothing. The *maiba* sprinkled *tairen* water on each of these and placed them at the foot of the altar. Then the *maiba* and *maibis* busied themselves in arranging special ritual objects for *Lai Ikoba* (to call the *Lai* from water).

Lai Ikoba

The preparation for *Lai Ikoba* necessitated the following objects:

1. *Khaiyong:* Offering on a plantain leaf. Rice mounds with duck's eggs and *langthrei* leaves.[73]
2. *Ihaifu:* An earthen pot decorated with plantain leaf, *langthrei* leaves and flowers. There is a specific pattern of decoration. It looked like a long shape going straight up from the opening of the pot. The *ihaifu* or *ishaifu* is for the purpose of carrying the souls of the *Lais*.
3. A solution of rice powder. This is a substitute for wine, *yu*, used in the past.
4. Preparation of a shredded vegetable called *sinju*, a popular salad in a Meitei meal. *Haibimana* herbal leaves are also added.
5. Fruits: Oranges and bananas.
6. Hollow pieces of bamboo used as rice measures, *ootong*. There should be sixteen of these, nine for *Lai* and seven for *Lairembi*.
7. Sacred thread: Freshly spun thread called *hirila*. There should be nine lines of thread for *Lai* and seven lines for *Lairembi*.
8. *Chong:* Huge white umbrellas to hold over *Lais* during a procession.
9. *Alwar:* Huge palm-leaf fans.
10. *Thang:* Two swords designed according to the particular style of the *Lais*.
11. Several utensils.
12. *Sumbul:* Rice-pounding pestle.
13. *Faida:* Seat carpets for *Lais*.
14. Palm fans of standard size.

The principal *maibi* asked a group of men and women to stand in two rows. Two men in white dhotis, large white turbans, and shawls on bare chests, came forward and stood on two plantain

---

[73]Leaves of a herbal bush considered sacred.

leaves placed in front of the altar. The order of the procession was as follows:[74]

From the farthest row from the temple:

First row: Two *pakhangs* (bachelors) holding *thang* (sword).

Second and third rows: Four *laishabis* (maidens) in two rows carrying fans and wine goblets.

Fourth row: Two *mous* (married women) carrying seat carpets and *sumbul* (rice-pounding tool).

Fifth row: *Lai-pubas*, two men as bearers of *Lais*.

Sixth row: Two men holding two *chongs* (huge white umbrellas) over the *Lais*.

In front of the first row one elderly woman stood in the middle, holding an earthen water pitcher over her head. The group of *maibis* stood on a line in front of the procession (Figure 6).

The two men who were chosen as *Lai-pubas* were of good social standing. A man married to a widow or a divorced woman is disqualified for this role. A divorced or widowed woman cannot participate in this procession. In a *sagei* temple, the *piba* (*sagei* head) and his wife were supposed to carry the *Lais*.

Married women wore bright-coloured *maiknaiba* over their breasts and white transparent *inafis*, their hair put into buns decorated with flower bunches. Each of the married women wore a special coloured cloth, *khoangchet* (small cotton shawl) indicating the special colour of her husband's clan.[75] The *laishabis* wore *maiknaiba* on their waists along with blouses and *inafis*, their hair brushed down and crowned with an encircling tiara. All the women were adorned with gold and gold-plated jewellery. The *pakhangs* wore all-white *dhotis* and *kurtas* and turbans, with shawls tied around their waists, and flower garlands.

After a short *Loichang Jagoi* (awakening the *Lais* or welcome to the *Lais*) to *pena* music, the principal *maibi* gave two *ihaiphus* (earthen pots) to the two *Lai-pubas*. Now the *maibis* walked forward leading the procession with dancing steps, along with *penakhongba* and *maiba* as *pena* played. Where the procession reached an adjacent pond, the principal *maibi* sat on a bunch of paddy straw

[74]The number of people in each of the rows could be much more, sometimes four to eight during Khoriphoba *Harouba*. The order in Radhagram and Thambalkhul followed the textual minimum.

[75]In some *Haroubas* all married women follow this rule, though in others it is relaxed. Each clan has a different colour of its own, e.g., black for Khuman.

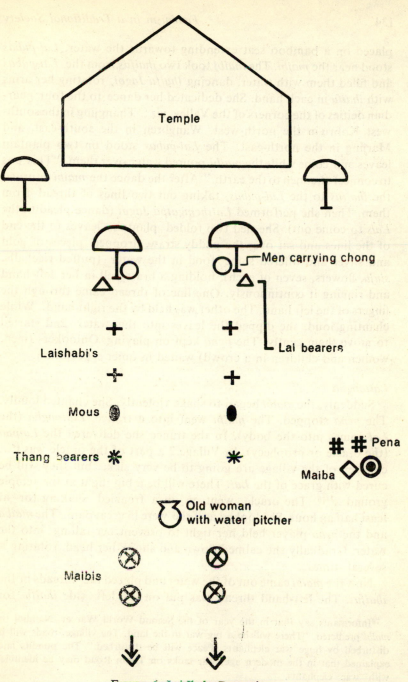

FIGURE 6: Lai-Ikoba Procession

Temple

Men carrying chong

Laishabi's

Lai bearers

Mous

Thang bearers

Pena

Maiba

Old woman
with water pitcher

Maibis

placed on a bamboo seat extending towards the water. *Lai-pubas*
stood near the *maibi*. The *maibi* took two *ihaifus* from the *Lai-pubas*
and filled them with water, dancing *Ihaifu Jagoi*, rotating her arms
with *ihaifu* in each hand. She dedicated her dance to the four guardian deities of the corners of the Valley, viz., Thangjing in the southwest, Kobru in the north-west, Wangbren in the south-east, and
Marjing in the north-east. The *Lai-pubas* stood on two plantain
leaves and coins while the *maibi* poured water over them. "This was
to connect the men to the earth." After the dance the *maibi* returned
the *ihaifus* to the *Lai-pubas*, taking out two lines of thread from
them. Then she performed *Laithemgatpa Jagoi* (dance pleading the
Lais to come out). She tied two folded plantain leaves to the end
of the lines and sat over the paddy straw, dropped pieces of gold
and silver and offered some food in the water (puffed riceballs,
sinju, flowers, seven of each), holding a brass bell in her left hand
and ringing it continuously. One line of thread came through the
fingers of the left hand. The other was held by the right hand. While
chanting loud, she dipped the leaves into the water and started
to move them gently. The *pena* kept on playing. Onlookers (men,
women and children in a crowd) waited in quiet expectation.

Laitongba

Suddenly, the *maibi* began to shake violently. She chanted loudly.
The *pena* stopped. The *maibi* went into a trance, *Laitongba* (the
Lai comes into the body). In the trance she delivered the *Laipao*
(the oracle or prophecy). In Village 2 a part of the oracle was "...
children of the village are going to be very sick, but they will be
cured with grace of the *Lai*. There will be a big fight at the temple
ground..."[76] The oracle went on in a frenzied shaking for at
least half an hour. She looked as if she were in great pain. The *maiba*
and the *pena* player held her tight to prevent her falling into the
water. Gradually she calmed down and shook her head, rotating it
several times.

Now the *maibi* came out of the water and placed the threads in the
ihaifus. The left-hand thread was put on the left side *ihaifu* for

[76]Informants say that in the year of the Second World War at Nambol the
maibi predicted, "There will be a big war in the land. The village roads will be
disturbed by huge war elephants. Peace will be disturbed." The pundits later
explained that in the modern age, war tanks on Tidim Road may be identified
with war elephants.

Lairembi, and the right-hand one to the right side *ihaifu* for *Lai.* The water pot of the old woman was filled by the *maibi.*

The *maibis* proceeded back to the temple and the procession followed in exactly the previous order. The *pena* started to play again. On the way back the *maibis* stopped three times and performed dances in dedication, called *Khunjao Laichao Jagoi.*

Before reaching the temple, the procession had to jump over several objects, e.g., fire, a basket of rice, duck's egg, dried fish, salt, iron and brass. The *maibis* were the first to jump over, followed by the old woman and then the rest of the members according to their order.

The old woman took the water pitcher inside the altar room, the *Lai-pubas* following her. Two *maibis* took the threads out of the *ihaifus* and placed them over the navels of the images, hidden inside the clothes.[77] The *maibis* exclaimed, "*Hiri*" (ritual thread); others replied, "*Hiri*". This ritual is called *Hirifanba.* The *ihaifus* were placed on either side of the altar. A group of married women performed a short dance to *pena* music, using rotating palm movements and gentle steps, typical of Vaisnavite rituals.

The *pena* player then sang a beautiful tune praising the virtues of the retiring *Lais.* At this point the *maibis* carried several offering trays for *Saraikhangba* (to feed the devil) ritual. They carried the offering, with a bell ringing to the left hand of the principal *maibi,* to the outskirts of the village. During *Lai Harouba, Saraikhangba* was performed on the first, third, fifth, seventh, and ninth days, or more after, i.e., on every odd-numbered day. The entire ritual of the evening was called *Lai Loukhotpa* and lasted about four hours.

Daily Schedule of Rituals

Morning Rituals. Early in the morning the *pena khongba* sang specific songs awakening the *Lais,* and the curtain was drawn open. As the devotees gathered with their offerings, a *maibi* sat in front of the altar. After singing and chanting and ringing bells with the left hand, she went into *Laitongba* and delivered an oracle. A large crowd gathered to listen, microphones amplifying her voice. At Khori-

---

[77]The textual instruction is that the thread carrying the *Lai* will be placed by a *maiba,* supported by three men, and the thread carrying *Lairembi* will be placed by a *maibi* supported by three married women (Pundit Kulachandra: 1963). This rule is still followed in some other villages, according to my informants.

phoba temple six *maibis* delivered their *Laipaos* one after another, their voices greatly amplified from the hill-top. People could hear it from Nambol and surrounding villages.

After the *Laipao* session around mid-day, the curtain was drawn.

Evening Rituals. In the late afternoons, during the festival period, one can sense the festive mood of the villagers. Every family must send its offerings to the temple. In Radhagram, all married daughters are obliged to send their offerings to the temple of their natal villages. In Radhagram, every day in the late afternoon, we met streams of men, women and children walking towards the temple ground. We could hear the band party playing traditional *Lai Harouba* tune, from a distance. This was broadcast through an amplifier. Women and girls wore their best in bright-coloured *maiknaiba*, gold and gold-plated heavy jewellery and fine white transparent *inafi* specially made for the festival, often rented from professional costume suppliers in Nambol. Little girls were brilliantly dressed with dazzling gold-plated jewellery. Their noses and foreheads were finely decorated with *chandana*, and they had flowers in their hair. The *mous* wore special bouquets of orchids with shining green leaves on their buns. The *laishabis* tucked flowers behind their ears and let their shining hair down, looking crisp and clean. Men wore white *dhotis* and *kurtas* with shawls over their shoulders. Many young men wore western clothes; little boys, everyday clothes of shorts and shirts.

Hundreds of men, women and children gathered on the temple ground of Village 1. The huge courtyard was surrounded by bamboo groves. The sheds on the right and left side of the ground were packed with spectators: males on the right, females on the lett. Several small umbrella-decorated bamboo poles dedicated by devotees were erected in front of the temple. Four huge *chongs* (white umbrellas were fixed in front of the temple porch. The village *pradhan* (head) sat on the right side of the porch with several other important men. The left side of the porch was reserved for the *maibis*. Other women could sit there too. The *maibis* wore special ritual costume over their everyday white dresses; green velvet blouses, gold and gold-plated jewellery, with armband, sash and necklaces indicating their status in the *Loishang*. Their hair was put into buns with long hairpieces hanging from them. Each was beautifully decorated with flowers and fine *chandana* designs. The *maiba* wore a *dhoti* with *pakhamba* motif (coiling snake design) printed on it, and *kurta*, and a turban. The *penakhongba* wore a *pakhamba*-design *dhoti*, velvet jacket, gold-plated jewellery and an elegantly decorated turban with a fan shaped on the top.

Many of the *mous* again wore the cotton *khoangchet* (wrapper), indicating their husband's clan. On the right side of the temple ground the band party was seated. The two *pena* players were accompanied by a *dholak* (drum), their soft melody often drummed down by the band music. Occasionally there were announcements over loudspeakers regarding the special events, like *Shumangleela* play on a certain date or the coming of the Speaker of the State Assembly. Local M.L.A.'s (Members of the Legislative Assembly) and several candidates for the post of *pradhan* for the oncoming Panchayat election were present in the audience. Everyone came to bow to the deities before taking their seats.

The evening ritual started around 3.30 p.m. and went by the following sequence:

Lai Lashingfa. Every day the *Lais* were dressed in new clothes by the *maibis*.

Lai Langba. Several elderly men of distinguished status offered flowers to the *Lais*. The flowers were then distributed, first to the men and then to the women.

Punglon Jagoi. A dedication dance was performed by five *maibis* facing the altar.[78] No one was allowed to dance before the *maibis*. The band was quiet and the *pena* players played a melodious tune. While the *maibis* danced, a group of *macha nupis* joined them trying hard to imitate the *maibis*. Gradually young *laishabis* joined. As the *maibis* started to move towards the right side of the temple, all the women joined them in groups for *Thougal* (dedication) dance. The *maibis* were followed in order by the group of *hanubis*, *mous*, *laishabis* and *macha nupis*. The women and girls formed two rows and danced with gentle movement encircling the ritual ground. The *maibis* performed five different movements with walking steps. Women danced these with real skill, without any previous rehearsal, little girls imitating their elders. The audience on the female side was a bit relaxed. Many commented *"Fajari"* (beautiful) in praise of some dancers. Several men came forward and offered

---

[78]In other *Lai Haroubas*, *Loiching Jagoi* or *Jagoi Okpagi* is sometimes performed to begin the ritual.

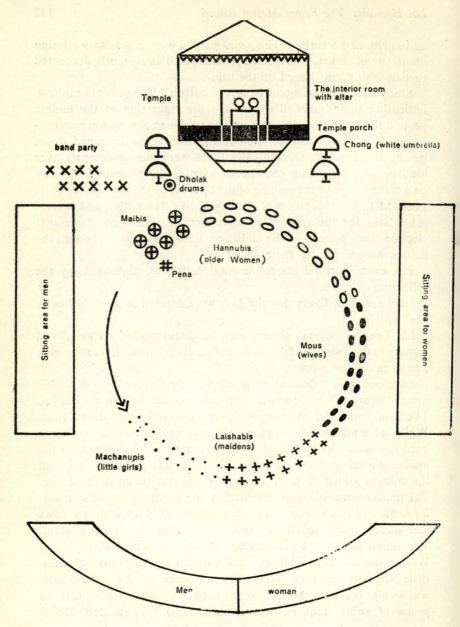

FIGURE 7: Thougal Dance

dakhshina.[79] (Figure 7.)

Hoi Lauba. Immediately after the *Thougal* (which lasted for about half an hour), a group of men in Meitei dress, the *maiba* the *pena-khongbas* and *maibis* gathered at the south-western part of the court-yard and sang accompanied by the clapping of hands and *pena* and *dholak* music. The song started with exclamations "Ho-ho-haya-ha..."[80]

After *Hoi Lauba*, the regular ritual was interrupted by a dance performance of *Leima Jagoi* (dance of the *Lairembi*), presented by a group of village *laishabis*. The *laishabis* are trained by a professional teacher. Although this particular dance was not a part of the core programme, such performances were part of traditional *Lai Harouba* custom. Good performers often rehearsed for months to be able to perform during the annual *Lai Harouba*. I observed several dances to *langol* legends, especially the theme of *Khamba-Thoibi* in different *Lai Harouba* festivals.[81] The performers hired costumes from pro-fessional suppliers.

At Radhagram, as the *laishabis* danced, the candidates for the post of *pradhan* (in the coming election) competed with one another in offering money as *dakhshina*.

Panthoibi Jagoi. After a series of recreational dances, the *maibis* started *Panthoibi Jagoi*, dedicated to the divine mother. This was another important dance commonly observed in the *Lai* rituals. Again, the women and girls joined the *maibis* for a *Thougal*, each age group dancing in order in procession.

Anoirol: The *penakhongba* sang with soft stepping, raising legs and swaying movements. The *maibis*, the *maiba*, and women (in different age groups) followed the *penakhongba*'s swaying movement. After making a circle around the courtyard, they came to the temple.

Laibao: This is the most important part of the daily ritual. No one

[79]At this moment, the present anthropologist was requested to join the *Thou-gal*, and she ended up collecting some *dakhshina*. The women were planning for this request for quite some time. They had never had a non Meitei woman join their *Lai Harouba Thougal*. Seeing me skeptical, the woman said, "If you want, we will get a written permission from the *pradhan*."

[80]Pundits and some informants say that women can also join *Hoi Lauba* but prefer to join the *Thougal* dance over *Hoi Lauba*.

[81]In the ballads of Khamba-Thoibi, there are beautiful descriptions of the couple performing together in front of Lord Thangjing of Moirang during a *Lai Harouba* ritual (N. Tombi Singh, 1976:136).

was allowed to leave the ritual ground after *Laibao* had started. The *maibis* made arrangements for the *Laibao* procession which is very similar to the procession I described for the *Lai Ikoba* ritual on the first day of *Lai Harouba*. When all members of the procession appeared in front of the porch, the *Lai-pubas* stood on two plantain leaves and a *maibi* brought out the *hiri* (ritual thread) carrying the *Lais*' souls and placed them inside the shawls of the men, pressed to their chests. The procession stood in the following order:

From the immediate front of the altar:

First row: *Lai-pubas*

Second row: Two *pakhang chong* bearers stood on the ground in front of the temple porch

Third row: Two *mous*

Fourth row: Four *laishabis*

Fifth row: Four *laishabis*

Sixth row: Two *thang* bearers—*akhangs*

Seventh row: Five *maibis* in a row

Two *penakhongbas* and *dholak* drummers accompanied the dancing *maibis*. As the procession started, the *Lai-pubas* went ahead of the *chong* bearers under the huge white umbrella. The members of the *Laibao* carried the same objects as they did for the *Lai Ikoba* ritual.

However, there was a striking change in female attire in the *Laibao* at Radhagram. In several other places[82] and in Thambalkhul, I observed women dressed in brilliant-coloured *maiknaibas* adorned with shining gold jewellery. The text (Kulachandra, 1963) also recommends that women dress in their best in the traditional style. In Radhagram, women in *Laibao* wore very plain-looking *pungo fanek*, familiar in Vaisnavite ceremonies. The *Lai Mapu* explained: "In the past, women always wore *maiknaiba*. They still wear them for the *Thougal*. We have recently changed the rule, because *maiknaibas* cannot be washed so easily and cleaned after a woman menstruates. *Pungo fanek* can be cleaned easily. In *Laibao* we have to be one hundred per cent sure that the *faneks* are really clean." He added, "We think women are already taking a very important part during *Lai Harouba*. During *Laibao*, the *Lai-pubas* should stand

---

[82]I observed women at *Laibao* in traditional attire in places like Chajing, Oinam, Thanga, Moirang, Hiyangthang, Khurai, Laiputhiba, Chaning Leima, Langpok, and in several other *Lai Haroubas*.

out not the women. They should dress less and play down their role.[83]

Before bringing out the *Lais'* soul, a *maibi* performed a ritual with dedication to the four *Lais* in four directions. The procession stood with its back to the temple. The five *maibis* faced the *Lais* and performed *Loichang Jagoi*, holding *langthrei* leaves between their fingers and making specific gestures of touching and stepping on the soft, newly-created earth. After the dance, the procession moved on (Figure 8).

The principal *maibi* exclaimed, "*Ho Lai-ningthou Madaremsha*" (Oh, the servants of the *Lais*).

The procession answered, "*Haan*" (Yes).

Maibi: Hoirou Haya Laugodari (We are going to sing. Do not move).

Group: *Hoi, hoi* (Yes, yes).

The procession stood quietly and the *penakhongbas* sang, "*Hoiro Hoya... Hoi Lauba...*"

The text explains this expression of *Hoi Lauba* as an expression of the joy of creation. During *Lai Harouba* the *pena* players are supposed to sing expressing Sanamahi's joy. They follow certain songs prescribed by the text.

Khayom Jagoi. Now the *maibis* danced *Khayom Jagoi* with palms joined in the front with gentle swaying movements and walked forward in a circle. The steps were choreographed. As the *maibis* led the procession, *hanubis*, *mous*, *laishabis* and *macha nupis* joined in groups. Some men joined in. Women followed the *maibis'* steps. Men walked. The members of the procession followed the *maibis'* dancing rhythm.

Hakchangshaba Jagoi (dance of the creation of the human body):
Maibi: Oh servants of the *Lais*, let us create the human body.
Women's group: *Hoi, hoi*, (Yes, yes). *Saroshe* (We will form).
Maibi: Jagoi Louri (Do it through dance).

---

[83]Later, in Khoriphoba *Harouba*, I found the complete exclusion of *mous* and *laishabis*. Only pre-pubecent girls joined the procession and an old woman joined the *Lai Ikoba*. I gathered that a few years ago, a *laishabi* started to menstruate during *Laibao*. Because of the danger of pollution, all members of the *Laibao* had to take baths and change their clothes. The *Laibao* ritual had to be repeated. Since then the temple committee has banned any woman of menstruating age to participate in the *Laibao* procession. One member said, "We know the textual instruction, but we do not want to take the risk anymore!"

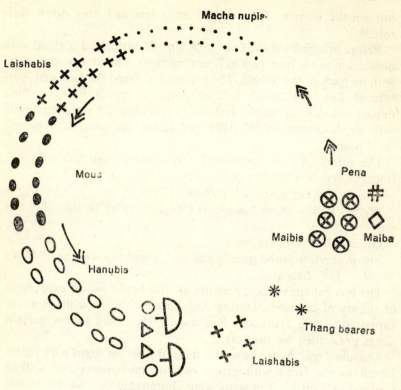

Macha nupis.

Laishabis

Mous

Pena

Maibis

Maiba

Hanubis

Thang bearers

Laishabis

Lai and chong bearers

FIGURE 8 : Daily Procession for *Laibao*

Women's group: *Hoi, hoi.*

Khut tek Mathek (*khut*-hand, *thekpa*- bend): The *maibis* perform-med *Khut tek Mathek* dance to offer the sixty-four sequences of the *Hakchangshaba* (creation of the human body). Each of the move-ments was performed with specific hand gestures, the procession following with gentle steps. Women of different age groups followed the procession with a gentle dance step and rotating palm movements. The sixty-four sequences of *Hakchangshaba* were movements show-ing:

1. birth canal and womb
2. roof of the head
3. forehead
4. two sides of the head
5. front part of the head
6. Eyebrows

7. corners of the eyes	8. eyes
9. bridge of the nose	10. nose
11. nostrils	12. cheeks
13. upper lip	14. lips
15. teeth	16. chin
17. ears	18. earholes
19. back of the head	20. throat
21. shoulder	22. back of the shoulder
23. entire shoulder	24. arms
25. elbows	26. inner forearms
27. wrists	28. tops of the palms
29. palms	30. fingers
31. nails	32. lines of palms
33. circular lines on the tips of the fingers	34. spinal cord
35. pulse at the wrists	36. breast
37. touching of the left and right fingers and touching of the left and right thumbs with middle fingers	38. breast-plate
39. heart	40. abdomen
41. waist	42. buttocks
43. anus	44. womb
45. sacrum	46. lower thighs
47. groin	48. upper thighs
49. knees	50. shin bones
51. calves	52. ankles
53. ankle bones	54. heels
55. tops of the feet	56. soles of the feet
57. toes	58. points of the toes
59. toe nails	60. lines under the toes
61. arches of the feet	

Then the maibis added a finishing touch to the entire body and performed a dance asking for the soul of the body from Guru Sidaba.

A dance to transmit the soul to the body.

After completing several circles by performing each of the above sequences, the *maibi* exclaims, "Oh servants of the *Lais*."

Group: *Ha-a-n* (Yes).

Maibi: The body has the soul and it is time for the baby to be

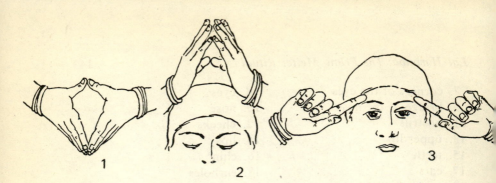

1

2

3

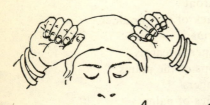

4

6

5

7

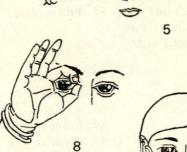

9

8

10

11

12

13

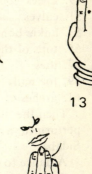

14

15

16

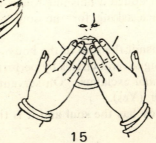

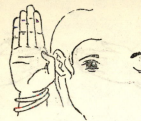
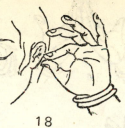
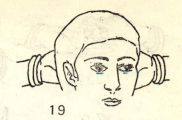

17

18

19

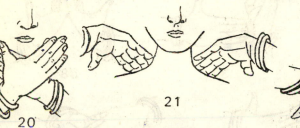

20

21

22

23

24

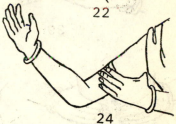

25

26

27

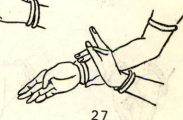

28

29

30

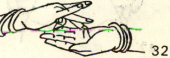

31

32

33 34 35

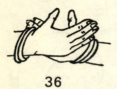

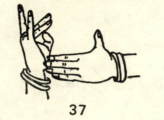

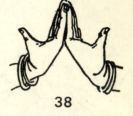

36 37 38

39 40

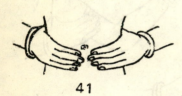

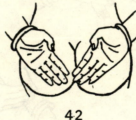

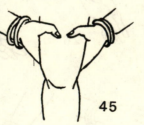

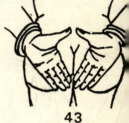

41 42 43

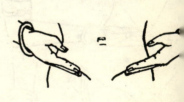

44 45 46

47 48

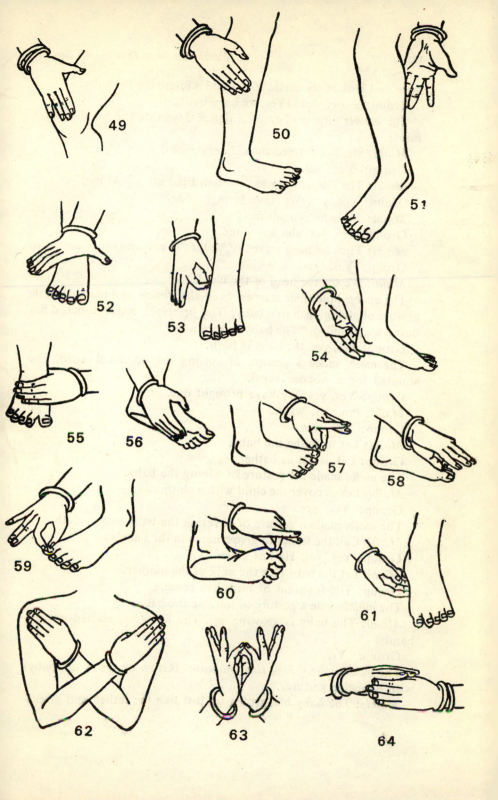

born and look at the earth. You build a house for the baby.

Group: *Share, share* (Yes, we have built).

The *maibis* now performed a dance depicting the building of a house.

Maibi: She has entered the delivery room.

Group: Yes, yes.

Maibi: The labour pain has started. Find me a gold mat.

Group: Yes, yes. We have brought one.

Maibi: Midwife, go inside.

Group: Yes, yes, she has gone.

Maibi: Time to have waves of water. The membranes are torn.

Group: Yes, yes.

Maibi: We see the head of the child.

The *maibis* hold their scarves over the *fanek* and made a subtle gesture of giving birth to a baby. The principal *maibi* touched her buttock and yelled, "The baby is born now!"

Group: Yes, yes, the baby is born.

The *maibi* made a gesture of cutting the umbilical cord. She shouted for a wooden bowl.

Group: Yes, yes. We have brought one.

Maibi: Pour the water.

Group: Yes, yes.

Maibi: Let us bathe the baby.

Group: Let us, let us bathe.

The *maibi* made the gesture of wiping the baby.

Maibi: Let us cover the child with a cloth.

Group: Yes, yes.

The *maibi* made a gesture of covering the baby with a cloth.

Maibi: Call the father to give a name in the baby's ears.

Group: Yes, yes. He has given.

Maibi: Let the baby face the milk of the mother.

Group: The fountain of milk has come.

The *maibi* made a gesture of nursing the baby.

Maibi: The baby is growing up. The baby has started moving hands.

Group: Yes.

The *maibis* sing, *"Ting ting chaorow"* (Grow up, grow up, baby) with bouncing gestures.

Maibis: The baby has grown up just like the father and grandfather.[84]

Maibi: He wants to dress up.

Group: Clothe him. Yes, yes.

The *maibis* danced with gestures of clothing a baby. They sang in a melodious tune.

Group: *Ho-ya-ya-yaya*.

Yumsarol Kuttek (hand movements of house building).

Maibi: Oh servants of the *Lais*.

Group: Yes, yes.

Maibi: Let us build a house for our lord.

Group: Yes, yes.

Maibi: Let us find a suitable plot.

Group: Yes.

The *maibis* make gestures of choosing a plot.

The main *maibi*: Let us find an auspicious day for the foundation.

Group: Yes, yes.

Maibi: Let us level the ground.

Group: Yes, yes.

The *maibis* made gestures of levelling.

Maibi: Oh servants of the *Lais*.

Group: Yes, yes.

Maibi: Let us make a design of a room.

Group: Yes, yes.

Maibi: Let us measure with thread.

Group: Yes, yes.

Maibi: Now we fix the pillars of wood.

Group: Yes, yes.

The *maibis* danced with movements enacting the fixing of pillars.

Maibi: Now we have fixed the pillars.

Group: Yes, yes.

Maibi: Now let us start to build.

Group: Yes, yes.

The *maibis* danced showing the plastering of a house. They came forward to the altar. *Penakhongbas* sang a special song of offering

---

[84]Until this moment, there was no reference to the baby's sex. Meitei writers like Jogendrajit Singh and Rajo Maibi refer to the baby as Guru's son, Pakhamba (Jogendrajit Singh, n.d.; Rajo Maibi, 1977). In another text, *Kakching Haraoba*, there is mention of babies growing up as *Pee* and *Paa* (parents). The book also indicates that the mother takes ten months and the father takes two months, altogether 365 days, to complete the creation of a baby.

while the *maibis* opened their folded scarves in front of the altar with a gesture of offering a house.

Maibi: We have completed the construction of a golden house. Let us perfrom *Panthoibi Jagoi* (*panthoibi*: divine mother; *jagoi*: dance — dance dedicated to the divine mother) for the prosperity of our community.

Group: *Hoi, hoi.*

The *maibis* started dancing *Panthoibi Jagoi* and the people of the procession sat down on one side of the arena. Two *maibis* performed the dances, enacting the sequences of fruit gathering, hoeing, sowing of seed, harvesting, sowing of cotton seed, picking of cotton, spinning and weaving, all in detailed dramatic action. The *pena-khongbas* and *dholak* drummers accompanied their dance all along from the beginning.

The principal *maibi* exclaimed, "*Lai* and *Lairembi* have matured now. It is time for them to become a couple."

The two *maibis* danced, running, jumping, sitting, depicting all kinds of domestic activities, e.g., washing of clothes, carrying of water, drying of clothes. Sometimes the *maibis* went close to the *dholak* drummer and danced ecstatically. Several people offered *dakhshina* to the *maibis*; they then enacted an offering of clothes to *Lais*.

Two more *maibis* joined the group and the procession started to move again. Many women and girls joined the procession and performed *Thougal* dance movements. After one round, the *maibis* left the procession and came to the middle of the ground and holding their sashes made a gesture of bowing. The group now stood quietly. The *maiba*, the male priest, then came to the middle of the ground.

Nikonthakonba. As the *maiba* stood along with the *maibis*, several men joined them. The men touched a tray of offering and the *maiba* chanted, calling all the souls of the villagers and even those who were away from their homes. The *maiba* prayed loudly for the peace of the community. Immediately after the prayer, a man and a *maibi* raced to reach the *Lais*. The *maibi* won. Again they ran and again the *maibi* won. The young girls clapped, singing rhymes, "*Lairembi ne thoire*" (*Lairembi* has won). The men teased, "No, the *Lai* has won!" The spectators giggled as the mock fight continued.

My informant said, "It is good for the *Lairembi* to win. Otherwise there will be no peace in the community."

The *Laibao* was going on for over two hours now. People had begun to relax by this time. The *maibis* sang erotic songs symbolizing sexual union of the *Lai* and *Lairembi*. One *maibi* sang, "One catches *ngamu* fish, another catches *nghao*."[85] People seemed to understand the erotic connotation. A *maibi* made a gesture of offering the fish to the *Lai*. Another *maibi* sang, "Be careful. The *ngamu* fish has become very wild." People laughed. This was the time for *pausha ishei*,[86] songs suggesting the romantic as well as the erotic relationship between the *Lai* and *Lairembi*. The *maibi* said, "Choose your partner." A pundit says, "In the past this was meant for husbands and wives dancing as couples. Nowadays, people are too embarrassed to dance, so the *maibis* themselves act as couples."[87] In Radhagram, the *maiba* and *maibi* sang as a couple. When the *maibi* was teasing the men, one man with a beautiful singing voice came into the arena and answered her. The spectators loved the dramatic exchange of songs and many offered *dakhshina* to the singers.

Now the *maibis* performed *Pafal Jagoi*. One *maibi* explained the dance as the movement of sexual union of the divine father and mother. While performing the dance, one *maibi* had *laitongba*. Her head was covered and she delivered *laipao*. The musicians stopped playing and two men ran to bring a notebook to write down the oracle.

[85]The *ngamu* fish is associated with the male sex organ, while the *nghao* fish is associated with the female sex organ.

[86]Informants gave me some examples of *pausha ishei* as follows:

Woman: "You are throwing the stone to my house. There will be a broken jug. Can you return the jug again?"

"The horns of the deer have not come out yet, they are only seen a bit on the surface."

Man: "The *ngamu* fish has not become mature yet. There is not enough hair. . . ."

Besides the suggestions of virginity, immature breasts and the male organ, there is often mention of public hair and labia minor ("leeches"). In the past, men and women used to stand in two rows facing each other. They clapped, going forward and backward. There are actually eights stanzas of *pausha ishei* but people could add new stanzas to them. They are sung like rhymes and the language is in riddles.

[87]The custom of husbands and wives dancing together in *pausha ishei* is not extinct. My field assistant informed me of watching it in 1978 in Thiyam village adjacent to my study area.

Chongkhongnaiba.[88] After the *maibi* came back to her senses, the *thang* bearers brought two more *chongs* and joined the two original *chong* bearers (Figure 9), all of them gathering in the middle of the

FIGURE 9: *Chongkhongnaiba*

[88]In one of the texts' interpretations, this dance demonstrates the cycle of creation. The four *chongs* are for *chuks* (ages). The two *maibis* represent *Pee* and *Paa*, the divine parents, Guru and Ima, in their sexual union. This creation method is eternal and is depicted in *Lairem Mathek* (Bharat Meitei, 1977).

arena. Two *maibis* took out the *hiri* (thread) with the *Lais'* souls. The four men held a piece of white cloth at four corners like a canopy, each holding a *chong* on a pole on the ground. Two *maibis* held the *hiri* in hand and started to dance, moving in and out under the canopy, coiling around each of the poles at the four corners in the direction of the four guardian *Lais* of the Valley. The coiling pattern of pakhamba created a complex movement. While the two *maibis* were dancing to depict the coiling of the snake, the other *maibis* sang to *pena* music and drum. They sang in a frivolous mood, hitting each other's buttocks with erotic gestures. The two *maibis* returned the *hiri* to the *Lai-pubas*. The members of the procession stood up and the *maibis* and *maiba* joined them, the *maibis* forming another Pakhamba pattern. Gradually the tempo increased. The *maiba* and *maibis* led the procession, rapidly encircling the four *chongs*, going in and out of the white canopy, following the complex of the Pakhamba design. Only *penas* were played. Dancers covered a much larger arena to create a huge Pakhamba coiling, and moved continuously. This ritual is called *Lairemmatek*. After the ritual had proceeded for about half an hour, the band party started to play a joyous tune. The solemn dignity of *Laibao* suddenly changed to exuberant celebration. Young boys and girls started *Thabal Chambi*, encircling the huge ritual arena, keeping the ritual of *Lairemmatek* going on in the centre. The *maibis* and *maiba* gradually went back to the original procession lined in two rows. Amidst the drum beat, *pena* and band music, the two rows took two different directions. The *maibi* exclaimed, rhyming, "*Lai, Lairembi nekhainaba, khainaba ne khainaba*" (*Lai* and *Lairembi* have a divorce). The *maiba* led the row with the *Lai* and the *maibis* led the line for *Lairembi*. After coiling in two different directions the leaders came back together standing side by side. The *maiba* sang, "*Lai* has come back because *Lairembi* is greatly in love with him. He wants to be united (*punsinba*)." The *maibi* answered, "No, no. *Lairembi* has come because *Lai* is deeply in love." Both sang, "*Lai* and *Lairembi* have *punsinba*, oh, they have *punsinba* (union)." After the two rows joined, the procession took a calm appearance, stopped moving and stood still. All the music stopped. The spectators remained silent. The *maibis* now led them back to the temple, and took the souls of the *Lais* back to the images. The *Laibao* was over.

Oakol Lauba: A group of men and women stood on the porch and started to sing "*Oakolo, Oakolo*" in praise of the *Lais*, clapping in joyous mood. While the song continued, the young boys and girls went on dancing *Thougal Chambi* to band music, *dholak* and *pena*. They danced forming a huge ring surrounding the actions of the core ritual.

The crowd became quite relaxed. It was past midnight. Men and women sat in their designated areas. They began to collect flowers from the *Lais*. As the band music stopped, *penakhongbas* started a gentle tune for the Lais. The curtain was then drawn in front of the altar.

From 3.30 p.m. to past midnight, the ritual went on without a break, beginning in solemnity, followed by a joyous and gentle devotion, and reaching an exciting peak. The mood of the audience changed along with the mood of the performance, from serious-ness to joyous frivolity. The spectacle of the solemn *Lairemmatek* encircled by exuberant youth dancing together in dramatic harmony produced an ecstatic expression on the onlookers. Men, women, young children—all appeared extremely joyous.

The *maibis* are trained in a vast repertoire of ritual dances. The variety and quality of their dancing depend on the expertise of the performers.

The *maibis* and *maibas* often offer a philosophical interpretation of the dances. About *Lairemmatek*, one older *maibi* (61) said, "It is like the never-ending creation method. Human beings are created and the population grows as children are born of the male and female. It is a never-ending motion, like Pakhamba's coiling."

In Radhagram and Thambalkhul only women joined the *Thougal*. Later in Khoriphoba *Harouba*, I found some men joining the *Thougal* forming an inner circle. Informants say that in some villages men still join the *Thougal* forming an outer circle (as prescribed in the text). This is also true in the famous Moirang *Harouba* and in areas near Thoubal. Pundit Kulachandra says, "In a *Lai Harouba*, men and women should join in equal strength. This was the traditional custom. Nowadays, men are too modern and embarrassed to dance like this. This is very wrong. The purpose of *Lai Harouba* will not be fulfilled if it is not participated in by both men and women equally."

Khoriphoba Harouba

Although the core programmes at all three temples (Radhagram, Thambalkhul, and Khoriphoba) were the same, there were some additional ritual dances at Khoriphoba. Khoriphoba *Harouba* also had an unusually long procession before the beginning of the evening ritual. For eight days, eight villages organized their own processions. On the other three days, the programmes were arranged by the committee and all the villages joined. The participants gathered on a village road. They vied with each other in presenting spectacular sights. Each of the processions was led by six *maibis*, two *penakhongbas* and one *maiba*, engaged by the committee.

On its *pali* (turn of duty) day at Sabal *Leikai*, fifteen horses with men and women in ancient costume led the procession. The horsemen wore huge decorative turbans like Khamba, and the horsewomen dressed in Thoibi style. They were followed by a band party. After this the *Lai Harouba Thougal* group joined, led by the *maibis* and *penas*. The *maibis* formed two rows with women following them in regular order in the four age-groups: *hanubis, mous, laishabis,* and *macha nupis*, all dressed in brilliant-coloured *maiknaiba*, white transparent *inafi*, gold jewellery and flowers. The four groups danced along with the *maibis*, a large group of young *pakhangs* walking quietly behind, all dressed in white *dhotis* and *kurtas* with shawls around their waists, each carrying a polo stick, used especially for Khoriphoba *Harouba*. They were followed by a group of young boys. After them came eight huge white *chong* bearers with two *Lai-pubas* and a large group of *mous* carrying *firup* baskets, and bamboo trays with fruit, vegetables and paddy. They were followed by another series of four age-groups of women and girls dancing in *Thougal* movements. When the long procession went past the Nambol bazaar, hundreds of traders left their stalls and rushed to watch the scene. Both sides of Tiddim Road were packed with women. Most of the older women of the procession were traders in the bazaar, and they attracted a great deal of attention from the crowd of fellow traders. Women onlookers made appreciative remarks, saying, "*Ah, fajare, yam fajare*" (Oh! beautiful, very beautiful). After about half a mile the procession climbed the steep hill. Against the setting sun of the monsoon sky it was a noble spectacle.

The procession of my host village, Nambol Awang, held a similar aura of grandeur with the added attraction of the inclusion of some *mayang* shopkeepers. Of eight villages under Khoriphoba, only two villages, Nambol Awang and Nambol Makha, have *mayangs* populating two sides of Tiddim Road. Next to the Meitei men and women, all dressed in sheer elegance, the *mayang* groups appeared clumsily dressed, clowning in Siva and monkey costumes. Two local groups consisting of drama parties, dressed in ancient costume, joined the procession. This was for their performance of some *langhol* legends. I was honoured at the invitation to join the group of *mous*.

The *Lai Harouba* of Nambol Awang attracted the largest crowd from the surrounding area because the *Shumangleela* immediately after the daily ritual acted as an attractant. A professional company from Imphal was invited to perform a popular play, "O.C. Saheb", on the temple ground.

After the procession reached the top of the hill, the daily ritual started in the usual order. The core part of the *Laibao* procession went up several steps of the temple to relax and the *maibis* led the long line of hundreds of women and girls in Thougal dance.

Special Ritual Dance: Kanglei Thokpa

In the origin myth, Lord Khoriphoba is described as a master horse-polo player. The legend says that Khoriphoba was not allowed to the game of the *Lais* because he was still a bachelor, so he set out to look for a bride. The ritual dance depicted his polo game and his searching for and finding a bride. In the past, the *maibi* went into the crowd and picked a *laishabi*. The *laishabi* was considered as the chosen one and she received *dakhshina* from the male audience. Informants said that people in Nambol area did not like *laishabis* taking such a conspicuous role and requested the *Loishang* to allow a *maibi* to act as a *laishabi*. In the rituals, I observed a *maibi* taking the part of the *laishabi*. The group of *maibis* sang, depicting Khoriphoba's search for a bride:

The goddess of the hills, my beloved.
The jewel, whom I am unable to part with.
On such a day I followed your footprints.
I failed to find you...
Sweet one, have you gone to another village?
Or, have you gone to fetch fire from your neighbour?
Or, have you gone to wash your hair at the river bank?
Or, are you combing your beautiful hair in the huge house of your
    father?
Perhaps, you have gone to a *Kang* game and seated between two
    village brothers as a piece of decoration, radiating...
Perhaps, a cloth is tied around your shoulder and slender waist
    and you are pounding rice.

My friend, I have not seen my beloved for a long time.
Please tell me where she is.

This romantic song and the accompanying gentle gestures gradually changed into vigorous dancing, enacting a horse-polo game. The *penakhongbas* and some *maibis* sang with *dholak* drums and a frequent shrieking sound, "Chi-hi-hi-hi ..." like a horse. One *maibi* held a polo stick in her hand and a ball in the left. She leaped across the ground and hit the ball towards the crowd. The crowd tried to avoid the ball. When she threw one ball, she was supplied with another. She danced with vigorous leaps and stamps throwing the balls one after another. Some young boys and girls were hit by the balls, and as this was considered a bad omen, the *maiba* sprinkled *tairen* water and chanted to ward off any evil effect on them. In an ecstatic performance, the *maibi* underwent *laitongba* and delivered a *laipao*. *Laipao* during a *Kanglei Thokpa* is considered very important for the prediction of the future of the community. The basic presentation of steps and gestures was similar in each performance, but the dancer's approach to presentation is quite innovative. Some *maibis*, like Ima Rajani Maibi (79), became well known for their vigorous and exuberant performance of *Kanglei Thokpa*.

Lamthokpa. On the ninth day of Khoriphoba *Harouba*, there was a *pali* (turn of duty) for Nambol Makha, where the permanent bazaar shed was located. Their procession went up the hill and carried the *Lais* on a *dolai* (a carriage carried by four men) back to the premises of the Nambol bazaar. The *Lais* were placed at the middle of the bazaar. Groups of men performed the *thang-ta* (traditional sword game) and women did *Thougal* dance around the *Lais*. After this, the procession went back to the temple and followed the usual ritual performances.

Lairoi: The last day of *Lai Harouba* is the most important. On this day, the ritual performance goes on until dawn. At Khoriphoba temple, *Lairoi* was organized by the temple committee, *Thougal marup*. The procession looked simpler than on most other days when different villages had their *pali*. Each village sent a few representative men and women to join the procession. At the temple there were a large number of offering trays and collections of coins dedicated to the deities. Men and women came to the *maibis* and asked for some flowers or garlands from the *Lais*.

The central part of the ritual followed the same routine as I had witnessed on the other days. In addition, there were several recreational dances performed by groups of young men and women from different villages ranging from *Langol* theme to a popular stage show of Naga dance. The spectators appeared immensely involved. All clapped along with *Hoi Lauba* songs. After *Hoi Lauba,* the *maibis* chanted to the deities and took *sharik* (offering plates) to the men and sang, "Don't say I have no money, you must give something to the *Lai.*" They took the plate first to the male and then to the female spectators. The *maibis* distributed flowers to the women asking them to fix them in their hair. The usual sequence of *Laibao* concluded with a spectacular *Lairemmatek* (Figure 10) at about 11.30 p.m.

FIGURE 10 : The Stages of *Lairemmatek*

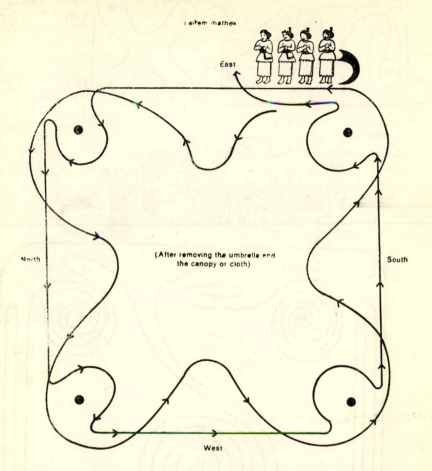

(tairem mathek)

East

North

(After removing the umbrella and
the canopy or cloth)

South

West

Thoiroi Hanjaba: The *maibis* arranged several ritual objects in front of the altar, e.g., *sham* (a paddy basket carried on women's backs among the Nagas), *ghat-chapu* (earthen pots), *iendou* (narrow poles from a bush that look like a bunch of white flags), bananas, heaps of paddy, a pot of water, *tairen* and *langthrei* leaves, poles for sailing boat, etc.[89] One of the *maibis* changed her dress and wore a Naga woman's costume, tying the *sham* (paddy basket) onto her back.

[89]Like the *langthrei* leaves, *tairen* leaves are considered sacred. The *langthrei* grows as a bush; the *tairen* from small trees. The *maibis* believe that both of these leaves have the scent of Guru's body. Both are used for medicinal purposes.

Phases of choreographic plan during *Lairemmatek*

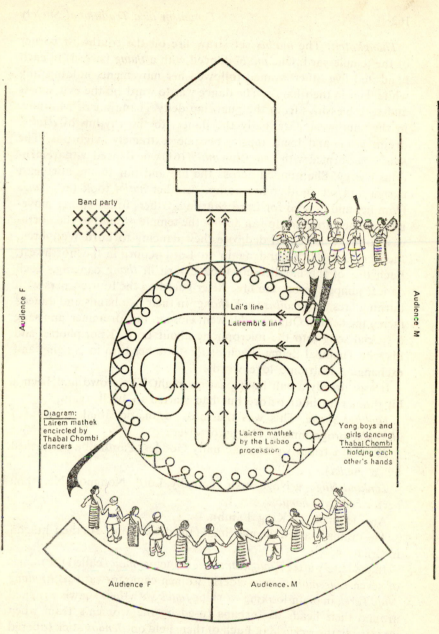

Band party

Audience F

Audience .M

Lai's line

Lairembi's line

Diagram:
Lairem mathek
encircled by
Thabal Chombi
dancers

Lairem mathek
by the Laibao
procession

Yong boys and
girls dancing
Thabal Chombi
holding each
other's hands

Audience F   Audience .M

Lairemmatek and **Thabal Chombi**

Thangkotpa: The *maibis* set straw fire on the southwest corner of the temple-yard. One *maibi* danced with a *thang* (sword) in each hand and five other women followed her movements holding tiny white flags in their hands. The dance was to ward off the evil spirits and seek blessings from the guardian deity Thangjing of Moirang, in the southwest. Gradually the dance, to the rhythm of *dholak* drum, *penas* and band music, became extremely vigorous. The *maibis* performed with a rotating *maibi* (61) who danced with tremendous energy. She jumped across the fire and ran to the northeast corner and set another fire going. Another *maibi* took the *thangs* from her and danced for Lord Marjing. Others followed her movements. The entire group ran across the temple ground to the northeast to make a fire and dedicate their dancing to Lord Wangbren, then crossed the ground again to Lord Kobru in the northwest. Each line of the flag-bearers took a turn in *thang* dancing. Each dancer jumped across the fire. After guarding the four corners with burning fires, two *maibis* took *thangs* in their two hands and danced facing the deities. Other *maibis* went close to the drummer and sang a special song into the microphone about Lord Khoriphoba and his wife Thambal Leima. Each *maibi* took her turn in singing and exchanging histrionic love words.

It was already a half hour past midnight. The crowd had been a bit thinner an hour before but had started to swell again.

Tankhul Shaba. This was the most dramatic ritual of all *Lai Harouba* programmes. The actors were:

Nurabi, a tribal woman (actually Goddess Panthoibi, performed by a *maibi*).

Tankhul Naga, a Naga man (actually Lord Nongpok Ningthou performed by a *hanubi*.

An old man, as King Lambu.

The drama enacted the meeting of the divine couple in their human incarnation.

Immediately after *Thangkatpa*, the principal *maibi* called the names of seven *Lairembis*. Seven elderly women came forward as *Khulong Nupi Tarek* in plain-looking working *fanek* with their shawls wrapped around their heads as turbans (used by the women's team when working in the ricefields). Each of them held one *iendou* stick (offered previously to the *Lais*). The women sang:

Ho Hailo Hoya Hairo

We are digging our father's paddy field,
　　Let us dig (refrain).
For the peace of the land,
　　Let us dig (refrain).
Our digging will bring long life to the king,
　　Let us dig (refrain).
Let us dig to expand our village land,
　　Let us dig (refrain).
To produce more crops,
　　Let us dig (refrain).
To make the lives long,
　　Let us dig (refrain).
To get the *Fourel Fouja*,[90]
　　Let us dig (refrain).
To grow coriander leaves, *Pakhol*,
　　Let us dig (refrain).
To grow *shingkha singhthum*,
　　Let us dig (refrain).

I was surprised at the reference to the "father's land" and "grandfather's land" by married women in patrilineal Meitei society. When I enquired about it, Pundit Kulachandra said that the dance was originally performed by seven *laishabis*. The *Tankhul Shaba* dance involves much frivolous behaviour, which people felt would be improper for the *laishabis*. So they requested the *Loishang* to change the textual rules and replace the *laishabis* with *hanubis*.

The women sang and danced with bouncing movements, banging their sticks on the ground. Then the Tangkhul Naga appeared shooting arrows in different directions in a clownish gesture. The audience broke into laughter. As Tankhul Naga started to sing, the *maibis* came forward and sang a romantic song from *Khulong Ishei*. Tankhul Naga and the *maibis* answered each other. Suddenly, Tankhul Naga chased a beautiful young *maibi* (22) dressed in tribal costume as Nurabi. He chased her from one corner to another in an awkward manner. Old women kept on dancing, bouncing and stamping the sticks on the earth. At last, Tankhul Naga and Nurabi confronted

---

[90]*Fourel Fouja* is the name of the best quality paddy. Other names are of different medicinal herbs.

each other. Tankhul said, "It is my land." Nurabi replied, "No, it is our land." Seven women sang a refrain, "Hoi," to the argument which sounded like a rhyme. Tankhul shot arrows again. People laughed. Now Nurabi appeared as a trader. Tankhul stopped her and wanted to know about her feeling for him. There was an exchange of romantic words. Nurabi sang, "I am an unlucky flower, if you pluck me I might fall apart...Woman's mind is steady, men are frivolous. With these songs the bachelors of the village will become wild." Men and women spectators alike enjoyed these erotic jokes.

Old women sang and walked in a circle around Nurabi and Panthoibi. Women sang, "We work on our father's land." Tankhul shouted, "No, no, this is my own land, not yours." In answer, the *maibis* jumped and stamped on the ground. Old women followed them and jumped and stamped their sticks. Tankhul came to attack them; the women scattered. The music of *pena* and *dholak* continued while the band music played off and on.

Nurabi came forward and said, "You are the ugliest man. You must not disturb me." A mock fight of chasing and teasing ensued.

There was an announcement that no one should leave the ground during this ritual. An old man as King Lambu came forward and tried to settle the dispute between the couple. Now Tankhul found a beehive and lighted a fire to get the honey out of it (performed in words and gestures). He was severely bitten by bees. Nurabi appeared to rescue him. Tankhul asked for food from Nurabi. Nurabi said, "I have food reserved for my husband." Tankhul snatched the food and ran away. Nurabi chased him with a stick, yelling, "Please give half of it back, please give some for my husband." Tankhul refused to share the food. Nurabi held a bottle of wine (nowadays an empty bottle is used). The young *maibi* performed a beautiful dance to the rhythm of a *dholak* and *pena* melody. Her movements were seductive as she lured Tankhul, who looked as if he were excited at Nurabi's appearance, and she offered him some wine. He then acted like a drunken man suffering from a stomach-ache. As the spectators roared with laughter, Tankhul in their midst squatted as if to defecate. Then he brushed his bottom with a plantain leaf placed on the ground. (Informants said that this method of cleaning is known among the hill tribes in Manipur. The Meitei use water and consider the other custom barbaric.) Tankhul then again chased Nurabi. The seven old women caught him and carried him to be judged before the old man who played the part of the ancient King Lambu. They shouted, "Panthoibi is a married woman." Tankhul apologized for his mistake and behaviour.

The next act showed Nurabi and Tankhul in love. Nurabi offered him food and he fed some of it to Nurabi. Then they started to dig, holding two hoes in their hands. The seven women and other *maibis* followed their movements. The dance continued with the vigorous movements of enacted terrace cultivation, the sowing of seed and the harvesting and gathering of paddy. As they danced, they slowly climbed the temple steps toward the altar. The moment the group reached the porch in front of the altar, the principal *maibi* put the *sham* (paddy) on the ground. People eagerly collected bits of paddy to take home. A *maibi* distributed paddy to them. The time was about 2.00 a.m. The ritual of *Tankhul Shaba* was over. The band music stopped, but *penas* continued playing. The preparation for the next ritual had already began.

Ougri Hongel Chongba: A *maiba* stood at the centre of the ground. A group of men and women held a rope (previously dedicated to the *Lais*) and stood forming a circle, in alternate positions according to sex. A *maibi* tied the two ends of the rope and fixed her bell on it. A *maibi* said, "This is the origin of *Thabal Chombi*." When Sanamahi wanted to attack Pakhamba, seven *Lairembis* guarded Pakhamba, forming a circle around him.

The *maibi* put pieces of plantain leaf in the hands of each person in the circle, chanted, and then took back the leaves. The rope was taken out and men and women held each other's hands. The *maiba* sang "*khenchore... khencho*" (meaning not known). The group sang a refrain and clapped. Two women and two men held each other's hands and moved in a spiral pattern. The *maiba* said that originally this dance had been performed by many men and women together. Now two men and two women act as couples. While the couples moved, the *maiba* sang a song teasing *Lairembi*. Women broke into laughter. Men and women clapped again, teasing each other. Next, men and women stood in two rows facing each other. They held *iendou* sticks in their hands and formed two straight lines. The *maiba* chanted for about twenty minutes. He exclaimed, "*Hee!*"; others answered, "*Hee!*" (an expression of joy). The *maibis* explained that the two lines of men and women represented the *Lai* and *Lairembi* coming onto a boat.

In the meantime, the *Laibao* procession was getting ready on the temple porch. The principal *maibi* led the procession with her bell. Other *maibis* and *penakhongbas*, followed by old women with *iendou* sticks, and the group of men and women dancing joined the procession. Only *pena* music played. After making two rounds, the two rows of people took two different directions similar to the dance of *Lai* and *Lairembi*'s *khainaba* (divorce) and *punsinba* (union) as described earlier. The two rows joined, and facing the temple climbed the steps to the porch. The principal *maibi* took the "souls" of the *Lais* out and placed them inside the images. Men and women went down the stairs and threw *iendou* sticks at the altar. The stick that lands nearest the altar is considered most auspicious. People rushed to collect the sticks. At about 4.00 a.m., two *maibis* carried trays of food and *thangs* to the outskirts of the hill for the *Saraikhangba* ritual. One of them walked ringing a bell. People fell silent. The *penakhongba* played a beautiful tune and sang. The *maibi* said, "With this music the *Lais* will go back to heaven." The white curtain was drawn in front of the altar, and the candles were extinguished.

In Radhagram, the images were dismantled immediately after *Lairoi*. At Khoriphoba temple, the images were set in place permanently and may be worshipped every weekend.

Men and women gathered near the temple porch to collect some flowers. After the exuberant all-night performance, the atmosphere grew calm. The spectators bowed to the altar and departed, leaving in their trail an aura of peace.

The day after *Lai Harouba*, athletic competitions were held in each village. There were many events, e.g., *mukna* (traditional method of wrestling), running race, coconut peeling competition, etc. At the conclusion of the events, the committee called for an auction of the huge amount of clothes offered to the *Lais*. The villagers were happy to get good bargains. Old informants said that in the past, the Maharaja encouraged boat races, *mukna* (wrestling), *thangta* (sword play), polo games and other competitions on the day after *Lai Harouba*. At Imphal, the Maharaja himself would come out to watch and in the villages, too, there was much enthusiasm for these traditional athletic competitions.

I asked some women, "When is another festival coming up?" They readily replied, "Oh, we have to wait two months. You must join *Kangchingba* and *Kanglen*. We will have those for eleven days." They were talking about the Meitei version of the Vaisnavite festival, *Rathjatra*. The *Lai Harouba* season more or less ends by the close of May. From June to the middle of August, people would be engrossed in rice cultivation, with very little time for festivities.

THE MAIBIS: AN INSTITUTIONALIZED ROLE FOR SOCIAL DEVIANTS

The rituals of *Lai Harouba* demonstrate an unusual prominence of the role of the priestesses, the *maibis*. There are at present 240 *maibis* formally initiated and registered with the *Pundit Loishang*. There are three groups of *maibis*: *Sanglen*, *Fura*, and *Nonmai*. Only the *Sanglen* group is allowed to worship Pakhamba. An ancient text, *Laichat*, prescribes rules for placing *maibis* in their proper categories. A novice belongs to her Guru's group. There are also many novices who have not yet passed through their tests at the *Loishang*. The *maibis* from faraway places like Jiribam, Cachhar, Silchar and Tripura are not registered with the *Loishang*. They maintain their practice privately through professional contacts.

In traditional Meitei society *maibis* were recognized as ritual specialists. Scholars refer to their high status in affairs of state (Hodson, 1908, reprinted 1975: 123; K. Singh Moirangthem, 1971: 80). A *maibi's* oracle was important to the king prior to any expedition, and in periods of crisis, he consulted a *maibi* to seek advice, addressing her as *ima* (mother). A *maibi* was responsible for performing propitiatory rites for the members of the royal family. Successful performance as a *maibi* often led to speedy rise in status.

At present, too, the *maibis* occupy an important position in Meitei social life. I have interviewed twenty-five *maibis* including some male transvestites, ranging in age from twenty-two to ninety-seven years. Their clientele often ranges from simple illiterate farmers to modern educated college professors and politicians. Both sexes, old and young, depend greatly on *maibis'* predictions or *senmit* (see below). Their clientele includes the Meitei and the Brahmans, the Loi and the hill tribes and the Pangam Muslims. I found *maibis* prescribing rites according to the religious faith of the client. A Pangam Muslim was asked to visit a Mullah, a Muslim priest. I, a Bengali Hindu woman, was asked to go to a Kali temple. A Meitei client was encouraged to worship some *Lais* in the traditional religious pantheon.

Senmit. Besides officiating for *Lai Harouba*, the *maibis* also act as diviners, performing propitiatory rites for their clients. Some of them have a reputation for *semjanba* (sorcery). Some are known for their ability to communicate with the dead at "seances". When a client asks for a *senmit*, the *maibi* asks the person to place some money (her fee) on a piece of plantain leaf. She chants in the archaic language from the scriptures, meditates for a while, and on throwing four ancient coins, the *maibi* predicts the future of the person. People visit a *maibi* early in the morning, for this time is believed to be the most efficacious for correct predictions. Sunday mornings are the most crowded times in a *maibi's* home. The number of clients depends greatly on her reputation in the field. Some *maibis* are known for their accurate predictions, others are favoured for their performing skills displayed during *Lai Harouba* rituals. I found an established *maibi's* income ranged from Rs. 200 to 600 a month, excluding gifts received, e.g., clothes, paddy, fruits. Successful *maibis* naturally expect more and earn much higher incomes.

The most interesting aspect of a *maibi's* role is that she holds a special ritual status outside the norms of the social framework for women. The two male ritual functionaries, discussed earlier, belong to the normal stream of life. But women who become *maibis* are, in fact, deviants who do not conform to the standard Meitei social roles.

When a woman or a girl experiences a trance or some such behaviour which is out of the ordinary it is customary for a Meitei family to summon a *maiba* (shaman and curer—different from a *Lai Harouba* priest) to treat her symptoms. The *maiba* tries to diagnose her ailment and performs the appropriate rites. If repeated trials fail and the patient's hair begins to coil in different places, the family is alarmed that her condition is incurable. My case studies demonstrate the daring and dramatic ways in which each of the women I interviewed who became *maibis* chose a Guru of her own and took up a new life-style and profession.

When a woman is accepted by her *Ima Guru* (mother Guru) she lives in her Guru's residence with other novices from one to five years. Here are the stories of five women which show their transition from a normal life to that of a *maibi*.

Rebati *maibi* (80) is the leader of a *sanglen* group. Even at eighty years of age she has a healthy shining skin and almost no grey hair. Her dark hair is brushed backward and neatly put into a bun in which fresh flowers are usually tucked. She has Vaisnava *chandan* on her forehead and nose. She wears white clothes and a large gold medal given to her by the former king, and came to greet us (a male informant, my daughter and myself) chewing betel-leaf. As she talked she intermittently smoked a water pipe. An infant was lying on the porch of the very well-maintained thatched roof Meitei home; she identified him as her great-grandson. Her daughter died many years ago; now Rebati lives with her grandson's family in her own house. She spoke about herself:

"I developed my symptoms when I was only ten. I was the eldest of three sons and three daughters. My grandfather had a high position in the palace. My insanity went on for three years. My parents arranged several rites, but none of them worked. Once I was ill and one day I predicted an exact date and hour that my *Ima Guru* would arrive. A night before the appointed day, my *Ima Guru*, Tanu *maibi*, had a dream of me. Next day, when *Ima Guru* arrived, my parents were convinced of their daughter's fate. They let me go with her...

"Raja Churachand's daughter Thampasana was very ill. In a *Laipao* I made a prediction that the princess would die in three days and named a *maibi* who should stand next to her bed. The King said that if I was wrong, I would be punished by *Ishing Tongba* (dipping in cold water all night long in winter). Princess Thampasana died and the King gave me the status of *hidang* though I was still a novice and very young. Later, I taught dancing to one of the queens of King Bodhachandra...When I kept in touch with my *Ima Guru*, my trance state was controlled. But whenever I visited the palace with her, I went into a trance and delivered *Laipao*.

"Later, I was married to a famous *sankirtana* singer and dancer. I had a flourishing career. I never learned any domestic work. I lived between my husband's house and my parents' house. In my regular life I was his wife, but when I went into trance I was someone else. I also travelled a lot and had my own profession. I had two children, one son and one daughter, but I lost them both. I lost my husband also. You know, *maibis* are very unfortunate women. They lose everyone of their own...

"*Ima Guru* was my caretaker for a long time. I travelled all over Manipur with her. My husband never minded my freedom. He did not take a second wife. When he came to live with my parents, my mother used to cook for him. We earned together with real understanding...

"Nongpokningthou is my guardian *Lai*. I slept separately from my husband on Sundays and Mondays...

"I trained many younger *maibis* as their *Ima Guru*..."

When I asked about the *chandana* mark, she said, "This is a fashion. You put it on even if you are going to worship a Meitei *Lai*."

Rebati *maibi* did *senmit* for me. She said, "You committed a sin in your last life. That is why you do not have a son. If you have a brass gong made and have your name and your husband's name engraved on it in a circle and present it to the Lai temple, you may be able to have a male child...your daughter is like a son and daughter both. She is going to take care of you in your old age... You have developed a backache since you came to Manipur... Your visit to Manipur will bring you success."

Rajani *maibi*, (79) popularly known as *Ima* Rajani, belongs to the *Fura* group of *maibis*. At present, she is one of the most well-known and established *maibis* of Manipur. She became famous because of her exquisite performances during *Lai Harouba* festivals. On recommendation from the Manipur State Kala Academy, she was honoured with a national award by the Government of India. She travelled to New Delhi to receive her award and performed *Panthoibi Jagoi* while there.

However, *Ima* Rajani's achievement has not changed her life-style. One informant said that when *Ima* was selected for the award, she really did not pay much attention to this honour. When she was invited, she said she would perform *Panthoibi Jagoi* in New Delhi. *Ima* came to the Dance College at Imphal to discuss the programme. The authorities of the Dance College and a *pundit* suggested to her that she should perform *Loiching Jagoi*, because of the time limit. *Ima* Rajani accepted their suggestion rather reluctantly. She looked rather unhappy during the meeting. Suddenly she went into a trance. The *pundit* ran out and got some *tairen* leaves from a bush and sprinkled water on *Ima* Rajani. He chanted hymns for a while and Ima Rajani came back to her normal state. Being alarmed, the authorities of the Dance College agreed to include *Panthoibi Jagoi* in the New Delhi programme.

Ima Rajani is always friendly and warm. She enjoys teasing people and makes jokes with erotic overtones. She has a smile and a twinkle in her eyes all the time. She narrates her story thus:

"I went into trance at twelve. I lost my mother in my infancy and was brought up by my mother's brother. He tried hard to suppress

my symptoms with the help of a *maiba*. I was married at twenty
and lost my husband when I was twenty-four. I was then seven months
pregnant with a girl. When I was about twenty-nine, I started to have
supernatural contacts. I searched hard for a good *Ima Guru* until
I met *Ima* Chunkhum *maibi*. She took care of me as her own daughter. I found a position in the palace *Loishang*. After a period of
training, I was assigned to attend *Lai Harouba* independently."

Ima Rajani worked in very close association with the palace and
often travelled in the company of Maharaja Churachand to different *Lai* temples. She told me of an interesting event in her life:

"Once I travelled to Sugnu, about sixty-six kms. from Imphal, in
the company of the Maharaja, three *pundits* and one *pena* player.
As we were resting by a river bank, a big *ngerthil* fish jumped out of
the water and hit a *pundit*. The *pundit* fainted. The fish came over
me and I caught it.... As we proceeded towards the temple at
Sugnu we talked about what a big catch it was and that after the
worship we would have a big feast. When we reached the temple,
the gate would not open. I realized that the fish should have been
offered to Lord Wangbren first; instead we had talked about our
own feast! However, when I performed a rite and they offered
some money to the temple in repentance, the gate opened. They
offered the fish to the *Lais* and had a feast afterwards anyway...."

Ima Rajani spoke a great deal about her association with matters
of the royal family. If the King dreamed of the *Yumjao Lairembi*,
a female *Lai* of the palace, who was the spirit of a previous queen
who died before fulfillment of her love, it was considered a bad omen
and the King might have died within three months. Once Maharaja Churachand had such a dream and *Ima* Rajani was recommended by her *Ima Guru* to perform a rite petitioning *Yumjao Lairembi*
on behalf of the King. The King awarded her a gold medal and a
traditional hand-woven blanket for this.

Once in a *Lai Harouba* at Chajing village, she predicted that the
King would leave Manipur for good to go on pilgrimage. She says,
"I never failed in my predictions. My predictions made me a favou-
rite of the palace. I also travelled with Maharaja Bodhachandra."

In her profession *Ima* Rajani is very busy in the six months of
the *Lai Harouba* season. During this period she has to travel up to
Cachhar, Silchar, Shillong in Assam State and Agartala in Tripura
State. I asked how she travelled. She said, "In the past I travelled
on horseback or on foot. Nowadays I travel by bus."

Bidhumukhi *maibi* (22) is one of youngest *maibis* I met in Manipur. She is also one of the prettiest and most graceful. She related her life story as follows:

"My husband took me by *thaba* when I was only fourteen. I fell in love with him, but I always had a sense of guilt because both of us belonged to the same clan. I left him when my son was thirteen days old. Now my son is four years old.

"During my married life I was insane for one year. I became pregnant then. Just after the birth of the child I got back my senses. I used to dream of a man dressed as a Naga. He behaved just like my husband. He touched me all over my body. Every Saturday and Sunday I would have sexual intercourse with him.[91]

"I prayed to *Ima Laimaren* to give me the power of prediction but I could not do anything. I used to look at the piece of *ngabang* (thick white cotton cloth) and eat the thread thinking of it as rice. One day my son looked like a *ngamu* fish and I was about to cut him with a *thang*. My relatives stopped me. After some days I started to search for an *Ima Guru*. When I met my *Ima Guru* my senses came back gradually. It took at least another year to become normal."

I met Bidhumukhi in Khoriphoba *Harouba*. She was a talented dancer and singer. She came there with her *Ima Guru*. I asked her whether she had trouble from men. She replied, "We go to unknown places and stay there for a period of time. Men often try to be intimate with me. If they are over-enthusiastic, I have to warn them, saying, 'Don't forget, I am dedicated to the *Lai*. If you insult me, the *Lai* will not forgive you!' This warning always helps."

Madhavi *maibi* (55) lives in Kwakeithal *Leikai* in Imphal. She is a slender, dark woman. I heard a great deal about her fine dancing skill in *Lai Harouba* rituals. As we arrived, she unlocked small door at one corner of the veranda. This was her shrine room having a mirror with a large black spot, new clothes, flowers and fruit. She said that the dark spot on the mirror appeared seven years ago. The *maibi* had a *laitongba*, saying that the dark spot indicated that the mirror belonged to the *Lai*. It was then dedicated to the *Lai*.

---

[91]Her description of a Naga man is similar to the Naga hero of Tankhul Shaba feature of *Lai Harouba*. Lai Nongpokningthou appears in Naga costume. Saturdays and Sundays are associated with the *Lai*.

She gave her life story as follows:

She had symptoms of a *maibi* at thirteen. Her parents were culti-vators. Her mother earned extra money by doing fine embroidery work. She was one of four children. At fifteen she got married. She said it was arranged after she fell in love with the man. She continued to have symptoms even after her marriage. She was no good at domestic chores. She could not weave. When she went to sell rice she gave it free to people. Her husband's family was disgusted with her and tried to separate them. She went back to live with her parents. The husband married another wife. But he died when Madhavi was twenty. Madhavi then married a *maiba*, a medicine man, but conti-nued to have symptoms (occasional trances and restlessness). During the ten years of her marriage with her second husband she had two children. When a daughter was born she became very ill. During the worship of the *Sagei Lai* she fainted. In her madness she wanted to be close to the *Lai*. Madhavi went to Kumari *maibi* and accepted her as her *Ima Guru*. Her life-style changed. She lived both in her husband's home and the home of her *Ima Guru*. Her in-laws took care of the cooking and the children.

At first it was very hard for her husband to accept her as a *maibi* but soon he recognized her inherent quality.

She was trained by her *Ima Guru* for ten years. The Ima Guru presented her to the *Loishang* and had her name officially registered. At first, she worked in her husband's locality only. She did *senmit* and accompanied her *Ima Guru* to faraway places on the occasions of *Lai Harouba*. *Ima Guru* took special care in teaching her dancing. Later she also took training in dancing from *Ima* Rajani *maibi*. Pundit Kulachandra taught her a great deal about the scriptures and the ritual procedure.

At present, Madhavi *maibi* has an established career. She lives with her own family, her husband, son and her son's family. I asked her, "Did you become happier in a *maibi*'s life?" She said, "This question puzzles me. In a way, I have a very joyful life in ser-ving the *Lai*; on the other hand, I realize that it is a very difficult life. A *maibi*'s life is full of pain. If you gain status, then it is worth it."

She has an almost equal number of clients of both sexes.

Chamu *maibi* (97).

I visited *Ima* Chamu *maibi* in her village, Nongdamba. Her only son, a *maiba* (priest) accompanied us. Chamu *maibi* looked extremely young for her age. She had occasional lapses of memory. She could not remember when she became a *maibi*. She said, "I guess when I was a *laishabi*. One day I walked for twelve miles and reached my *Ima Guru*'s house. I never met her before. Her name was Samukhambi. I stayed with her for a number of years."

Chamu has lived during the reigns of Maharajas Churachand and Bodhachandra. She walked with the King's party to Moirang (twenty-five kms. from Imphal). Chamu's son (57) told us a few more things about his mother's life.

Chamu was married according to the *kainakatpa* custom and had two children. One day a cobra spread its hood over the head of her five-year-old son who was sleeping. Seeing this, her husband killed the cobra. Both of Chamu's sons died that very night. Chamu realized it was the result of the sin her husband had committed by killing a cobra. The cobra could have been an emissary of *Lai* Pakhamba. She left her husband after this incident and later met a *maiba*, (priest), who eventually became her husband. The *maiba* already had two more wives, but he visited Chamu frequently. He bought a paddy field and built a house for Chamu and their son. The son took up his father's profession. Chamu achieved the status of a *sanglakpi*. Chamu's *maiba* husband also attained the status of a *pundit*. He died ten years ago, when she was eighty-seven.

Chamu *maibi* was very happy that we visited her. She volunteered to perfrom *Panthoibi Jagoi*. She sang and danced with remarkable strength and grace.

Chamu remembered eleven names of her disciples. She always mentioned the name of the village along with their names.

Chamu's village Nongdamba is about ten kms. from Imphal. Her disciples walk many miles from various areas of the Valley to reach her home. Chamu said, "I did not find any difference between my male and female disciples. They were all alike. She said that at present several new dance pieces had been added to Lai *Harouba*, which she had not seen in her youth.

From the day a woman is accepted as a novice, her life-style changes completely. She wears all-white dresses, *fingo ira tanba* or *fingo setpa* according to prescribed rules. She has to wear three pieces of cloth around the lower part of her body. A regular Meitei woman wears only a *fanek*. According to the text, (F.I. Sharma, n.d.) the white dress of a *maibi* symbolizes light from darkness before creation. The white coloured scarf around her waist signifies her femininity and her hair put into a bun indicates her marriage with the *Lai*. She cooks her own meals with special firewood and is forbidden to have certain kinds of fish, such as *ngkra*. There is a long list of foods which are taboo for *maibis*.

Under the supervision of the *Ima Guru*, the *maibis* trained in dance, music, chanting, and complex ritual procedure. After a period of arduous training, the *Ima Guru* takes the novice to different places to attend *Lai Harouba* ceremonies. The novice also studies the technique of *senmit* and the procedure for performing different rites. She has to learn to use the most important tool of her profession, a brass bell, which, whenever she chants in a *senmit* or *laitongba* or performs some particular rites, e.g., *saraikhangba*, she rings. It is wrapped with a white cloth at the handle. (It is believed that the bell represents the male and female organs. Others say, "The bell is the navel of the Guru.") A *maibi* never attends a ritual without her bell. When *Ima Guru* finds her ready, she is asked to appear for a test at the *Pundit Loishang*. The *Maibi Loishang*, a branch of *Pundit Loishang*, carefully examines her superior powers and her skill in the profession. Several experienced *maibas* and *maibis* are responsible for the selection. If she passes the test, she performs a ritual of *ipanthaba* (a ritual of birth performed during *shastipuja* after childbirth) to indicate her own birth into a new life. From then on she can practice her profession on her own. Her *Ima Guru* becomes the key person in her professional contacts. I came across names like Tanu *maibi* and Samukhambi *maibi* who were famous *Ima Gurus* of several old and established contemporary *maibis*. Most *maibis* return home after *ipanthaba*, but they maintain their contact with their *Ima Guru* all their lives.

A *maibi* is a full time specialist[92] and hers is a permanent status. There has been no case of a *maibi* returning to her normal life. Once a *maibi* enters the *Loishang*, she is exposed to a competitive world of hierarchy unknown in the Meitei women's world. There are four ranks distinguished by the Loishang: *hidang, hanjabi, sanglakpi* and *asukpi*. *Hidang* is an ordinary *maibi*, *hanjabi* and *sanglakpi* are

[92]During my stay I found only one *maibi* at Jiribam, at the border between Assam and Manipur, as a trader in the bazaar. But I found her talking to prospective clients during her time in the market-place. A hill Naga woman came to contact her for a rite to help recapture a stolen cow.

the next two higher ranks, and *asukpi* is the highest of all. At present there is only one *asukpi* in the *Loishang*. I often heard complaints from *maibis* against the partiality and corrupt practices of the *Loishang*, which many attributed to the absence of kingly authority.

A *maibi* always comes from a Meitei family. Brahman and R.K. women are not known to have symptoms that would indicate their potential to become *maibis*.

The path of a *maibi* is usually traversed only by a female. Pundit O. Bhogendra of the *Pundit Loishang* says, "A *maibi* has superpowers. The first symptom is the formation of the *jota* (hair coiling into a tangle) preceded by a serious illness.... Only an *Ima Guru* can recognize the prospect of a future *maibi* by unfolding the coils of her hair." Pundit Kulachandra says, "A *maibi* is a woman, because only a woman can be spiritually close to the *Lai*. Women have the steady mind (needed) for concentration. It is very hard for men." A *penakhongba*, Ojha Nongal Mera, says, "A *maibi* is ordained to be female since the beginning of history. A male is not fit for the role. A woman has more powers of concentration than a man." But according to Rajo *maibi* (a male transvestite *maibi*), "A *maibi* cannot be judged by sex. A *maibi* is sexless, outside the norm of life. A *maibi* is in between the *Lais* and a human being, like intermediaries."

A *maibi* is completely independent of men. If a married woman becomes a *maibi*, her husband accepts her as a special person. She stops all domestic work, and cooks only for herself. If she marries after becoming a *maibi*, she cannot have a *luhungba*, but only *kainakatpa*. Her husband has to offer bridewealth to the *Lai*, who is the guardian *Lai* of the *maibi*. She sleeps on the right side bed which in Meitei society is normally used by the husband. She also has special days when she must abstain from sexual intercourse with her husband. All *maibis* I interviewed have children who were born either before or after their initiation for becoming a *maibi*. They do not take care of the children as normal mothers do, but only contribute money towards their upkeep. Informants said that husbands do not dare interfere in a *maibi's* life. "Even if he does," (one informant used a typical Meiteiized English expression), "she damn care him. He cannot beat her, because if he does, he is sure to die very soon." No man can touch her without her consent, for the same reason. I was frequently told of a recent incident at Imphal: a lawyer slapped a *maibi* and died within a week.

Yumsang told her own story which perfectly exemplifies how a young girl deemed insane by society through her status of a *maibi* can be recognized as one deserving of social immunity to the extent of attaining protection from the King himself.

Yumsang *maibi* (56) became a *maibi* at fifteen and got married at twenty-six. Her mother was also a *maibi*. When she was only seven, her mother left home. She grew up with her father and stepmother. When she acted strangely, people thought she was insane. Some said her blood was impure. At the age of twelve, her hair coiled up in three places. But her father thought that she was afflicted by the *heloi* spirit. She had attacks like epilepsy. Often she fell into water and did not care about her clothes. At fifteen, she became violent. She would beat doors, slam things against the wall. Her father thought that the stepmother was responsible for some evil act against his daughter, as she had no child. Her father started to beat her, accusing her of witchcraft against his daughter, whereupon she left him. After this her father felt helpless. He cried, worrying over what had befallen his only child. People said that she was possessed. He called a famous *maiba* to help, who performed a rite several times. Yumsang would be all right durihg the rite, but she had convulsions in between the ceremonies.

Once during a ceremony Yumsang had a strange vision: she looked at the *maiba* and he metamorphosed into a horse. She jumped over his shoulder to ride on him. She was forced by some people to come down. The *maiba* left and refused to work with her.

People began to tease her for this behaviour. They called her names. Late one night she slipped out of the house and walked for a long time until she reached a *tairen* tree. A pack of dogs came barking towards her and she climbed the tree. The dogs turned into tigers in front of her eyes.

From there she crossed a shallow river and reached the home of her *Ima Guru*, Tonu *maibi*. Yumsang had heard of Tonu *maibi* but had never met her before. Tonu *maibi* was sitting on her front porch performing *senmit*, She looked at Yumsang and said, "Here is the daughter I dreamed of. She has come to see me." Tonu took Yumsang on her lap. They both began to cry. People who had assembled for the *senmit* session left, knowing that no work would be done that morning. At this time Tonu *maibi* was very old. She was doubtful whether she had the strength to train a novice. She called upon her oldest disciple, Lairen *maibi*, and told her to train Yumsang. Lairen had taken over Tonu *maibi*'s role in different *Lai Haroubas*. She accepted Yumsang as her disciple and took her to her home at Kwakeithel.

Over the years, Yumsang gained renown for her graceful dancing in *Lai Harouba*. She married her partner *pena* player and had five children by him. She stayed as his wife for a long time, but then decided to separate. Although she still lives in the same compound, she does not share her bed with him. When asked the reason, she said, "I was attracted to him for a long time, but I was never a good wife or mother. His mother took care of the children and did all domestic chores. I did my own cooking. Gradually I lost my attachment to him. There is no particular reason for it. The love just faded away.... In a *maibi*'s life, there are a lot of opportunities for meeting men. But I did not want any complication in my life. So I did not allow any other man in my life.... a *maibi* is ruled by her free will. As she goes about life, she may suddenly be seized with a wish or desire to go somewhere else and will drop everything to fulfil that."

Yumsang travelled all over Manipur and never encountered any trouble with men. The King and the *Loishangs* organized the ceremonies of *Lai Harouba* and ensured the safety of the *maibis*. Once Yumsang was going through an army camp during the Second World War. The white soldiers stopped her for interrogation. She went into a trance and in confusion they called the Meitei soldiers. The Meitei men apologized to the *maibi* and asked her to forgive them. They bowed to her to show respect. When the King heard of the incident, he issued an order to leave the *maibis* alone.

Yumsang performs weekly rites in the temple of Okmaren at Ningthoukhom. She stays there for the weekends as a guest of the temple caretaker. When we visited the temple she invited us to have lunch with her. She asked us to stay overnight. She said, "We three (Yumsang, my assistant and myself) can share one bed. After all, we are all women."

Almost all *maibis* I met were well groomed and sophisticated in their behaviour. Old *maibis* look unusually young for their age. They are well travelled and accustomed to talking to strangers freely. Some of them are charming in their manner of speech. Once a beautiful fifty-year-old *maibi* said to me, "I know you are coming from a distant land, but how can I look upon you as a stranger. You belong to the same species of human race as I do. One day we will sit down sharing the same mat, we will share flowers from the same cluster and share food from the same plate...."

Older *maibis* who lived during the time of King Churachand talked a great deal of their travels, sometimes on horseback, to faraway places for *Lai Harouba* ceremonies. Some of them accompanied the King's party on foot for distant journeys.

Socially, a *maibi* must be called *Ima* as a sign of respect. Common people talked about being awed by the *maibis*. An old man (85) said, "We are afraid to ignore her." Without *maibis*, people feel helpless because they are the only ones who have *Laitongba* (*Lai* comes in the body), through whom the *Lais* mediate with the people. *Maibis* are known for their eccentric behaviour. I found them extremely warm and friendly with a fine sense of humour. When men are not present some *maibis* feel free to discuss their sexual lives. One of them (69) said, "We are not like common women. When we need sex we do not wait for the man to come to us. We just hold his thing and ride on top of him." Some embarrassed men by teasing them with words having erotic connotations.

However, in public appearance the *maibis* are always dignified and conspicuous in their crisp white dress.

The attractive feminine presence of *maibis* exposes them to many men as potential lovers. During extensive travels *maibis* come across many men and are constantly interacting with them in the professional field. Some experience a series of romances. A beautiful *maibi* (47) in my area is known to have had thirty marriages. The number might be an exaggeration indulged in by the informants, but it is indicative of her attraction among the male populace. I also found several *maibis* who settled for one husband. *Maibis* work and travel closely with other ritual functionaries like *maibis*, *pundits* and *penakhongbas*. The *Pundit Loishang* recommends a *maibi* to look upon a *maiba* as the father and a *penakhongba* as a brother. In spite of the prohibition, some *maibis* are married to *maibas* and *penakhongbas*. One *penakhongba* has been ostracized by the *Pundit Loishang* and is not allowed to work in *Lai Harouba* because he married a *maibi*. However, the *maibi* involved in the case was not hurt by the *Loishang's* rules.

The Meitei have an ambivalent attitude towards a *maibi*. A family always tries to suppress her symptoms with the help of a *maiba* until it becomes inevitable that they must adjust to her new life-style.

Maibis are known to have difficult deaths, with prolonged suffering. It is believed that a dying *maibi* keeps on breathing until another *maibi* comes and makes a hole in the roof of her room and chants a particular hymn. After this ritual, *lainonggaba*, the soul of the *Lai* residing inside a *maibi* goes to heaven. After the death of a *maibi*, her family performs a special funeral ceremony called *Chukshaba*, so that no other *maibi* is born in the future in the family. The same ritual is performed for a person dying an abnormal death.

One *maibi*, a mother of eight children, said, "It is very hard to become a mother when you are a *maibi*. One of my children was drowned because I could not look after him. My husband did not leave me and my mother-in-law brought up the children." The positive answers were: "It is a very hard life, but people show a lot more respect to a *maibi* than they do towards other women," or "But people will never treat you with disdain as a crazy woman; they will recognize you as a servant of the Lai."

None of the *maibis* wanted their daughters to become *maibis*. A *maiba* (56), son of a famous *maibi* said to me:

"It was very hard growing up as a *maibi*'s son. Mother never had her mind in domestic duties; she was always on the move. Sometimes she took me with her to different *Lai Harouba* festivals. She used to be very busy in those days. She always took another woman to accompany her to take care of me. I travelled all over Manipur with her... *Maibis* have *shakti* (a super power of feminine energy). You should never make them angry. Once they are angry it is difficult to calm them down. I used to be afraid of my mother when she had *laitongba*, sometimes for more than half an hour. I never wanted to marry a *maibi*. A *maibi*'s husband has to follow all her rules."

However, children of a *maibi* do not suffer from any social stigma. All the *maibis* I met had children who led normal lives, and are usually raised by the *maibi*'s mother or some other relatives. Traditionally, as a mother of a groom, a *maibi* cannot participate in *kujabawa* (groom's mother in special ritual). However, these rules are being relaxed nowadays.

During *Lai Harouba*, one can observe the expressions of *maibi* behaviour which varies from a solemn presence to extreme frivolousness. Some of the *Lai Harouba* dancing demands a bold and energetic presentation. Women's Vaisnavite ritual dancing uses rather restricted and subtle movements. In Vaisnavite dancing, women are required to keep their knees close together with feet hidden under the *poloi* skirt. In *Lai Harouba* too, *Thougal* dancing for women is extremely gentle with soft steps. Also, *maibi* dances, like *Loiching Jagoi* or *Panthoibi Jagoi*, express a delicate gentleness typical of Vaisnavite female dancing. But a *maibi's* dancing in *Thangkotpa*, with swords in both hands and *Kangleithokpa*, enacting the polo game, involves several knee-turned-out positions, high leaps, feet stamping, all of which project an exuberant and vigorous personality. Meitei male dancing is marked by a powerful masculine vigour, but in no other sphere of Meitei dancing does one observe such a bold vitality of feminine expression.

WOMEN AS PRIESTS IN OTHER AREAS OF MEITEI RELIGION

Lai-ibi: the High Priest

Women are highly recognized for their spiritual power in different spheres of Meitei religious world. During the reign of Maharaja Churachand, the royal temple of Pakhamba had a woman as *Lai-ibi*, the high priest.

To be qualified for the post of a priest at the Pakhamba temple a woman had to be from an R.K. family and over fifty years of age. She must have the standing of an ideal woman, e.g., not been divorced or widowed, have a living male child as her first-born, and a reputation for good behaviour. After becoming the priest she has to remain celibate and live in special quarters within the temple compound. She walks in front of a *dolai*, the wedding carriage of a princess.

Kithumpuba or Sadhika: Holy Female

I also found several women (as well as a male transvestite) as another kind of religious specialist. They were called *kithumpuba*, or by a Hinduized name, *sadhika* (holy female). They were known to have got sudden power and received *mantra* in a dream or trance. Sometimes people referred to them as *maibis*. They became self-styled holy people without any formal training or recognition from the *Loishang*. They can only perform *senmit* and some propitiatory rites, and cannot attend *Lai Harouba* festivals. Nonetheless, they attract a large clientele from all social strata. Unlike the *maibis*, these people do not make public appearances. These women (and the male transvestite) never go out of their homes and look upon the outside world as taboo. They wear normal clothes, but each of them has personal idiosyncrasies concerning food, colour of dress, or some other aspect of lifestyle.

One fifty-year old woman was married and had a son. She left her husband at thirty and went to serve the *Lai* of her parents' family temple. She said, "I heard voices all the time. I started having a large number of clients. My parents gave me the charge of the family temple of *Lai* Khurembi." I heard a great deal about the efficacy of the prediction of this woman. The temple of *Lai* Khurembi at Uripok *leikai* in Imphal is also famous. The *sadhika* mentioned names of at least half-a-dozen well known politicians who came to her for prediction. Because of the growing number of clients, the *sadhika* at *Lai* Khurembi temple is now building a rooming house to lodge the visiting clients. She does not use the method of *senmit*, but requests that her clients ask questions. After listening to these questions she meditates for a moment and starts answering. The youngest *sadhika* (17) also draws immense respect from her clientele. It was interesting that her guardian *Lai* was not a Meitei *Lai* but the Hindu goddess of knowledge and art, Saraswati.

Saraswati's (17) story was narrated by her step-sister:

"She was normal until she was fourteen years old, when she met a Hindu goddess, Saraswati, in her dream, who asked her to worship her. Next morning, the girl spoke about her dreams to all in her family. We did not pay any attention to that. But soon she started to have trances. My father, a *maiba* (medicine man) treated her in all possible ways but failed. One night, she met the goddess again in her dream, who asked her to go out to the backyard and look for a sign in the shape of a cross. She went to the backyard along with her younger brother. Both searched for the sign. After about two hours of searching, she found a piece of wood exactly in the required shape. She immediately went into a trance and chanted in praise of goddess Saraswati. When she recovered, she told my father that she would like to perform *senmit*. My father realized that this was not an ordinary illness. My sister gave up her former name and took the name of Saraswati herself. Her *senmit* was so successful that my father built a small temple for her adjacent to the house. Visitors crowded our compound. She cooks for herself and takes strict vegetarian meals. On her prediction days, twice a week, she fasts all day until her work is over. My father collects her money, about Rs. 50 to 80 or more a week, and deposits it in her bank account.... Saro says she will go out of the house only when she is thirty-five."

When I visited Saro, she appeared as a very modern *laishabi*. Her eyebrows were plucked and her hair cut short. She had lipstick on. Such grooming was most unusual for a village girl. Her appearance did not give the slightest hint of her lifestyle. I found her listening to a transistor radio on her bed. It was one of her workdays. Some young men and women had already started to gather at the family *sangoi*. Saro changed into a nice crisp *fanek* and went to meet them inside the temple one by one.

During the *yaoshong* festival we could hear the festive dance music from her room. I asked her, "You are such a young girl! Don't you feel like joining *Thabal Chombi* dances?" She said, "No, I am now a servant of *Ima* (mother Saraswati). I have no time for such things."

Saro's family accept her as a special person. They do not interfere in her lifestyle. She shares her bedroom with her half-sister. When I described Saro as a gentle person, the sister said, "If you had seen her in her trance you would not have said that. She was very violent then. Only after she found the sign and started to worship regularly did she become all right. Now she has become very well known. Her clients are from all over the Valley.

About her modern style of grooming, the sister remarked, "She picked up the style from some of her city clients."

8
Analysis and Conclusion

Meitei society can be viewed as a field of conflict and compromise operated upon by two diametrically opposing forces, the process of "Hinduization" and resistance to it by Meitei cultural tradition. Recently, the latter has been spurred on by a burst of energy, with a concomitant rise in Meiteiization. In the previous chapters we noted three important forces of change in Meitei history: male depopulation, Sanskritization, and colonization. I shall show how Meitei society adjusted itself to the forces of change and how traditional values persisted, especially in the area of the sex roles of women.

An overview of Meitei society leads to the conclusion that a woman's role in Meitei culture is very unusual, especially compared to other South Asian societies. The traditional roles of Meitei women are too deep-rooted in society to be subverted by Brahmanic influence.

There is an expression of feminism in Meitei patrilineal culture which encourages women to be individually self-reliant and collectively powerful without necessarily involving a sex war. I shall focus on this distinctive power base in a woman's role in Meitei society. Arising out of a collective spirit, it acts as a moral backing to men. It is an integral part of the patrilineal social system and does not act against it, unlike cases recorded in anthropological literature on the subcultures of women. (I.M. Lewis, 1971)

With an understanding of Meitei culture and of the social position of Meitei women, I then proceed to analyze the ritual repertoire of *Lai Harouba*. In addition to the community-based *Lai Harouba*, I shall also focus on lineage of a community. Although this is not a common form of ritual, it reveals some interesting aspects of women's role in traditional Meitei religion. The analysis of non-Hindu Meitei rituals gives an insight into the traditional cultural ethos of sex roles and inter-sex relationships, which are based on mutual dependence, respect, and co-operation. It also draws atten-

tion to the two contrasting sex role models for women, viz. the primary social roles of women and the alternative ritual role of the
priestesses. The recognition of a woman's social role as an economic
contributor (whether she is a daughter, a mother, or a wife) and the
tolerant acceptance of the high ritual status of priestesses in the core
religious system are two features most unusual in a male-oriented
society. How a patrilineal society could accommodate the existence
of an elevated important female status and leadership in religion is
indeed a problem in this study. However, the informing ethos of
Lai Harouba may serve as a key to the understanding of the people
and how they have sustained their basic character throughout a
long history.

PERSISTENCE OF TRADITIONAL SEX ROLES: THEIR SURVIVAL POTENTIAL

Depopulation
The demographic imbalances of the sexes caused by the *Chahi
Taret Khuntakpa* (seven years of catastrophe) in 1819-1826, preceded
by sixty years of warfare against Burmese invaders may be considered a major cause of change in social relations among the Meitei.
The historian Gangumei Kabui (1974:54) writes: "The repeated
Burmese invasions had uprooted the social and economic life of
people.... Thousands of people fled to Cachar for refuge; and many
more (were) taken prisoners and deported to Ava. Francis Hamilton
(Hamilton in *Account of Assam*, 1807, Calcutta) records that about
300,000 Manipuri prisoners were taken to Ava...." In the last
century Johnstone referred to this event (1896:86): "Manipur at
this time contained 2,000 inhabitants, the miserable remnants of a
thriving population of at least 400,000 or possibly 600,000 that
existed before the (Burmese) invasions."
One result of such massive depopulation was an even greater
emphasis on male progeny. In addition, there was the growing
popularity of polygyny (Yambem, 1976).[93] However, the system of
polygyny is detrimental to the monogamous ideal based on romance

[93]Here we may recall a similar historical event in Paraguay at the time of the
dictator Francisco Solano Lopez when, in 1865-70, the Paraguayan army fought
against the Triple Alliance (Brazil, Argentina, and Uruguay). As only 13
per cent of the male population survived the war (*Encyclopaedia Britannica*, Vol.
17, 1967: 309) the custom of polygyny became popular after this period. (Professor Conrad Arensberg, personal communication.)

as depicted in Meitei rituals and folklore. In *Lai Harouba* I did not
observe any polygynous implication, nor is there any place for
polygyny in the vast literature of romantic love in Meitei culture.

The demographic imbalance of the sexes most probably resulted
in two distinct changes in women's sex roles: (1) it affected the importance of the wifely role and the husband-wife companionship
in a monogamous union, and (2) it enlarged the work sphere of
women with increased opportunity and responsibility in subsistence
because of the absence of a sufficient number able-bodied males.

Sanskritization

Sanskritization started much earlier than the "catastrophe" mentioned above, but gained impetus following the large-scale depopulation. It is a process which continues to this day.

Sanskritization in the Manipur Valley was introduced in an extremely organized way. The king, royal officers, and immigrant
Brahmans developed a complex strategy to mould the lifestyle of
the people in the state. Vaisnavism was presented in a grand and
aesthetically attractive manner, and in effect worked as a political
force in disguise.

But in the Manipur Valley, mass Hinduization did not submerge
the simple folk religion; instead, it had to accommodate itself within
a strongly established and highly sophisticated religious culture.
The ancient texts of Meitei religion date back to A.D. 33, and the
philosophy is based on well-developed intellectual dogmas. The
religious system was organized under complex hierarchical institutions with different councils of learned scholars, office bearers,
musicians, dancers, priestesses, etc. under the control of the state;
the process of Vaisnavization (though under the royal patronage)
was confronted by this extremely powerful force in the existent
religious system. In this respect, the Meitei case contrasts with other
South Asian societies.

An important point in issue is the extent to which the process of
Sanskritization has integrated Meitei society with the Brahmanic
socio-religious system, and in what areas the society has resisted.
To be sure, the Meitei have adopted several caste values, e.g., the
rules of commensality, pollution taboos on food and water, and
vegetarianism. They have also integrated numerous Hindu rituals
and ceremonies into their socio-religious framework. Hodson remarked at the beginning of this century: "It is very difficult to

estimate the precise effect of Hinduism on the civilization of the people; for to the outward observer, they seem to have adopted only the festival, the outward ritual, the caste marks, and the exclusiveness of Hinduism, while all unmindful of its spirits and inward essentials" (Hodson, 1908, reprinted 1975:96). I found that the most conspicuous failure to integrate Hindu values concerned women's sex roles in the socio-economic and religious spheres. Equally conspicuous is the failure to diminish the strength of women's public role.

Anthropological literature on India is replete with theoretical formulations on the issue of Sanskritization, but there is very little substantive literature on the changes in women's roles effected by this process. Following Srinivas (1952, 1971, 1976), anthropologists explain (Ornstein, 1963 on the Sagar Rajput; Mayer, 1956 on the Bhilala weavers; Sinha, 1971 on the Bhumija, etc.) how a lower caste "translates" the high caste values. Perhaps the most important aspect is the emulation of the upper-caste custom of controlling women by curtailing their socio-economic freedom. Subsequently, women are made completely dependent on men, which results in a society with strict polarity of the sexes. Anthropologists sometimes refer to specific indication of these changes, e.g., the removal of women's labour from agriculture, the introduction of the dowry in place of the bride-wealth, the barring of widow remarriage and divorce, the prohibition of women's participation in festive dances in public, etc. (Epstein, 1973 on the Okkilaga of Mysore; Berreman, 1966 on the Pahari low caste; Sinha, 1971 on the Bhumija of West Bengal; Bailey, 1957 on the Boad distillers, etc.). But none of these writers discusses how far the changes in women's roles might bring an overall change in economic-social relationships.

Anthropologists (Apte, 1975:43; Boserup, 1971:47) have indicated how the value of women is often determined by their economic role in society. Miller's (1978) study shows a marked difference in the value placed on female children in the societies of northwestern and southern India.[94] The custom of bride-price is also often associated with the female role in the economic sphere. The curtailment of direct participation in the economy induces a higher dowry rate in

[94]Miller correlates the low mortality rate of female children in South India with the prominent female participation in the wet-rice agriculture of the region. It should be noted that in the wheat-growing area of the North, there is little need for female labour and female babies are considered a liability.

North India.[95] Epstein points out (1973) that in the past, a peasant wife of the Okkilaga caste was an economic asset. In order to emulate the upper-caste lifestyle, Okkilaga women were removed from the agricultural labour force: in place of bride-price, the Okkilaga have adopted dowry. Srinivas (1976:16) points out that the emulation of upper-caste lifestyle influences family relationships: "It immures them (women) and changes the character of husband and wife relationships." Thus a conjugal asymmetry eradicates egalitarian partnership. Srinivas (1962: 46-47) also states that Sanskritization emphasizes the prominence of patrilineal values in kinship and the conjugal relationship. However, writers have noted that this ritual escalation will not be successful unless the entire caste-group achieves considerable economic gain which would then enable the system to exclude women from the economic sphere. From Fuchs' study (1968) we may infer how the effort to Sanskritize the Gond by caste association failed because of the lack of economic gain for men and because of the social and economic independence of Gond women.

If the success of Sanskritization is correlated with economic dependence and the seclusion of women, the failure of Sanskritization in Meitei culture is easily understood. Meitei women's economic role has proved to be too valuable and pervasive to be replaced through any of the processes of historical change that the society experienced.

Socially, the upper-caste behaviour model faced strong resistance from women. The Brahmans of Manipur made numerous attempts to introduce Hindu codes of conduct, e.g., the prohibition of widow remarriage, the prohibition of divorce, the encouragement of pre-puberty marriages. Zealous Brahmans encouraged even the custom of *sati* (G. Kabui, 1974).[96] None of these efforts succeeded in Mani-

[95]The large number of spinsters in Sind and Punjab and of suicide cases among unmarried girls in Bengal (Karve, 1965: 105-14) may also be associated with the absence of an economic role for women and the high rate of dowry. At present increased rate of unemployment (scarcity of suitable males) has created a social attitude towards extreme monetization of marriage customs all over India among the higher castes, as well as those wishing to imitate them. Ironically the pressure of dowry is now felt by both fairly educated employed brides and less educated and un .nployed ones. Incidents of suicidal dowry deaths among young brides frequently feature in Indian newspapers.

[96]Kabui (1974:61) quotes from the royal chronicle *Chaitharol Kumbaba:* "In 1698 Saka (1777 A.D.) on Friday.... Yaiskullakpa died. His wife ran away as she failed to die along with him. She was exiled to Sugnu (a Loi outcaste village)."

pur. One good reason for this failure might have been the dearth of upper-caste Hindu women. A majority of immigrant Brahmans arrived in Manipur as bachelors and married Meitei women hyper-gamically. There was thus no class of upper-caste women to set a standard of behaviour for the rest.[97]

There is no major reflection of Hinduism in the customs of marriage excepting *luhungba* (the Brahmanic ceremony of marriage), and even there everything except the *sampradana* ritual is tradition-ally Meitei. In *sampradana*, according to Brahmanic tradition, the woman is treated as a passive object. Three men (the bride's father, the groom, and the Brahman priest) monopolize the scene.[98] The bride's father has to touch the knee of the groom while offering his daughter as a gesture of his inferior position as a daughter-giver.

The distinctive position Meitei culture occupied in Indian society can be recognized when compared to the dramatic change in marriage ritual among the Tiyas of North Malabar, a matrilineal and viri-local people, under the influence of Sanskritization (Rao, 1972: 126). Rao describes how matrilineal kin and women (the bride's mother's brother's wife, and the groom's sister) have been completely replaced in prominence by patrilineal kin. Now in the core Sans-kritic ritual, instead of women members of the matrilineage, the bride's father takes the most important part, bestowing the groom with the high status of the receiver of *kanyadan* (the gift of a virgin).[99]

[97]Incidentally, Pangan Muslim women in Manipur did not accept the Islamic rule of purdah, and continue to enjoy considerable freedom in the socio-economic sphere.

[98]Perhaps an extreme degree of female inferiority is ritualized in the high caste marriage custom of the Hindus of the Sylhet district of East Bengal (at present in Bangladesh). Here the bride circumnavigates a throne, on which the groom is seated, seven times (Sanskritic ritual *saptapadi*) offering flowers at his feet, worshipping him as a deity. Later she has to wash his feet and wipe them with her hair as an expression of dedicated servitude. Such an extremity of the expression of female inferiority is rare in marriages in the other areas of Bengal. However, the bride is often carried on a wooden seat in *saptapadi* (thus making her rather a commodity) and the bride touching the groom's feet (denoting obedience) eat-ing from her husband's used plate (a ritually inferior act among the Hindus) etc., all symbolize the wife's status as that of a ward of the husband.

[99]The Tiyas underwent a radical socio-religious change directed toward Sans-kritization under the leadership of a religious leader, Sri Narayan Guru Swamy (1854-1929). The religious group, Sri Narayana Dharma Paripalana (S.N.D.P.), brought a considerable imbalance to the traditional matrilineal culture. (Rao, 1972: 126.)

In Meitei in spite of the introduction of the Hindu ritual of *kanyadan*
one notes the highly important role taken by the groom's mother and
to some extent by the bride's mother;[100] such prominence of women
is indeed very non-Brahmanic.[101]

Marriage in Brahmanic culture is a hypergamic alliance, the family
of the groom enjoying the higher status (Dumont, 1961; Karve,
ibid; Mandelbaum, 1970), and the daughter-giver being of inferior
status. The superiority of the groom's family is seen in its demanding dowry and other gifts, requiring no reciprocation. A son-in-law
is always treated as an honoured guest without any expectation of
reciprocity.[102] In contrast, there is no such status-asymmetry between
the bride's and the groom's families in a Meitei marriage, and son-
in-law and sisters' husbands have reciprocal obligations.

In other types of marriages, the bride and the groom are on an
even plane; as consenting adults. The custom of *chelhong* (*luhungba*
after *chenba*) defies the very concept of *kanyadon* (gift of a virgin)
enjoined by Brahmanic tradition. *Chenba, lokhoutpa*, and *kainakatpa*
all allow a woman to choose her own partner. This is contrary to the
Hindu ideology of marriage. Repeated threats of ostracism and the
loss of royal rank failed to reinforce Brahma Sabha rules regarding
women. The customs of *khainaba* (divorce), remarriage, and widow
remarriage all testify to the persisting social freedom enjoyed by
Meitei women.

Even though Sanskritic rituals were introduced into Meitei society,
they were later replaced or modified by those more in tune with the

---

[100]Incidentally, in Bengali high-caste weddings a bride's mother is barred from
even watching the core ritual, and thus deprived of her role in *sampradana*.

[101]Non-Brahmanic traits may not necessarily be indicative of social advantages
for females. Besides *sampradana, saptapadi* and *jagna* (ritual before sacrificial
fire), in Bengali high caste Hindu weddings the rest are of non-Brahmanic and non-
Vedic origin (Roy, 1980: 608). In Bengal the Brahmanic culture, which proclaims
a strong patriarchal ideology of male superiority, is further supported by a series
of women's rituals of non-Brahman origin. Women are socialized to accept their
inferior roles which are glorified with an aura of womanly chastity (also called
sati). This attitude is similar to that of the Tamil women who are the "staunch
supporters" of female inferiority (Wadley, 1980). But the non-Brahmanic rituals
of the Meitei, participated in by both sexes, do not emphasize such convictions of
female inferiority.

[102]An annual feast given as a ritual for the son-in-law (*Jamai Shasti* in Bengal)
symbolizes his position as an honoured guest. There is no corresponding ritual
among the Meitei.

Meitei ethos. A case in point is the replacement of *Bhratridvitiya* (brother's ritual and feast) with *Ningon Chakoba* (sister's and daughter's feast) in the mid-nineteenth century.[103] *Bhratridvitiya* and also the ritual of *Rakshabandhan* (tie for protection), or its variant in some North Indian societies, allow women to establish alliances with brothers, male cousins, and other, non-kin, males (as fictive brothers). Brother-sister alliances can be recognized as bonds for women's security in a rigidly male-dominated society. If we correlate the presence of *Bhratridvitiya* with women's need for security, we can well explain its replacement by *Ningon-Chakoba*, an appropriate ritual reflecting women's bonds with their natal home and the valuable role of daughters in a family.

A striking non-Sanskritic feature in Meitei Hinduism is women's participation in central rituals, especially women's ritual dancing in public. Anthropologists have often referred to cases where various caste groups stopped their women from participating in public dancing because of its association with low-caste or tribal behaviour (Sinha, 1971 on the Bhumija of West Bengal; Berreman, 1966 on the Pahari low caste; Dube, 1956 on an Andhra Pradesh village society).[104]

Meitei women not only participate in simple folk dancing, they take prominent part in spectacular classical Vaisnavite ceremonial dances in public *manadapas*. The traditional dances of women and in *Lai Harouba* also reflect a highly sophisticated and fine aesthetic sense. The male spectators' respectful and warm response reflects a reverence for these roles of women in the socio-religious world.

In the *Kangchingba/Kanglen*, the Meitei version of the Hindu *Rathajatra* festival, the last day, called *ningonpali* (the day for the daughters' turn in the ceremony), has been added to the Vaisnavite religious complex, indicating a continuous effort of the society to accommodate its women's traditional role within the Hindu religious framework.

---

[103]In the South, owing to the absence of village exogamy, and the custom of cross-cousin marriage, women do not have to face an alien, insecure world after marriage like their North Indian sisters. There is no *Bhratridvitiya* or *Rakshabandhan* in the South. Nor is such ritual found among the matrilineal and matrilocal Nayars.

[104]Dube's study (1956:13) refers to the high-caste attitude toward women's participation in dance in public: "Women from the two highest castes, i.e., Brahman and Komti, do not participate in dancing. . . . Similarly, women from "respectable" families refuse to join in the dance. . . ."

Another important non-sanskritic aspect of Meitei culture is the spirit of male-female co-operation in religion. In the community *mandapa* activities, there is marked co-operation of the sexes in different age groups. Both sexes begin participating and cooperating in each other's activities from a very early age.

In the major Vaisnavite festivals, women's prominence in *Raslila* dancing and male prominence in *sankirtana* present complementary role models. The sexes have an equal opportunity to become musicians and teachers. The spectacle of women's *Raslila* performance in the Govindaji temple is paralleled by the exuberance of male *sankirtana* groups in a regale of colour during the spring festival.

There is very little stress on sex dichotomy among child participants. In *Gostharas*, or during the *Holi* festival at the royal temple, their roles are interchangeable. In Vaisnava philosophy, the devotional experience of the *gopis*, the milk-maids and companions of Krishna's consort, Radha, symbolizes the highest fulfillment of human spiritual pursuits. Meitei women dancing as *gopis* symbolize this essence of Vaisnavite faith. This, of course, is contradictory to the Brahmanic concept of the supremacy of the male. In the sixteenth century, Vaisnavism brought in a sense of egalitarianism which cut across sex, caste, and social divisions in Indian culture. In Bengali Vaisnavism, this philosophy is limited to religious scripture and sacred lyrics, and does not extend to the Hindu social framework.[105] Among the Meitei, the Vaisnava philosophical concept found a fertile social environment. Pan-Indian Vaisnavism has been absorbed in Manipur into an ethnic religious culture perhaps to be found nowhere else on the subcontinent.

The effect of Sanskritization on the Meitei male took a different pattern. Vaisnava ideology (as indicated in the political context) was incompatible with the male cultural traits of a martial society. The new religion did not offer a real substitute for the glorious martial activities of the past. It promoted the ideas of vegetarianism, humility, and non-violence, and tabooed liquor—in total contrast to the traditional martial habits of the Meitei. The traditional forms of masculine energy are found only in the ecstatic dancing and singing of *sankirtana*, singing sessions of groups of males (*nupapala*). The loud emotional crying of males in the audience during

[105]In Bengal, there are Vaisnavite religious cults, with male and female membership (*bostom, bostomi*). These groups are looked down upon by the upper castes because of their so-called lax moral behaviour.

these ceremonies is not found in Meitei traditional rituals like *Lai Harouba*. Could this be explained as an emotional outlet for the repressed feelings of men who had to surrender their martial ego and pride to the Vaisnava idea of humility? Crying and dancing in sheer ecstasy thus replace the exuberance of pride and power in a heroic people.

Colonization

The British authorities made valiant efforts to strip Meitei men of their pride and independence. Several important male activities, e.g., membership in the *lalmi* (organization of the men of war), the martial art of *thang-ta* (sword-play) and various other heroic displays were banned by the British government. The absence of the *lalmi* and *lallup* (free labour to the state) took away a male's direct individual responsibility to the state. Gradually, several male activities, e.g., *keirup* (tiger association), and the use of *langshoi* (a method of taming wild elephants), became extinct. This was the time when the *Brahma Sabha* became extremely exploitative, with the active support of the King, who had by then lost a great deal of his political authority.

Colonization reduced the political status of Meitei women by ignoring the function of the women's court. However, it did not adversely affect their economic role which, unlike that of women in other Third World societies (Boserup,1970; Pala, 1976; Leacock, 1972; Sachs, 1974; Smock, 1977; Mullings, 1976),[106] increased in importance with colonization. Before contact with colonial India, the traditional weaving industry of Meitei women catered mostly to domestic and local markets. A colonial report of 1882 (*Report on the Administration of Assam for the Year 1981-82*, Shillong, 1882: 133-134) on Manipur's cottage industries indicates an awareness of their activity:

[106]Boserup states (1970:54): "Virtually all Europeans shared the opinion that men are superior to women in the art of farming; and it seemed to follow that for the development of agriculture male farming ought to be promoted to replace female farming. Many Europeans did all they could to achieve this." Mullings notes (1976:247): "Colonization often resulted in differentiation of social and domestic labour, the introduction of large scale production for exchange, and the transformation of productive resources into private property—processes that significantly altered the status of women."

The manufacture for which Manipur is chiefly famed is that of different kinds of clothes, which besides being used in the Valley, are exported to Cachar and Assam, and eagerly bought up by all surrounding hill tribes. Not only has Manipur obtained a ready sale for her particular kind of cloths, but the people have, with energy worthy of all commendation, imitated the different clothes of adjoining hill tribes and succeeded in many cases in taking the trade out of their hands.... Every woman in Manipur weaves.

This description of the role of women was given ten years before British rule began in Manipur. However, Manipur had been in contact with colonial India much earlier and this created a wider market outside Manipur for the women's weaving industry. The economic opportunities of the colonial period expanded a great deal with the advent of modern facilities in communication and transportation. Meitei women appear to have taken full advantage of their contact with North Indian traders for the export of their products.

WOMEN'S SEX ROLE: A POWER BASE WITHIN A PATRILINEAL FRAMEWORK

In a patrilineal social atmosphere, women of the Meitei society stand as a collective body. Women's sense of solidarity is overtly demonstrated in all phases of their lives. The social structure offers men the position of authority, as fathers and husbands, but women's socio-economic power often counteracts socially sanctioned male domination. This power base springs from a collective spirit among women and from the options available to them for economic autonomy, both of which are based on a woman's identity with her age-group within a community, with a further support provided by her own kin and mother. Anthropologists today recognize the concept of *shakti*, the superior feminine energy as a "covert power" e.g. that of Tamil women in South India as opposed to an "overt" expression of male dominance in the society (Wadley, 1980). This power is based on women's acquired capacity for self-denial, penance and complete submission in her oppressed position.[107] Meitei women's power is not founded upon such a concept of self-denial and self-

[107]We can also recognize the deep veneration for the custom of *sati*, (self-immolation of widows) among the higher caste Hindus, which was looked upon as the utmost expression of self-denial in a chaste woman. A widow had to accept a social death being deprived of basic rights of life, but a "*sati*'s physical death deified her for the future generation." (Chaki-Sircar: 1978.)

effacement, but rather on a capacity to control their own lives. Furthermore, the traditional Meitei religious ideology recognizes in women a "superpower", *shakti*, but does not deprive her of the basic social privileges enjoyed by men. In the life cycle of Meitei women, we note two types of bonding: (a) the mother-daughter bond, and (b) the age-group bond. Anthropologists have often remarked on the mother-daughter relationship in non-Western societies (Dwyer, 1973: 261 on Moroccan society: Nash, 1965: 51-54 on Burmese society; Strathern, 1972:93 on Mt. Hagen society; Jacobson, 1977:34 on a Central Indian society). Among the Meitei, this bond appears to be very strong.[108] A Meitei mother is the social and professional mentor of her daughter, her support emerging secure and effective because of her own standing in the socio-economic sphere. The mother-daughter relationship provides a secure base in a woman's life in a society where the marital bond is rather brittle. Several of my case studies reveal how the mother becomes the crucial figure during a girl's *chenba* or *thaba*. Besides being in charge of her moral behaviour, a mother is also responsible for the development of her daughter's economic skill. It is the mother who gives shelter to her daughter after a divorce and, if the latter remarries, raises any children of the first marriage without subjecting the young woman to feelings of guilt. My case studies suggest that through the frequent occurrence of a woman going through successive marriages and moving back and forth between her mother's (or parent's) residence and the husband's home, the former is deemed a permanent base. Although a woman gives birth to her child in her husband's compound, (an allegiance to the patrilineage) her mother is present during the delivery. The mother's *stridhan* (women's wealth) is inherited by the daughters, and the inheritance of market plots by women can often be traced matrilineally. What is striking about the mode of socialization of Meitei women is that although the mothers oversee their daughters' moral behaviour and discipline (which is often more severe on the girls than on the boys), the young girls are socialized to be self-reliant and independent, and not crippled into a passive model of sheer dependence on the male. Through life's joys and sorrows, successes and failures, the mother-daughter relationship of Meitei women is sustained and strengthened.

---

[108]A Meitei proverb expresses a mother's feelings toward having a daughter: "Who will cry for me when I die if I do not have a daughter?"

Another noticeable aspect of Meitei culture is the collective spirit of women in different contexts, a bond which can be traced throughout their life cycle. I described various forms of bonding such as the *marup* credit associations, *khulongs*, the rice cultivation teams, *nupipalas*, associations for religious singing and dancing, and many others in economic and socio-religious spheres, each attached to a particular phase of a woman's life. In anthropological literature, one comes across woman's bonding either as a defence mechanism for emotional security within the domestic domain, or as an economic or political power in the extra-domestic domain against male domination. In both cases, bonding provides a power base that serves women exclusively. In societies with strong polarity of the sexes (Dwyer, 1978 on the Moroccan; Murphy and Murphy, 1974 on the Munduruccu; Wolf, 1968 on the Chinese; O. Lewis, 1958 and Karve, 1965 on the North Indian), women's bonding develops as an "insulation" from male interference in a male-dominated social system.[109]

Economic or political bonding expands a woman's world greatly beyond her familial environment. Such cases are found, for example, in several African societies, where women's economic life extends beyond the home (B. Lewis, 1977 on the Ivory Coast women; Levine, 1970, Van Allen , 1976 and Okonjo, 1976 on the Igbo women; Falade, 1974 on Dakar women; Levine, 1970 on the Yoruba women; Nelson, 1979 on the *buzaa* beer brewers in Kenya, etc.). Women's secret associations, mutual aid associations, and political groups of several African societies (especially those with large numbers of women in trade and in the market economy) provide an economic

[109]Dwyer describes (1973:48) how the emotional ties of the Moroccan woman can be broken by her just moving out of the street or immediate neighbourhood and how bonding is dependent on her access to an extremely isolated social world. Wolf (1968) shows how young Chinese brides in a rural society establish a group identity of subservient females, which may act as a social defence against dominating mothers-in-law and men. In North Indian societies, all married women come as outsiders to the alien environment of their husband's village. Young married women of different caste groups, living extremely subordinate roles, hold on to each other in a "vertical solidarity" (Marriott, 1955). However, Ursula Sharma (1979), in her study of a village in Himachal Pradesh, shows an opposite situation, where women are isolated in their own patriarchal families without any sense of bonding with other women of the community. She attributes this to the sense of powerlessness of women in a rigidly male-dominated social system.

and political stronghold. These associations give their members an economic and political role independent of men, and additionally provide the emotional support of a sorority.[110] To some extent, there are parallels of African women's associations in the Meitei situation. However, in Meitei society, the influence of bonding and associations is perhaps more pervasive and includes social causes involving both sexes. Women's collectivity does not even form a "subculture" (I.M. Lewis, 1971): it plays an important role in the social universe of both sexes. Its interest does not exclude men. Women are *not* "...always a potential source of disruption to the unity" (as per Tiger and Fox, 1971:57); instead, they co-operate with men and provide them with true supportive strength.[111] Age group bonding accommodates itself to the different socio-economic options available during the life cycle of a woman. And for a Meitei woman, an exciting life begins at forty with greater opportunities with her social radius and as extended horizons to her economic pursuits. Unlike some of their sisters in the western world of the U.S.A. women of Manipur do not face the so-called crisis of aging and do not feel the need to question their self-worth in a male-oriented society. This may perhaps be best exemplified in their attitude toward menopause; Meitei women feel no loss of self-worth or sexuality or any form of the depression associated in the West with

[110]For example the traditional social and political organizations in several West African societies such as the Yoruba, Igbo, and Nupe of Nigeria, supplied various opportunities to women to act with considerable social and political power. Among the Yoruba, market-mothers, titled *Iyalode*, were elected to oversee women's judicial and social affairs with an all-women administrative body and police force (Awe, 1977). Similarly the western Igbo elected an *Omu* (town-mother; female counterpart of the male monarch, *Obi*) from amongst the commoners to rule the women. The eastern Igbo villages had two women's associations, daughters' association and wives' association, both taking care of the social and religious affairs of women. Village women's associations among the eastern Igbo also exercised considerable social control over dominating husbands. For example, women's groups used to perform a special ritual called "sitting on aman" (or "to make war)" to punish a recalcitrant husband, reciting offensive and abusive poems about him, dirtying his hut, demonstrating in their ritual dress (signifying the wrath of their ancestress) until the man came out to apologize for his misdeed. This custom was approved by the village elders, who were all men (see Van Allen, 1972).

[111]This study may dispel the naive notion of the "inevitability of patriarchy" (as per Goldberg, 1973), and of the universal subordination of females (Young, 1965; Tiger, 1969; Tiger and Fox, 1971).

menopause. On the contrary, many look forward to their post-menopausal lives, free from the burdens of childbearing and other biological constrictions.[112] A woman's self-worth is not dependent on her sexuality or youth, but on her personal achievement in life as a mother and a provider for the family. In fact, a woman, *hanubi*, is respectfully addressed as *Ima* (mother) by both sexes, indicating status and a recognition of the mature feminine qualities.[14]

Women in Politics

We observe that women not only brought a humane element into the masculine world of justice and law, but that they also wielded considerable political power which influenced state politics. An esteem for women is patent in the traditional judicial system where women controlled their legal affairs, and both Brahmans (having the highest status) and women were exempt from capital punishment.

To this day, female solidarity based on the market centre acts politically to influence affairs of state. The validity of women's collective representation in the King's court and the recognition of the power of the collective voice of women against an execution suggest their socially sanctioned political power. While men hold political authority through competition and a rigid hierarchy, the unassigned power of women works from a rather egalitarian base. Although the political participation of women is very unusual in traditional Indian societies, it is familiar in many African ones.[114] The events of the *nupi-lan* (women's war) are very close to the experience of Igbo women in 1929 in Nigeria. Anthropologists take a

[112]My observation was supported by Dr. Y. Satyabati Devi, a Meitei woman gynaecologist who found depression only among some sterile women who finally lost all hope of having a child.

[113]This is very much in contrast with the situation in American society today. On the U.S. television and other media older women as mothers and mothers-in-law are often presented as clownish and stupid. Even in children's literature old women are frequently described as witches and hags. There is also no veneration attached to the very address, "Mother" for an older woman, as it is found all over the Indian subcontinent. In several African societies also, women gain more prestige with age (Smock, 1977 on the Ga and Ewe tribes of Ghana). Barbara Lewis discusses how menopause helps an important mode of social promotion with more extended possibilities of economic autonomy and social contact among the women of Ivory Coast (1977:187). The older women are also addressed as mothers indicating a veneration of their old age.

[114]See Awe-Bolanle, 1977 on the Yoruba political system and Smock, 1977 on women's corporate identity in Ghana.

critical view of British colonial indifference to the political role of women in Africa. The British experience with Igbo women (Van Allen, 1972; Sacks, 1976; Pellow, 1977) in the women's war showed the traditional power of women in the market centres of the *mikiri* association (Ifeka-Moller, 1976; Van Allen, 1976 and Okonjo, 1976).[115] Market centres of several African societies remained sources of strong political power (Lebeuf, 1963; Levine, 1970; Sanday, 1974).

The two *nupi-lans* (women's wars) and several other political activities in recent years developed in the market centres of the Manipur Valley, and the continuity and perhaps increasing strength of this political power base became evident during these women's movements. It may be that the extremely powerful statewide mobilization of women during the women's wars in the first half of this century gained real impetus from the increasing economic strength of women during the colonial period. In the past, there was collective representation of women in the court, but there is no record of any large scale rebellion similar to the women's wars before the beginning of the twentieth century. During the colonial period, the alien government failed to respect the collective voice of women and, as a result, the conflict took a severe form.

Traditionally, only mature women in the market became involved in political action. The recent incident in the village Panchayat election (described in Chapter 2) marks a new trend involving young unmarried girls. Here, too, perhaps the recent progress of the weaving industry offered the community of unmarried girls a political awareness which is based on their economic standing.[116]

[115]Igbo women's market associations developed strong political power bases in the twenties and early thirties. In Aba, eastern Nigeria, an outburst of women's political power occurred in 1929 when ten thousand women were united, representing *mikiris* of a large region to protest against the tax-policy of the colonial administration. The British armed forces subdued the upheaval with a death toll of fifty women marchers (Van Allen; 1972).

[116]Incidentally, in South India today, one comes across evidence of women's political involvement which is directly related to their work-role in agricultural labour. There are cases of increased political consciousness and militancy among women agricultural labourers in Kerala and Tamil Nadu. Although the leadership of the union (run by CPI-M) is still in the hands of men, 80 per cent of the members are women who actively protest the oppression not only of the landlords but also of male domination in their families (Mencher and D'Amico, 1979: 8-9).

Women's solidarity as a veritable political power may be observed in the recent event of "the night patrollers of Manipur" in 1975 (Yambem, 1979)[117] and the two incidents during my stay in Manipur in 1978 (see Chapter 2).

There were incidents of food riots with women's active participation in Europe in the seventeenth and eighteenth centuries and in early twentieth century America. But *nupi-lan* cannot be described only as a food riot. Its impact was much wider and it evoked a deep respect for and recognition of women's collective power for the benefit of the entire society.

It is noticeable that in none of the cases is the women's group in competition with men. Both sexes thus still perform complementary roles, in keeping with tradition. In fact, men's reliance on women's political support is symbolized in the public recognition of the date of *nupi-lan* as "women's day".

Socio-Economic Context

The political power base of Meitei women may be considered a social power in the socio-economic sphere.

In Meitei society, a man, as head of a household, rarely bears the economic brunt alone; he usually works together with a woman, who provides a supplementary income. Where women are household heads of uterine families, they are the sole earners. Female labour in family and community is thus an indispensable part of Meitei agriculture. In addition, weaving and trade guarantee women several options throughout their life cycle. However, women are not to dispose of their income as they see fit. In the past, the absence of land rights for women was compensated for by their legal right to their own and their mother's *stridhan*. A woman's dowry, which is often collected from her savings during her unmarried years, is considered her wealth, which can often serve as capital for future economic activity, and is returnable on divorce.[118]

Two important aspects emerge in relation to the economic role

---

[117]Unpublished research data from S. Yambem.

[118]There is a real difference in the concept of dowry between the Meitei and North Indian societies. In North India the dowry is given to the groom along with *kanyadan* (the gift of a virgin). The woman has no right to the dowry except for her personal jewellery. Among the Meitei, unmarried girls are even members of a *luhungba marup* (credit association for marriage) enabling them to collect a lump sum of cash at their wedding.

of women: (*a*) self-reliance and the potential for economic autonomy, and (*b*) collective strength based on co-operation and mutual dependence.

As a wife, a woman provides a supplementary income, but she can also use her capital for economic autonomy in times of need. The family recognizes women as providers and many families are dependent on their earnings. Any possible tension between mothers-in-law and daughters-in-law, familiar in many patrilineal societies (Wolf, 1965 on Chinese society; Karve, 1965 on North Indian societies) is eased by economic partnership between the two.

Male-female partnership and mutual co-operation are observed in many aspects of Meitei society: in romance, in marriage by elopement, and in the interdependence of conjugal life.[119] Yet we can detect the existence of sex antagonism embodied in the secret male rite of ancestor worship (the ritual of *Sagei Apokpa*) which excludes women. The comment of *maiba* about the female violent destructive power of "one of seven daughters of Durga (benevolent Hindu goddess) suggests a fear of women's *shakti* similar to that found in South Hindu communities (Wadley, 1980). This reflects a typical Hindu anxiety about women's inherent power (ibid). Tension is also evident in the traditional belief in witchcraft and in accusations against so-called women witches, the *hinch-habis*, and the female witch spirits, the *helois*. Such beliefs find a place in societies where women are economically dominant; anthropologists interpret it as an expression of men's hostility towards the economic role of women and their dependence on it (Nadel, 1970 on the Nupe; Hochsmith, 1978, Morton Williams in Mair, 1973 on the Yoruba; Epstein, 1967 on the women moneylenders of a Mysore village in India; Spiro, 1967 on the Burmese). Given women's opportunities for economic autonomy in Meitei society, accusations against them of witchcraft may well arise from men's discomfort about women's sense of independence.

A fear of the spirit from the beautiful maiden (found in the belief in *helois*) also exists in Burmese society, where pre-marital romance with a girl is discouraged by a strong sexual taboo (Nash, 1965: 179). It is significant that the affliction caused by the *helois* (appearing as a young temptress) is mostly observed during the period of

[119]Sixty-seven per cent of the people in my samples have monogamous and apparently stable marriages.

the spring festival, *yaoshong*, the prime time for social encounters of unmarried girls and boys. This is also the busiest season for *chenba* cases. However, the women accused of witchcraft are not attacked directly; when a suspicion of witchcraft arises, a preventive rite is performed without the knowledge of the person who is suspect.

At present, the most noticeable area of conflict is in individual sexual relationships. The male-female confrontation and clash occur frequently in polygynous marriages, in *khainaba* (divorce), and in *thaba* (abduction). These conflicts are contradictory to the sex role ethos of the society.

The most frequent tension in conjugal life is caused by the husband's desire for an additional wife and the wife's refusal to take it in her stride. Here polygyny may be observed as a means by which a husband curtails woman's power within the nuclear family. Eventually, it leads to marital conflict, separation of the couple, and formation of a matrifocal household headed by a single woman as a divorcee, or a "second wife." The social environment encourages strong emotional ties between the husband and wife, so the institution of polygyny has not been well-received by the Meitei. Many men and women end up with a series of monogamous unions.

Among the urban elite, polygyny appears to have a stronger hold. This is probably a result of the adoption of Sanskritized values by women, which inculcate the indissolubility of the marital bond. Nevertheless, disruption of family life is quite common in urban polygyny too.

In rural areas polygynous households are rare. Women, conflicting with their husbands in different situations, must form uterine families or find new husbands. Sometimes, even a mother-in-law allies with her daughter-in-law and grandchildren, against her son. Here again, we see the importance of the two-woman economic team. The most contradictory attitude in male-female behaviour is found in the tradition of *thaba*, the abduction of a virgin. Meitei society promotes a very tender, romantic attitude between the sexes. Social ceremonies like the *Thabal Chombi* dance, the *likkol* game, the *kang* tournament and others, encourage romantic relationships. Yet customs such as *thaba*, though rare, could be used by men as instruments to terrorize and subjugate women. The custom of *nambothaba* (marriage by intrusion), now extinct, could also in the past be used by men as an "oblique strategy" to overcome a woman's independent will. It should be remembered that *thaba* is a custom often supported by the abductor's family, a fact which therefore makes it more legitimate. Although it is not an honourable act among the Meitei, it is not a socially condemned offense either. When a group of men, however small in number, can use the power of force to exploit the valued sexuality of unmarried women, it indeed symbolizes expression of the desire to assert that, no matter how independent women may be, men can still control them if they so choose. Once married, women are not subject to *thaba*. They are left alone because they no longer possess their sexuality independently of men. The unmarried girl appears to be extremely vulnerable in a *thaba* case; often she surrenders and marries her abductor. But it is interesting to note that once women accept themselves as *mous* (non-virgins or wives), their fears and inhibitions are overcome. A majority of women married by abduction leave their husbands shortly after marriage.

Although actual abduction is not frequent, unmarried women live in constant fear of it. This restricts their social freedom but it forges a strong sense of solidarity among them from a very early age. A young unmarried woman, a *laishabi*, is vulnerable as an individual, but she can be powerful collectively in social, political, and economic spheres of the community. Their sense of oppression can yet be recognized in the "ritual of rebellion" by unmarried girls, who reverse their controlled role during the five days of the *yaoshong* festival and harass and dominate men in provocative ways. Such features are not unknown to patrilineal societies (see Gluckman, 1954 on the Zulu).

Meitei social structure ensures the superior status and authority of the husband and father. Even the traditional architectural plan of a Meitei house reflects the patriarchal ideology, with priority of place assigned to the father, the eldest son, the wife, and the daughter-in-law.

However, though a woman relinquishes her jural and ritual rights on her parental home upon marriage, there is a marked leniency in the patrilineal rules. The right of residence of widowed, unmarried, and divorced daughters and sisters in the natal home offers a strong security to women from their own kin. A married woman has several social obligations (offering at the *Lai* temple of the natal village and joining the *ningon pali*—daughter's day—during the *Rathajatra* festival, etc.) which tie her to her own kin group. The role of a daughter as an only child is equated to that of a son, a feature very unusual in the Hindu societies.

The absence of rules concerning village exogamy and the small radius of the marriage circle allow married women to be close to their own mothers and kin and to maintain the friendship bonds of their unmarried years. Here again, Meitei women, unlike their North Indian sisters, enjoy a social advantage.[120] A newly married woman in North India occupies a subservient position, is surrounded by strangers, and is shielded from any close contact with her own kin. The strict separation of the sexes does not even allow her much opportunity to meet her husband (unknown to her until her wedding day). The *purdah* system prevents her from meeting men of her husband's village, except the young ones.[121] Here again we can see the social freedom of a *mou anobi* (new bride) among the Meitei, who will soon find a strong power base among other women of the community.[122] The absence of a joint family allows a newly married woman to be in charge of a nuclear household within her in-laws' compound soon after her marriage. Her relationship with her mother-in-law is often based on partnership rather than on the latter's domination over her.

The *nupi mamal* (the price of a wife) has become extinct,[123] and the system of the return of the dowry upon separation offers economic security to the woman. Although the law gives custody of older children to the father, the social norm is for the children to follow the mother, enabling her to develop a uterine family.

[120]The studies of Northern Indian societies by O. Lewis (1955), Marriott (1955), Karve (1965:117), Mandelbaum (1970), and Sharma (1979) discuss the large marriage circles extending over a wide geographic area. Some show how a small village of two hundred households can have affinal links with four hundred different villages (see Lewis, 1955; Marriott, 1953). It is also considered preferable not to have more than one bride in a family from the same village.

[121]*Purdah* persists among both Hindu and Muslim high status women. In Haryana, 72.6 per cent of the women observed this rule, in Rajasthan 62.18 per cent, and in Delhi 60.7 per cent (Government of India 1974: 61).

[122]In North India, there is a clear distinction between a daughter and a daughter-in-law in a family. The former is treated with compassion and indulgence, whereas the latter is bound by strict rules of behaviour (Karve, 1964: 114).

[123]The system of bride-price is very rare in my study area. Where money is accepted by the girl's family, it is expected to be returned on divorce. However, this rule is followed only if the divorce occurs soon after the marriage. After some years, a woman can leave her husband without any obligation to him. Even when there is a family obligation a young bride can leave her husband at her own will.

A leniency in the rules of patrilineage in favour of daughters, the daughter's social and ritual rites with her own kin, the absence of village exogamy, the small radius of the marriage circle, the absence of the veil and segregation of the sexes, the freedom to divorce and the subsequent return of dowry all combine to allow women a social freedom within the family and the community.

Extensive socio-economic freedom can endow women with the power to defy the socio-structural authority of men. A daughter can defy her father's authority by *chenba* (elopement) and a wife can defy her husband's authority by initiating *khainaba* (divorce). Both of these allow women to choose lives of their own, independent of men's control.

SEX-ROLE ETHOS IN TRADITIONAL MEITEI RITUAL

The preceding discussion of the traditional role of women in Meitei society can be further understood through an analysis of the traditional ritual of *Lai Harouba*. This embodies a cultural ethos which is not only ancient and traditional but has also remained resilient, surviving past changes.

I have described two types of *Lai Harouba*, both performed annually. The first, *Kabok Chaiba*, a one-day family-based ritual is supported by the community. The other, *Lai Harouba*, is organized all over the Valley by an entire community or village. While the regular community *Lai Harouba* represents a "moral community" with sex roles and social relationships of both male and female, *Kabok Chaiba* represents only the woman's role in the society.

Kabok Chaiba

Kabok Chaiba (the sprinkling of puffed rice/festival of puffed rice) celebrates the abundance of a harvest, for the prosperity of society. The ritual signifies women's responsibility for the production and distribution of food, and links it to the benefit of the wider community and the state.

Still, *Kabok Chaiba* is a ritual for the benefit of the patrilineage. Only wives and married daughters are eligible to participate: through marriage these women support the value of the patrilineage and its kin-groups. The presence of the wife of the lineage head, the *piba*, also emphasizes the priority of the patrilineage.

The male members of the lineage are involved in the organization but they are excluded from the activities of the ritual because basically it celebrates women's sex role. The *maibi*'s prophesies at the temple and at the palace during the women's activities indicate the importance of the ritual and the high status of women's contribution as recognized by the state.

Community Lai Harouba

Lai Harouba proclaims "the paramountcy of patrilineage." But its recognition of and emphasis on the female role is rather unexpected in a patrilineal society. The ritual recognizes the dichotomy of the sexes. Both sexes fulfil their obligations in their own areas, yet they need to depend on and co-operate with each other for this.

The main focus of *Lai Harouba* is on the perpetuation of the patrilineage. The rules of the *piba*'s (lineage head) eligibility, the model of the "ideal woman" as a participant in the core procession, married women's lineage identity in the colour of their wrappers (*khoangchet*), the birth of a male baby and finally his naming by the father—all this clearly supports the patrilineage and safeguards its interest.

The organisational structure of *Lai Harouba* is community-based. It is linked to the central state organization through the *Pundit Loishang*, the council of religious office bearers, which is exclusively male and has a formal and rigid hierarchy. The *Lai Harouba* committee reflects the contemporary political model of the community; the educated young are taking the place of the older, uneducated leaders, a feature also seen at village *Panchayat* elections. Women are not included in the organisational structure of *Lai Harouba*, nor do they have any formal authority in the political leadership. Nevertheless, it would be wrong to conclude that *Lai Harouba* is a male-dominated ceremony. The following list of the major activities and rituals show the extent of male and female participation and their relative prominence.

Organisation: all men.

Participants: both sexes.

Seating arrangement: men on the right and women on the left. No rules for children.

Ritual functionaries: both sexes.

Rituals

1. *Lai Ikoba* procession (calling of the *Lais* from the water): *Lai*

bearers—both sexes: wives, maidens, old women, bachelors, *maibis*.

2. *Leilangba* (flower distribution): to men first, according to status hierarchy; then to women.

3. *Loiching Jagoi* (awakening the *Lais* to begin the afternoon ritual): *maibis* open the dance floor.

4. *Thougal* dance (dance of dedication performed in between several sequences of the ritual repertoire): *maibis* are followed by women representing four age groups. In some villages, men join to make an outer circle. More popular among women.

5. *Hoi Lauba* (song in praise of creation): men and the *maibis*. The text prescribes both men and women, but I never found women taking part in it.

6. *Panthoibi Jagoi* (dance in dedication to the female deity Panthoibi): a dance performed only by the *maibis*, which is often followed by the women's *Thougal*.

7. Entertainment (enactment of the *Langol* legends to depict the incarnations of the divine couple and their ideal love for each other): both sexes.

8. *Anoirol: penakhonba* (the male instrumentalist) leads the dance of the *maibis* followed by the women's line in order, as in the *Thougal*.

9. *Laibao* (core ritual procession—the most important part of the daily rituals): *Lai* bearers: both sexes—wives, maidens, bachelors, *maibis*.

10. *Khayom Jagoi*: the above procession is joined by women in order of age groups.

11. *Hakchangshaba* (formation of a human body in the mother's womb and the birth of a male child): core procession and women—sometimes men join in.

12. *Thougal*: procession rests—women and men join the *Thougal*.

13. *Nikonthakonba* (praying for the souls and protection of the villagers): *maiba*, *maibis* and men.

14. Acting out the battle of the sexes: *maiba*, *maibis*, men; sometimes women participate.

15. *Pausha Ishei* (dance of the husband and wife as a couple): both sexes.

16. *Chongkhongnaiba* (dance enacting the sexual union of the divine couple): men as *chong* (parasol) bearers and *maibis* as dancers.

17. *Lairemmatek* (enactment of never-ending creation in a coiling snake motif): core procession and *maiba*.

18. (*a*) *Thabal Chombi* (dance encircling the ritual of *Lairemma-tek*): young men and women.

(*b*) *Oakol Lauba* (songs in praise of God): both sexes.

19. *Kangleithokpa* (*maibis* dance showing Lord Khoriphoba's polo game and search for a bride): only *maibis*. (Originally one young woman joined the *maibis*.)

20. *Lamthokpa* (performance of the sword game and *Thougal* at the market centre): both sexes.

21. *Lairoi* (the ritual to end *Lai Harouba*):

(*a*) *Thangkotpa* (dance with sword and fire): *maibis* only.

(*b*) *Tankhul Shaba* (dramatic presentation of the legend of incarnation of the divine couple): *maibis, maiba*, seven women (originally performed by unmarried girls), old man.

(*c*) *Ougri Hongel Chongba* (men and women in equal numbers stand in a circle holding each other's arms): both sexes, *maiba*.

(*d*) *Hijing Hirao* (men and women in equal numbers enact rowing of a boat, racing, etc.): both sexes.

22. *Saraikhangba* (rituals to drive off evil, performed on the third, fifth, seventh, ninth, eleventh and other odd numbered days): *maibis* only.

23. Day after *Lai Harouba* (athletic competition): traditionally all men—nowadays, sometimes, women join in.

The series of rituals promotes the glory of the patrilineage, but it does not support male dominance and female inferiority, a feature of the rituals of many patrilineal societies (Srinivas, 1952; Bateson, 1967; Wilson, 1957).

As far as women's participation is concerned, the most prominent of all the rituals is the *Thougal*, in which large numbers of women participate, standing in order of their age. The *Thougal* dances predominate the ritual spectacle throughout the entire period. Traditionally, the *Thougal* was always performed by women within a circle formed by men, an arrangement that is understandable in terms of male-female sex roles in the society. The *lallup* system (compulsory free labour), the *lalmi* (organization of men of war), and continuous warfare, hunting, and other activities often forced men to be absent from their community while women held control over subsistence and the market economy. At present the *Thougal* is often performed exclusively by women independently of men.

The first ritual, *Lai Ikoba* is very important for an understanding of the sex roles of men and women among the Meitei. In the procession of a lineage temple, (see diagram), the presence of the clan head and his wife as *Lai* bearers ratifies the principles of Meitei patrilineage. Both these bearers must conform to the clan rules of the ideal man and woman. The two men as *chong* (parasol) bearers represent the male status. The young maidens and wives delineate their roles of providing nourishment and nurture. The *thang* men (sword bearers) signify male responsibility as warriors and protectors from external attack. Ahead of them all walks an old woman, as the mother of all men, the giver of the life-sustaining force symbolized by water. The presence of the *maibi* leading the entire ritual and the highlighting of her prophecy underline a reverence for and reliance on female spiritual power to communicate with the other world.

At the beginning of the daily ritual of *lai langba* (distribution of flowers), the male status is evident. But this is balanced immediately with a series of *Thougal* dances, representing women in the various stages of their life Men's admiration and adoration of these women, very old to very young, are often expressed in warm and dignified exclamations and the offering of *dakhshina*, an expression of respect and appreciation.

Dances depicting love legends reinforce the model of romantic love and the ideal relationship between husband and wife. They serve other social functions as well. There is often a mood of competition among the performers for social status and recognition, and village politicians take advantage of the occasion to demonstrate their patronage by offering *dakhshina* to the performers.

Women's sexuality and fertility are a high point of the core ritual of *hackchangshaba* (formation and birth of a baby). In a solemn ritual the *maibis* lead the dance followed by the core procession. The detailed description of the anatomy of the human body, labour pain, the role of the midwife, reference to amniotic fluid as waves, the appearance of the baby's head in the birth canal, the birth of the baby, the cutting of the umbilical cord—the entire presentation has a dramatic and mystical aura that transcends the facts of mere biological truth, reaching, ultimately, a metasocial level. "The fountain of milk," the life giving energy, is provided by the mother. The father's role is providing for the baby's name and his lineage identity.

After birth comes the problem of survival of the society. The *maibis* perform a series of theatrical dances enacting the phases of progress of civilization. The activities represent the male and female division of labour:

House building:	Male occupation
Fruit gathering:	Female occupation
Hoe cultivation:	Both sexes
Sowing and harvesting:	Both sexes
Cotton cultivation:	Both sexes
Spinning and weaving:	Female occupation
Domestic chores:	Female occupation

and so on.

The remarks of pundits, *maibis*, and informants concerning several rituals are self-explanatory and strongly emphasize the sexual aspects of the rituals. The ritual objects in *Lai Ikoba* suggest their association with food, sex, fire, and fertility.[124]

The performance of *Chongkhongnaiba* signifies sexual union. The continuous coiling motion in *Lairemmatek* as explained to me is the timelessness of creation in its infinitude. The two lines of male and female deities separate to meet again, acting out a battle of the sexes in a playful encounter of divorce (*khainaba*) and union (*punsinba*). The choreographic patterns as shown in the sketch suggest the form of the womb and the birth canal. While the continuous coiling motion proceeds smoothly in the middle of the courtyard, unmarried men and women hold hands to form a ring around it and perform the *Thabal Chombi* dance. The whole spectacle represents the "moral community" transmitted from one generation to the next.

[124]Some of the ritual objects may be explained as follows:

Rice:	food, prosperity, land
Plantain:	fertility—a perennial, known for its excessive growth
Duck's egg:	fertility
Sinju:	vegetable, medicinal herb
Utong:	a rice measure
Thread:	umbilical cord
Chong:	hierarchy, status—white colour is associated with the male; in some temples red flags are used to indicate the presence of a female deity
Thang:	male role in warfare, use of metal
Sumbal:	rice pounding tool, female role of nurturance, wealth. Gold, silver—wealth

In *Lai Harouba*, the mutual cooperation and dependence of the sexes are highlighted. The inter-sex behaviour in *pausha ishei* (dance and song of the husband and wife team), *ougri hongel* (men and women of equal number), *hijing hirao* (men and women in equal number), *tankhul shaba* (enactment of the legend of the divine couple) is full of friendliness, love and romance.

It is seen then that in Lai Harouba, women are represented not only in terms of their reproductive power, but also in their roles as daughter, wife, and mother. The four age grades in a woman's life cycle are associated with the different socio-economic roles that women play in different phases of their lives.

The productive role of unmarried girls in the agricultural economy is highlighted in the dramatic representation of *khulong nupi taret*, a team of seven daughters, *khulong* (possibly associated with the seven clans of the Valley), cultivating rice, an indispensable part of Meitei agriculture. The *khulong* song refers to paddy, vegetables, and medicinal herbs, and while working in the field, the maidens sing in praise of their "father's land," "their grandfather's land," and for the peace of "the King's land." One can hardly call this labour restricted to the domestic domain. Such recognition of the daughters' collective labour in the community is indeed a rare patrilineal ritual. Here we may also recall the role of married daughters of the lineage in the ritual of *Kabok Chaiba*.

In *kangleithokpa* (the ritual polo game), the emphasis is on romance and marriage in a man's life; hence the hero's bachelorhood becomes unacceptable. In fact, the romantic relationship between the sexes is repeatedly expressed in different ritual songs, e.g., the song of *pausha ishei*, Khoriphoba's search for a bride, and love songs of the divine couple. The deities, *Lai* and *Lairembi*, as husband and wife, present a model of the monogamous conjugal bond, and their songs are charged with vibrant sexuality as well as romantic love.

In *Lamthokpa*, the ritual at the women's market, an exuberant sword play by men is followed by the women's gentle and graceful *Thougal* dancing. The sex role balance is ritualized here by emphasizing the masculine role (warrior) in a social arena dominated by women.

In *Tankhul Shaba*, the hero (the incarnation of the divine father) presents a barbaric aspect with a comic tint. The woman as Nurabi introduces the man (Tankhul Naga) to agriculture and they both farm together in the rice field. One might wonder why the martial glory of the male is so much reduced in the main part of a ritual of a society where warfare used to be a frequent affair. It is possible that the martial pride of Meitei men needed to be mellowed in a ritual where the "life-sustaining force", not the life-taking power, is celebrated (Schlegel, 1977 : 263). It is also possible that excessive aggression was a necessary evil for the defence of the land and the maintenance of law and order, but in the ritual sphere the Meitei worshipped the life-activating energy for the survival of the society. A similar attitude is found among the matrilineal Hopi, who minimize the role of warfare and amplify the life-sustaining force (Schlegel, *ibid*). Like the Hopi, the Meitei believe that "productivity is a major social goal" (*ibid* : 263). After the mock battle of the sexes, one Meitei informant remarked, "It is good for the *Lairembi* (female deity) to win. Otherwise there will be no peace in the community."

In fact, throughout *Lai Harouba*, the wife's role is presented as that of a sexual partner as well as an economic contributor, and in the latter productive role, women outside the home are so elevated that, beside them, men sometimes appear inexperienced and awkward.

Here Meitei culture is different from another patrilineal martial society in India, the Coorg, among whom martial glory and the hunting spirit are at the centre of the ritual complex. Women are recognized only in domestic ritual, for the importance of fertility for the perpetuation of the patrilineage, and are totally excluded from community ritual and collective dance. Of women's share in production, the ultimate word of the Coorg is, "A woman may not be head of an *Okka* (patrilineal joint family), and a bitch may not be given a share of the game it helps to kill in a hunt" (Srinivas, 1952 : 45). Such masculine arrogance in Coorg society is based on a patriarchal ideology of the absolute superiority of males over females. Similar attitudes can be found in several complex societies (Fustel-de-Coulanges, 1864, on ancient Greece and Rome; Mace and Mace, 1960, on India, China, Korea and Japan; Yang, 1946, on China; Luzbetak, 1946, on Caucasia).

In Meitei society, we can assume the vital importance of male babies as future warriors for defending the society from hostile neighbours. But the absence of a sufficient number of males during warfare and the decrease of the male population in the beginning of the nineteenth century enhanced the importance of women's role in the economy. Thus the male priority nowhere supersedes the female productive role; rather than asserting male dominance, the ritual exalts the mutual partnership and interdependence of the sexes.

The athletic feats on the day after *Lai Harouba* are essentially a gala of male splendour. Here, men enter again the world of competition for status and rank.

Lai Harouba thus presents prototypes of the male and female cultural models, encapsulating an ideal relationship between the sexes and painting a picture of intersexual harmony. It highlights women's contribution to the perpetuation of society, and a remarkable feature is the recognition of women's roles as providers and economic partners, as well as sexual partners and mothers.

Maibis: ALTERNATIVE STATUS FOR WOMEN

Says a Meitei proverb: "Stubborn women are destined to become *maibis.*"

Lai Harouba represents two opposing models for women. On the one hand, there is the model of the "ideal woman"—the woman as daughter, wife, and mother. On the other, there is the "stubborn woman's" alternative: the role of the *maibi.* I also call the latter a model in the sense that it reinforces a standard pattern of behaviour that can be followed in a socially approved manner.

The *maibis* are the most spectacular presence in a *Lai Harouba* ritual. From the beginning to the end, the principal *maibi* and her companions, as priestesses, not only conduct the ritual procedure, but are also the most energetic performers who run the entire celebration in an intense and convincing manner. They attract the undivided attention of the spectators, and their ecstasy reaches a climax in trance, *Laitongba* (*Lai* coming into the body). A *maibi*'s oracular power has a tremendous effect on the audience and sometimes exerts far-reaching influence upon the society. The power of prophecy uplifts a *maibi*'s status, and her role is thus extended far beyond the village boundaries. This is also the only role for women in traditional Meitei society which involves rank and competition for professional success, both of which belong generally to the man's world. The two male ritual functionaries perform their prescribed role, but none have the opportunity to gain such prominence as the *maibis.* They remain rather passive as accompanying participants.

Each of the "stubborn" women somehow rebelled against the

family and the existing social order and found her way into a *maibi*'s life, a life which promised her immense freedom in the extra-domestic domain, considerable social status, and the prospect of good livelihood. These cases suggest a standard pattern of behaviour, and none conforms to the normal sex roles of Meitei women. Once a woman is ordained a *maibi*, she achieves a ritual status outside the expected norms of the society, and her ritual immunity allows her a most liberated lifestyle unthinkable for an ordinary woman. She is her own master, having only the *Lai*, the god, as her guardian.[125] A *maibi* is never called a "proper" or "ideal" woman. Nor do people accept her role comfortably: it is accepted as the destiny of parti-cular women. Yet a *maibi* is considered a chosen woman, a vehicle of supernatural power, and she communicates on behalf of earthly people with the divine world. People are afraid to ignore her, and often have an awed and ambivalent attitude toward her. Conven-tionally, a *maibi* should be addressed as *Ima* (mother), evoking respect from all. Her ritual role as *maibi* is supposed to be asexual, yet men are attracted by her sexuality: a *maibi* enters into sexual relationships at her own discretion.

Veneration for female spiritual power is formally recognized in the institution of *maibis*. Their professional world is directly attached to the central organization of ancient Meitei religion, and the impor-tance of their role is indicated by the entire procedure for the initiation ceremony, their affiliation with the council (*Loishang*) of *maibis*, the assignment of rank, the use of rank insignia, the nature of professional contact, and the standard of fees and overall strict supervision by the *Loishang*.

Peripheral vs. Central

Female spirit possession and female shamans are known to exist in several patrilineal societies. But anthropologists do not consider them as part of the core religious system except in the simpler, less stratified societies just above the hunting-gathering level.[126] Spirit

---

[125]According to Meitei custom, a married woman's guardian is her husband, who is called *mapuroiba* (her caretaker).

[126]Professor Arensberg in a personal communication referred to spirit pos-session cults in simpler societies where the shamans have the central position in religion. It is only when a society becomes stratified that the religion gives priority to permanent priesthood and relegates the role of shaman to the lower stratum of society.

possession cults have been explained as an expression of rebellion or frustration of oppressed females in a male-dominated society (I. M. Lewis, 1971; Potter, 1974; Harper, 1969; Horton, 1969; Beattie, 1969; Spiro, 1967).

I. M. Lewis (1971) cites examples of spirit possession and shamanism from different cultures and explains these phenomena as a "feminist subculture," which men may tolerate but do not respect. He suggests a dichotomy between a "main morality possession cult" and a "peripheral cult". The former is observed in simple homogeneous societies: "In highly atomized societies without secure and clearly defined political positions, the shaman comes into his own as an omnicompetent leader, regulating the intercourse both between man and man and between men and spirits" (Lewis, 1971: 34). By contrast, "peripheral cults" remain outside the main morality religion. Women with a peripheral role themselves hold onto this peripheral religion. Lewis looks upon the spirit possession cult as "an oblique aggressive strategy," "a mystically complex feminist movement," a "sex war". He argues that the pervasiveness of trance among women is indicative of their powerlessness in a male-dominated society. Anthropologists, e.g. Lee (1969) on the Zulu of South Africa, Beattie (1969) on the Bunyoro women in East Africa and several others (see Beattie and Middleton, 1969), recognize an almost universal pattern of female rebelliousness in the institutionalized behaviour of spirit possession. As Horton (1969:42) comments on Kalabari society: "In adopting this complex of roles a woman is enabled from time to time to really 'be' what she has always yearned to be but never can be in ordinary normal life." Spiro's (1967) study on Burmese supernaturalism depicts dominating women shamans as a despised class who practise a cult involving amoral *nat* spirits. He recognizes this as beneficial towards Burmese society, because the cult helps to release women's sociopathic symptoms. Potter (1974) speaks of the Cantonese shamans, the *mann seag phox*, in an extremely male-dominated society. He describes the shamans as "the most downtrodden group in a village society" (*ibid*:229). But the shaman's function in rural life is not at all negligible. "She rules over the dark world inhabited by the malevolent ghosts of the unsuccessful, the discontented, the abnormal and the exploited and ...her major function in the village society is to deter these discontented and dangerous beings from wreaking their vengeance on the living villagers" (*ibid* : 231). Jordan (1972 : 163) speaks of the Taiwanese *tang-ki* : "...the voice of the medium can be that of the moral community when it deflects structural irregularities and declares that their associated ghosts must be pacified." Among the South Indian Tamil communities, one medium "...had the gift of extraordinary *Shakti* only because she belonged to the class of the downtrodden, the uneducated, those of low castes, married women oppressed by their husband..." (Egnar, 1980:15).

Iris Berger (1976) lends a different perspective to this subject. In her study of spirit mediums in the Interlacustrine and Nyamwezi area of East Africa, she criticizes the "sex war" hypothesis as one of rather limited utility, and develops an alternative thesis showing that, in addition to supplying an anti-male outlet, cults also offered "religious leadership" in the central system of the society.[127] Kendall (1979 : 52) shows that the Korean shaman is more than "a cultist seeking the recurrent satisfaction of salving ecstasy. She is a professional ministering to the needs of a broader clientele which often includes the male... The shaman (*mansin*) is no agent of subversion... (she) stands with the community" (*ibid* : 54-55) though deprived of a recognized status in the ideology of the Confucian religion. There are striking similarities between the *maibis*, the life experiences of the Korean *mansins* (Kendall, 1979), the Cantonese *Mann seag phox* (Potter, 1974), the Taiwanese *tangki* (Jordan, 1972), and the East African cult leaders (Berger, 1976).

Lewis finds that women shamans are mostly unattractive old women. He also associates trance with humble and oppressed people. In Meitei society, high status R. K. and Brahman women do not experience trance, but unlike the women of Lewis' description (Lewis, 1971 : 95), *maibis* have attractive and well groomed feminine personalities. Most of them start their careers at a very early age. Their professional skill, acquired through a period of rigorous training, is highly valued by both sexes of all social strata. We may also mention the fact that recently one of the established *maibis*, Ima Rajani, was given the President's Award by the Government of India for her contribution to and skill in the field of dance.

---

[127]It is interesting to note that in the People's Republic of China, former sorceresses at times transformed their mystical roles into political leadership in a socialist environment. These women carried their oratory skill and charismatic performing personalities into this new role in the women's movement against patriarchal values (Yang, 1959:132).

The most unusual feature in the institution of the *maibis* is that these women are ordained as priests of the Meitei core religion. Shamanism is only a part of the *maibi*'s total role, and not a necessary one: many work solely as ritual priests in *Lai Harouba* and other *Lai* ceremonies. In a *Lai Harouba*, the *maiba* and the principal *maibi* act as high priest and high priestess. The *maiba* follows a literate tradition based on his scriptural learning, a sphere exclusively reserved for the male, and the *maibi* follows an oral tradition in the history of human societies for formal scriptural studies with valuable knowledge to be a male prerogative. But in Meitei society, status and power might not have been invariably associated with scriptural studies. In fact, the most powerful and culturally accomplished king, Bhagyachandra, is known to have been almost illiterate. In the ritual field, the *maiba* and the *maibi* depend on each other's knowledge as colleagues. In the eyes of the society, the *maibi*'s esoteric knowledge is by no means less valuable than the scriptural knowledge of the *maiba*. The respect and recognition of the *maibi*'s mystic power among the *maibas* and pundits confirm this view. Unlike her Korean sister *mansin* who "...shares in the ambiguous status of other glamorous but morally dubious female marginals: the actress, the female entertainer, and the prostitute" (Kendall, 1979:250), the *maibis* enjoy a central position in the Meitei ideological system. When challenged by Brahmanic culture, the *maibis* stood their ground and retained their prominent role. Ironically, it is the Brahmans who now on occasion depend on *maibis* for special propitiatory rites.

The proverbial stubbornness of a *maibi* suggests Lewis' concept of the sex war. We can assume a strong possibility that some strong-willed women in Meitei society do revolt against the social system. Following Berger (1976), we may also recognize *maibis* as status seekers. The professional world of a *maibi* is indeed based on professional competence and competition for status within the hierarchy which cannot be achieved through the primary sex role of a woman in Meitei society. But what makes the institution of *maibis* different is that these rebellious women are given an elevated permanent status in recognition of their superpower. They do not form a subculture; rather, they are an integral part of Meitei culture. *Maibis* are not considered social deviants; their role is accepted in the existing social order. A *maibi*'s role can be seen as an alternative lifestyle for women who are non-conformists.

It can be argued that this is an adjustment Meitei society makes by according ritual status to gifted and uncontrollable women in an institutionalized way. It does not hamper the social standard of Meitei male-female behaviour, nor does it affect the ideal of a proper woman in the society. The *maibi*'s liberated behaviour does not pose any threat to the male, who enjoys the advantages of the patrilineal system in the socio-political sphere. Women's spiritual superiority is thus accepted in an institutionalized manner and men do not have to lose their superior standing in the social system.

Another interesting sphere of women's religious roles in Meitei society was the position, in the past, of the royal high priest, *Lai-ibi*. During the reign of Maharaj Churachand (1892-1941), the position of this royal high priest was occupied by a woman of royal family. She was no ordinary woman nor was she a social deviant like a *maibi*; on the contrary, being royal, she personified the "ideal woman". Her post-menopausal age and an ideal life reflected the esteemed image of older women as *Imas* (mothers) of Meitei society. (We may recall that during *Lai Harouba* in the *Lai Ikoba* procession, in front of all, walks an old woman (an ideal woman) with a pitcher of water signifying the life-sustaining force.) *Lai-ibi*'s presence ratified the interest of the royal patrilineage for the benefit of the state. This also indicated the high regard for women's spiritual power and the valuable role of women necessary to the survival of society.

A different kind of religious specialist are the *kithumpubas* or *sadhikas*. Here again we note a natural acceptance of and tolerance for women (or male transvestites) who claim, and are believed to be endowed with, divine power, bestowed by traditional divinity as well as those of the Hindu belief system. Although not recognized by a traditional institution like the *Pundit Loishang*, these self-styled diviners play an important part in people's religious lives. All of them ritually isolated themselves to remove any possible threat to the social norms of women in a male-oriented society.

RECENT CHANGES IN *Lai Harouba*

Most of the changes in the ritual repertoire of *Lai Harouba* occurred in the recent past. Alterations in some ritual sequences reflect a discomfort and anxiety on the part of the present society with regard to the sex-role models of women found in the ancient ritual. I believe most of the changes can be explained in the perspective of social changes discussed in the beginning of this chapter.

The textual prescription for the ritual requires men and women in equal numbers as participants (Kulachandra, 1963). At present, in general, many more women than men join the *Thougal* dances in *Lai Harouba.*

In *Laibao* (the core ritual procession) in Nambol area at Radhagram, the gorgeous Meitei dress of the women has been replaced by a very plain-looking *pungofanek,* the attire worn in Vaisnavite ceremonies. The temple caretaker's comment explains the obvious attempt to downgrade the women's role in the most important part of the daily ritual. In the Khoriphoba temple, women's role in *Laibao* is further de-emphasized by replacing married women and maidens with pre-pubescent little girls so as to avoid the fear of possible menstrual pollution. However, the traditional textual rules are followed in the other *Lai Haroubas* I observed.

Pausha Ishei (dance and song of the husband-wife team), at the Khoriphoba temple are performed by the *maibis* acting as couples. But these are still performed by husbands and wives, in other villages in the area.

In *Kangleithokpa* (ritual dance depicting Khoriphoba's polo game and search for a wife), the role of Khoriphoba's bride was previously given to an unmarried girl, but now this is assumed by a *maibi.* People do not want a maiden to be so prominent in public. Similarly, in *khulong nupi taret* (ritual of seven women in a rice cultivation team), the roles were hitherto taken by seven unmarried girls; now they are taken by older women.

However, some of these charges are rather superficial in the Nambol area. Being an important stronghold of Vaisnavism, Nambol tends to preserve the Hindu cultural standard more persistently than other areas farther away from the Brahmanic influence.

The comments of informants regarding the undermining of the role of women and the increasing obsession with menstrual pollution both point to a conflict with the traditional Meitei attitudes as found in ritual texts and as observed in the *Lai Harouba*. The exclusion of unmarried girls mentioned above is significant, denoting as it does, the influence of the Hindu upper caste custom of attempting to safeguard unmarried daughters. This over-protective attitude towards virgins is not confined to the Hindus, but is an essential trait of a patriarchal system found in many cultures with a strong notion of male dominance (Schneider, 1971 : 21; Dwyer, 1978 : 174; Tiger, 1970 : 191; Karve, 1965 : 72). Similarly, men's reluctance to join the *Thougal* and *Pausha Ishei* is a further instance of how Hindu cultural behaviour is still haunting Meitei society.[128] In those places where female prominence is patently contrary to Hindu values (e.g., the seven unmarried girls' team in agriculture), a compromise has been struck. Old women acting as unmarried daughters remove the potential danger of making a virgin's sexuality too prominent in public. The *maibi* who dons the role of Khoriphoba's bride, though feminine in appearance, can be tolerated because of her sexual ritual designation.

Is it possible now to identify the forces under which such changes in the ritual could have occurred? The continuous compromise of the two opposing forces of Meitei and Hindu cultures may be observed in both Vaisnava and *Lai Harouba* ritual complexes.

SEX ROLES IN MEITEI SOCIETY: A PARADOX?

The foregoing discussion underlines the paradox of sex roles and inter-sex relationships in Meitei society. We cannot find a pure harmony in social relationships, nor can we observe conflict as a major concern. Male superiority is institutionalized in the family structure, but religious ideology emphasizes female superiority in the spiritual realm. Manifestations of the social ideology of male superiority often confronts female defiance. The problematic co-existence of the ideological social superiority of men and an absence of actual subordination of women creates a varying degree of harmony and conflict.

Areas of harmonious interdependence of the sexes are found in socio-economic, political and religious spheres. Women as a collective group stand next to men and co-operate on an equal footing. There are also features of deep reverence for the female spiritual power in the belief system. In conjugal life, partnership is based on mutual dependence. But the tradition of women's potential self-sufficiency challenges and contradicts the socio-structural value of the husband's superiority, a tension further accelerated by Hindu Brahmanic ideology. Thus conjugal life frequently ends up as a battleground for the sexes.

[128]N. Tombi Singh (1976:132) gives an account of the intersex behaviour in a traditional *Lai Harouba*. "Husbands and wives were encouraged to present duet items before the deity. One can imagine the fun and mirth that might have emanated from duet presentations by extremely old couples with bent waists. There was another category of duet in which unmarried boys partnered unmarried girls of their age."

Paradoxical as all this may appear, there are several analogies with the Meitei situation in Southeast Asia, especially the Burmese, Javanese and Malaysian societies (Spiro, 1977 and Nash, 1965 on the Burmese; Geertz, 1961 on the Javanese; Firth, 1966 on the Malaysian). In these societies, the individual and collective strength of women offers a material self-sufficiency and ensures a degree of equality in cooperation with men in the social sphere. This cooperation is often juxtaposed with conflict in an instability of marital relations because of the ideology of male domination (Spiro, *ibid*; Geertz, *ibid*; Firth, *ibid*).

An examination of divorce rates and their possible causes in these societies throws further light on inter-sex social behaviour. Divorce is rather infrequent among the Burmese, Spiro finds (1977:288). "An important difference between Burma with its low divorce rate and Malaya and Java, which have high divorce rates, is that in Burma marriage is based on free choice, while in Malaya and Java (first) marriage is arranged." Firth comments on a Malaysian society (1966 : 29): "One of the undoubted reasons why divorce is not the disaster for a woman which it might be is her ability to earn her own living". Of the Javanese, Hildred Geertz (1961 : 144) states, a "...divorced girl always has a place in her parents' family". About the Javanese matrifocal household she says: "The mother has no such urgency to maintain a marriage if she can take the children with her, since it is not thought that a child *must* have a father or that a stepfather is bad" (*ibid.*, 143). A Javanese woman has a full range of options for "fully supporting economic occupations", "to be independent of her husband".

However, the divorce rate among the Meitei is much lower than that among the Malaysian or the Javanese.[129] I suspect that, in the Meitei case, a man's desire for polygyny ends in divorce with his first wife because of the concept of love associated with marriage. Almost all first wives, now divorced or remarried, expressed a deep feeling of hurt when their husbands took another wife. Perhaps there is always a possibility of tension in the sexual relationship in a male-oriented society where the marital security of women does not depend on material security but rather on the emotional

[129]In my samples, I found that 33 per cent of all marriages ended in divorce in my study area. From a personal communication with Professor Clive Kessler, Barnard College, I gathered that in the Malaysian case the divorce rate is as high as 70 per cent of the marriages performed every year.

tie. In *Lai Harouba*, the battle of the sexes and the issue of *khainaba* (divorce) and *punsinba* (union) are ritualized in a "play of forces" (Turner, 1969 : 84). *Lai Harouba* reinforces the harmony of the conjugal bond by resolving a problematic relationship between the male and the female. The emphasis on the model of the "ideal woman" in the core procession of *Lai Harouba* is also indicative of possible tension in the social system.

It is also possible that the forces of change, discussed earlier, have upset the sex role equilibrium in the society. Inter-sex conflict can arise from the resulting imbalance.

Women's age group bonding is still vital in Meitei society, as symbolized in *Lai Harouba*. Similarly, we can still find cooperation and mutual dependence of the sexes rather overtly in different cultural contexts. Women as providers are still an integral part of the family. Monogamy based on an emotional tie is always the preferred type of marriage.

One recognizes the ambivalence of men's perception of the women's role in relation to what we see in real life and gather from the women's viewpoint. Based on structural superiority, Meitei men internalize a superior self-image and accord themselves as having a higher status in relation to women. Women usually show a formal expression of deference to male authority: a widow head of the family would bring her young son with her as a formality when she had to deal with men, e.g., for the sale or purchase of a piece of land. A man is expected to behave with an air of authority. Men who make decisions after the approval of their wives (in public) are called *nupinaongba* or *odhamorh* (both meaning hen-pecked). For women, their self-sufficiency and social bonding provide a degree of autonomy. Like their Javanese sisters, Meitei women can conceive of a life without a husband. A woman's self-image is also very much influenced by her role as a mother, which provides her a superior status and stable security compared to her wifely role. Meitei husbands perceive their own dominance, but female defiance of male dominance is a profound feature of their culture.[130]

[130]Manning Nash (1965: 253-54) paints a similar picture of Burmese society: "In theory and in public the husband is supposedly dominant, but this dominance is so tenuous, so indefinite and ambiguous that its social visibility is virtually nil." A similar behaviour pattern is found in Javanese society by Hildred Geertz (1961: 46): "The wife makes most of the decisions; she controls all family finances, and although she gives her husband formal deference and consults

However, women are sometimes caught between two forces. On the one hand, they refuse to accept their husbands' denying them wifely status in a monogamous marriage; on the other, they also seek men as companions and wish for children. Hereby a woman who leaves her husband because of his second marriage may settle for the role of second wife to another man, for as such, she can lead the life of a single woman and can still have a legitimate sexual partner and children. It may not be an ideal situation for her, but the arrangement at least gives her independence from a man's domination.

In Meitei society several advantages are enjoyed exclusively by men. These include a superior authority image within the family structure, the right to have more than one wife, the right to the use of the plough (a prestigious tool) the ability to abduct a virgin with impunity (because of the absence of harsh condemnation). the right to tangible property, such as land which can be inherited and controlled by men, the right to the custody of children after a divorce, and so on. By contrast, women have the option and power to defy male authority within the family, the access to the use of the loom (a lucrative tool) and to their own earnings, the right to divorce a polygynous husband, the right to "women's wealth" (including land if it was given to her or purchased by her), the return of the dowry on divorce, the normative power to keep the children after divorce, and above all, the option to choose their marital partners and their occupation. In spite of the socio-structural superiority of men, women can conceive of their lives as independent of men.

In the economic arena, it is evident that women's control over production and resources may be, and frequently is extended beyond the home. The extent of their ability is clearly seen in the expansion of their trade and in their adaptability to mechanization (e.g., fly shuttle looms, rice mills, and bicycles). The traditional political power of the market network of women can paralyze the political or administrative system when the need arises. The religious world emphasises mutual dependence and cooperation of the sexes. Whereas in the patrilineal social system, a woman is still inferior in status to a man, this socio-structural superiority of men becomes ineffective when a woman has options to choose a life of her own,

---

with him on major matters, it is usually she who is dominant ...families actually dominated by men are exceedingly rare."

independent of a man. A woman in Meitei society is indeed a recognized citizen of the community by virtue of her own identity as a member of the *khulong* (the rice cultivation team), the *marup* (credit association), the *nupi-pala* (religious associations for women), and various other activities, regardless of her marital status.

Meitei society thus presents different spheres with male and female power often cooperating with, but sometimes confronting, each other. *Lai Harouba* attempts to resolve this by providing an idealized model of male and female interdependence, cooperation, and mutual respect to counter-balance the incongruity inherent in the patrilineal social system. The ritual establishes the legitimacy of male-female partnership, and the contribution of women is recognized in a magnified manner to justify the ethics of their high ritual status in a patrilineal framework.

A tremendous change was wrought in the social scene in the years since the 1950s. The growth of a new political consciousness and a movement toward Meiteiization have been inspired by a sudden education explosion, closer contact with modern Indian society, a rapid decrease of the power of the Brahma Sabha and the Brahmans, the abolition of native statehood and the assimilation with India. One may question whether Meiteiization would revive the ancient Meitei culture, or lead Manipur along a secular path of modernization. The recent popularity of *Lai Harouba* and the movement in favour of reinstating the original Meitei script, an anti-Brahman attitude and the reinstallation of ancient deities—all these can combine to develop into a political force rather than just regenerate old Meitei customs.

However, the process of Meiteiization can hardly be called a product of political awareness. In fact it started at the very beginning of the Vaisnavization of Meitei culture. My study clearly demonstrates how the patriarchal nature of Hinduism was adapted into the ethnic environment next to the autochthonous religious culture. The cessation of royal patronage to the Hindu religion and the diminished control of the Brahmans might well have contributed to a growing awareness of pre-Hindu culture. Regional political sensitivity against Indian domination is another contributing factor in this respect.

Nowadays anthropologists are questioning the functional interpretation that a ritual can reinforce harmony in social organization (Geertz, 1973). Geertz offers his example of a Javanese ritual to show that the dynamic elements in social change fail to be congruent with the cultural pattern. Rapid social change can create a tremendous hiatus between the cultural meaning of a ritual and the social scene. In the light of this, one may ask: How far does *ai Harouba* serve the traditional social function in Meitei society today? My data show how persistent is the cultural ethos of the Meitei and how it has sustained its character through many pressures of change. *Lai Harouba* represents the socio-moral world of traditional Meitei society. The ritual has survived as a powerful religious symbol through different phases of chaotic change. It would be rather simplistic to say that *Lai Harouba* reflects the sex roles and the social relationships of today, but it represents something the society wishes them to be—an idealized version of social life.

My data on Meiteiization indicate that *Lai Harouba* also serves as a political symbol in the wake of regional awareness. A trace of secularization of the sacred can be noticed in urban *Lai Harouba*. However, the role of the *maibis* (during *Lai Harouba* and other ritual activities) and the people's deep commitment to the indigenous belief system indicate that the sacred has not been transformed into the secular. In the past, *Lai Harouba* ensured the prosperity of the community. It still does in a different context. Politicians still depend on the traditional specialists as did the past rulers of the society.

The decline of the Brahmans has helped the dramatic rise to the surface of some Meitei cultural traits. A striking example is the recent breakthrough by women's *sankirtana* singing groups in an area formerly reserved for men. Despite strong resistance from Hinduized conservative quarters, women's *sankirtana* found ready acceptance from the people and approval by the court of law. The popular support indicates a revival of the sentiment for the role of women that is very traditional in Meitei society.

However, the recent incidents of exclusion of women from the core ritual, though limited to the Nambol area, show that Meiteiization probably has a long way to go to be able to overcome the Hinduized attitude of the Meitei male. Still, while the male organizers zealously curtail women's role in the core ritual, an increasing number of women representing four age groups now dominate the ritual ground, with spectacular *Thougal* dances.

As a microcosm of Meitei society, *Lai Harouba* still reaffirms the underlying cultural ethos. The political use of the ritual at present is, in fact, a reassertion of the traditional ethos which was confronted by alien cultures over the past two hundred years. Rather than being dysfunctional, the ritual, as I observed it, was experiencing a resurgence.

I have tried to demonstrate how, in the midst of immense political turmoil, social chaos, and the strategic spread of Sanskritization, Meitei culture has sustained its enduring traits in social relationships and sex roles. The increasing awareness of Meitei identity is thus reflected in a growing enthusiasm for *Lai Harouba* as the embodiment of Meitei cultural identity.

Bibliography

AHERN, EMILY M.
1975 'The Power and Pollution of Chinese Women', *Women in Chinese Society*, Margery Wolf and Roxanne Witke, (eds.), Stanford, Stanford University Press, pp. 193-214.

ANDORS, ELLEN B.
1976 *The Rodi: Female Associations among the Gurung of Nepal*, (unpublished Ph. D. thesis), Columbia University.

ANSARI, SULTAN AMED
1976 *Economic Geography of Manipur*, Imphal, P. Tikendrajit Singh.

AWE, BOLANLE
1977 'The Iyalode in the Traditional Yoruba Political System', *Sexual Stratification*, Alice Schlegel, (ed.), New York, Columbia University Press, pp. 144-159.

BAILEY, FREDERICK G.
1957 *Caste and the Economic Frontier*, Manchester, Manchester University Press.
1960 *Tribe, Caste and Nation*, Manchester, Manchester University Press.

BANERJEA, GOPA
1973 A Note on the Dancing Girl (*Nachni*) of Purulia, *Man in India* LIII, 3:279-293.

BASHAM, A. L.
1959 *The Wonder that Was India*, New York, Grove Press Inc.

BATESON, GREGORY
1967 *Naven*, Stanford, Stanford University Press.

BEATTIE, JOHN
1957 'Initiation into the Cwezi Spirit Possession Cult in Bunyoro', *African Studies* XVI, 3:150-161.

BEATTIE, J., AND MIDDLETON, J. (eds.)
1969 *Spirit Mediumship and Society*, London, Routledge and Kegan Paul.

BENNET, LYNN
n.d. "Sex and Motherhood among the Brahmins and Chhetris of East-central Nepal", *Journal of the Institute of Nepal and Asian Studies*, Tribhuvan University, vol. 3, special issue, pp. 1-52.

BERGER, IRIS
1976 'Rebel or Status-Seekers? Women as Spirit Mediums in East Africa', *Women in Africa*, Nancy J. Hafkin and Edna G. Bay, (eds.), Stanford, Stanford University Press, pp. 158-181.

BERREMAN, GERALD
1963 *Hindus of the Himalayas*, Berkeley and Los Angeles, University of California Press.

BETEILLE, A.
1974 *Studies in Agrarian Structure*, Delhi, Oxford University Press.

BETTELHEIM, BRUNO
1954 *Symbolic Wounds: Puberty Rites and the Envious Male*, Glencoe, The Free Press.

BHOGESWAR, OINAM
n.d. *Manipuri Lokasahitya*, (unpublished manuscript) Imphal, State Kala Academy.

BOSERUP, ESTER
1970 *Women's Role in Economic Development*, New York, St. Martin's Press.

BRIGGS, JEAN
1975 'Eskimo Women: Makers of Men', *Many Sisters*, Carolyn Matthiasson, (ed.), New York, Free Press, pp. 261-304.

CHAKI-SIRCAR, MANJUSRI
1972 'Community of Dancers in Calcutta', *Cultural Profile of Calcutta*, S. Sinha, (ed.), Calcutta, The Anthropological Society of India, pp. 190-198.

1977 *Dance in Modern India: Women in Transition*, Albany, State University of New York Press.

1978 'Widowhood among the Uppercaste Hindus: A Legacy of Sati', unpublished manuscript for *Woman's Place*, Flora Kaplan, (ed.), New York University.

COHEN, MYRON
1976 *House United, House Divided*, New York, Columbia University Press.

DAMANT, G. H.
1875 'The Two Brothers—A Manipuri Story', *Indian Antiquary* IV, pp. 260-264.

DAS GUPTA, S.
1952 *Sree Radhar Kramavikash*, Calcutta, A. Mukherjea and Co. Private Ltd.

DE SOUZA, ALFRED (ed.)
1975 *Women in Contemporary India*, Delhi, Manohar.

DRAPER, PAT
1975 'I Kung Women: Contrasts in Sexual Egalitarianism in Foraging and Sedentary Contexts', *Toward an Anthropology of Women*, Rayna Reiter, (ed.), New York, Monthly Review Press, pp. 77-109.

DUBE, S. C.
1955 *Indian Village*, Ithaca, Cornell University Press.

DUMONT, LOUIS
1959 'Dowry in Hindu Marriage', *Economic Weekly* XI, pp. 519-20.

1961 'Marriage in India', *Contributions to Indian Sociology* V, pp. 75-95.

DUNN, CAPT. E.W.
1975 *Gazetteer of Manipur*, New Delhi, Vivek Publishing House (1896).

DWYER, DAISY HILSE
1973 *Women's Conflict and Behavior in a Traditional Moroccan Setting*, (unpublished Ph. D. thesis), Yale University.

1976 Review of *Beyond the Veil* by M. Fatima, *Signs*, (Winter), pp. 470-472.

1977 'Bridging the Gap between the Sexes in Moroccan Legal Practice', *Sexual Stratification: A Cross-Cultural View*, Alice Schlegel, (ed.), New York, Columbia University Press, pp. 41-66.

1978 *Images and Self-images: Male and Female in Morocco*, New York, Columbia University Press.

ENCYCLOPAEDIA BRITANNICA

1967 Paraguay, XVII, pp. 305-311, Chicago, William Benton.

EPSTEIN, T. SCARLETT

1962 *Economic Development and Social Change in South India*, Manchester, Manchester University Press.

1967 'A Sociological Analysis of Witch Belief in a Mysore Village', *Magic, Witchcraft and Curing*, J. Middleton, (ed.), New York, The Natural History Press, pp. 135-154.

1973 *South India: Yesterday, Today and Tomorrow: Mysore Villages Revisited*, New York, Holmes and Meier Publications Inc.

FALADE, SOLANGE

1974 'Women of Dakar and the Surrounding Urban Area', *Women of Tropical Africa*, Denise Paulme, (ed.), Berkeley, University of California Press, pp. 217-230.

FIRTH, ROSEMARY

1966 *Housekeeping among Malay Peasants*, London, The Athlone Press, University of London.

FRIEDL, EARNESTINE

1967 'The Position of Women: Appearance and Reality', *Anthropological Quarterly* XL, 3 : 98-105.

1975 *Women and Men: An Anthropologist's View*, New York, Holt, Rinehart & Winston.

FUCHS, STEPHEN

1960 *The Gond and Bhumia of Eastern Mandala*, Calcutta, Asia Publishing House.

FURER-HAIMENDORF, C. V.

1962 *The Apa Tanis and Their Neighbours*, London, Routledge and Kegan Paul.

1969 *The Konyak Nagas*, New York, Holt, Rinehart & Winston.

FUSTEL-DE-COULANGES, NUMA DENIS

1901 *The Ancient City*, Boston, Lee and Shepard (1864).

GANGOPADHYAYA, BELA

1964 *Marriage Regulations among Certain Castes of Bengal*, Poona, Deccan College.

GEERTZ, CLIFFORD

1957 'Ritual and Social Change,: A Javanese Example', *American Anthropologist* LIX, pp. 32-54.

GEERTZ, H.

1961 *The Javanese Family*, Glencoe, The Free Press.

GLUCKMAN, MAX

1954 *Rituals of Rebellion in S. E. Africa*, Manchester, Manchester University Press.

1963 'The Role of the Sexes in Wiko Circumcision Ceremonies', *Social Structure*, M. Fortes, (ed.), Russell and Russell, pp. 145-167.

GOLDBERG, STEVEN

1973 *The Inevitability of Patriarchy*, New York, William Morrow and Co.

GOODY, JACK, AND STANLEY TAMBIAH

1973 *Bridewealth and Dowry*, Cambridge, Cambridge University Press.

GOSWAMI, M. G., AND CH. BUDDHI SINGH

1973 'Co-operatives of the Fishermen of Thanga Village in Panipur', *Man in India* LIII, 1:1-6.

GOVERNMENT OF INDIA

1882 *Report on the Administration of the Province of Assam for the Year* 1880-1, Shillong, 1882, Calcutta, Government of India Press.

1955 *Census of India, Manipur*, New Delhi, Government of India Press.

1971 *Census of India, Manipur*, New Delhi, Government of India Press.

1974 *Towards Equality—Report of the Committee on the Status of Women in India*, New Delhi, Department of Social Welfare, Ministry of Education and Social Welfare.

GOVERNMENT OF MANIPUR

n.d. *Manipuri Customs* (codified by the Codification Committee), Imphal, Government Press, Manipur Administration.

GRIMWOOD, ETHEL ST. CLAIRE

1891 *My Three Years in Manipur*, London, St. Clair.

GULATI, LEELA

1978 'Profile of a Female Agricultural Labourer', *Economic and Political Weekly* XIII, 2:27-35.

GUPTA, GIRI RAJ

1974 *Marriage, Religion and Society*, New York, J. Wiley and Sons.

HAFKIN, NANCY J., AND EDNA G. BAY

1976 *Women in Africa: Studies in Social and Economic Change*, Stanford, Stanford University Press.

HARPER, EDWARD

1964 'Ritual Pollution as an Integrator of Caste and Religion', *Religion in South Asia*, Edward Harper, (ed.), Seattle, University of Washington Press, pp. 151-196.

1969 Fear and the Status of Women, *American Anthropologist* XXV, pp. 81-95.

HASLUCK, MARGARET

1954 *The Unwritten Law in Albania*, Cambridge, Cambridge University Press.

HOCKSMITH, JUDITH

1978 'Radical Yoruba Female Sexuality', *Women in Ritual and Symbolic Rites*, Judith Hocksmith and Anita Spring, (eds.), New York, Plenum Press, pp. 245-267.

HODSON, T. C.

1975 *The Meitheis*, Delhi, B. R. Publishing Corporation (1908).

HOFFER, CAROL P.

1975 'Bundu: Political Implications of Female Solidarity in a Secret Society', *Being Female*, Dana Raphael, (ed.), The Hague, Mouton Publishers, pp. 155-163.

HORTON, ROBIN
    1969 'Types of Spirit Possession in Kalabari Region', *Spirit Mediumship and Society*, J. Beattie and J. Middleton, (eds.), London, Routledge and Kegan Paul, pp. 14-49.

IFEKA-MOLLER, CAROLINE
    1975 'Female Militancy and Colonial Revolt—The Women's War of 1929, Eastern Nigeria', *Perceiving Women*, Shirley Ardener, (ed.), New York; John Wiley and Sons, pp. 127-158.

ISHWARAN, K. (ed.)
    1970 *Change and Continuity in India's Villages*, New York, Columbia University Press.

JACOBSON, DOROTHY ANN
    1973 *Hidden Faces—Hindu and Muslim Purdah in a Central Indian Village*, (unpublished Ph. D. thesis), Columbia University.

JACOBSON, DORANNE, AND SUSAN S. WALEY
    1977 *Women in India—Two Perspectives*, Columbia, Missouri, South Asia Books.

JOHNSTONE, SIR JAMES
    1896 *My Experiences in Manipur and the Naga Hills*, London, Sampson Low, Marston and Co.

JONES, REX L., AND SHIRLEY KURZ JONES
    1976 *The Himalayan Woman: A Study of Limbu Women in Marriage and Divorce*, Palo Alto, Mayfield Publishing Company.

JORDAN, DAVID K.
    1972 *Gods, Ghosts, and Ancestors*, Los Angeles, University of California Press.

KABUI, GANGUMEI
    1974 'Social and Religious Reform Movement in Manipur in the 19th and 20th Centuries', *Bulletin of the Division of History*, Imphal, Centre of Post-Graduate Studies, Jawaharlal Nehru University, pp. 53-75.

KAPADIA, K. M.
    1966 *Marriage and Family in India*, New Delhi, Oxford University Press.

KARVE, IRAWATI
    1961 *Hindu Society*, Poona, Sangam Press Private Ltd.
    1965 *Kinship Organization in India*, Bombay, Asia Publishing House.

KATONA-APTE, JUDITH
    1975 'The Relevance of Nourishment to the Reproductive Cycle of the Female in India', *Being Female*, Dana Raphael, (ed.), The Hague, Mouton Publishers, pp. 43-48.

KELLY, JANE HOLDEN
    1978 *Yaqui Women: Contemporary Life Histories*, Lincoln, University of Nebraska Press.

KENDALL, LAUREL M.
    1979 *Restless Spirits: Shaman and Housewife in Korean Ritual Life*, (unpublished Ph. D. thesis), Columbia University.

KLASS, MORTON
    1966 'Marriage Rules in Bengal', *American Anthropologist* LXVIII, pp. 951-970.

KULACHANDRA, PUNDIT
  1963 *Meitei Lai Harouba*, Imphal, D. Gandhi Memorial Press.
LAMPHERE, LOUISE
  1975 'Women and Domestic Power: Political and Economic Strategies in
        Domestic Groups', *Being Female*, Dana Raphael, (ed.), The Hague,
        Mouton Publishers, pp. 116-130.
  1977 'Anthropology: Review Essay', *Signs* II, 3:612-627.
LANG, OLGA
  1946 *Chinese Family and Society*, New Haven, Yale University Press.
LEACOCK, ELEANOR
  1972 'Introduction', *The Origin of the Family, Private Property and the State*,
        by Frederick Engels, New York, International Publishers.
LEBEUF, ANNIE M.D.
  1963 'The Role of Women in the Political Organization of African Societies',
        Women of Tropical Africa, Denise Paulme, (ed.), Berkeley, University
        of California Press, pp. 93-120.
LEE, S. G.
  1969 'Spirit Possession among the Zulu', *Spirit Mediumship and Society*, J.
        Beattie and J. Middleton, (eds.), London, Routledge and Kegan Paul,
        pp. 128-158.
LEVINE, ROBERT A.
  1970 'Sex Roles and Economic Change in Africa', *Black Africa*, John
        Middleton, (ed.), London, pp. 174-180.
LEWIS, BARBARA
  1977 'Economic Activity and Marriage among the Ivorian Urban Women',
        Sexual Stratification, Alice Schlegel, (ed.), New York, Columbia Uni-
        versity Press, pp. 161-191.
LEWIS, I. M.
  1966 'Spirit Possession and Deprivation Cults', *Man* I, 3 : 307-329.
  1969 *Ecstatic Religion*, Harmondsworth, Penguin.
LEWIS, OSCAR
  1955 'Peasant Culture in India and Mexico: A Comparative Analysis', *Village
        India*, McKim Marriott (ed.), American Anthropological Association,
        Memoir 83, June, pp. 45-70.
  1958 *Village Life in Northern India*, New York, Vintage Books.
LIGHTFOOT, LOUISE
  1958 *Dance Rituals of Manipur, India*, Hong Kong, The Standard Press,
LITTLE, KENNETH
  1973 *African Women in Towns*, Cambridge, Cambridge University Press.
LLEWELYN-DAVIES, MELLISSA
  1979 'Two Contexts of Solidarity among Pastoral Maasai Women', *Women
        United, Women Divided*, Patricia Caplan and Janet M. Bujra, (eds.),
        London, Indiana University Press, pp. 206-237.
LUZBETAK, S. V. D.
  1951 *Marriage and the Family in Caucasia*, vol. 3., Vienna—Modling: Studia
        Institute Anthropos—St. Gabriel's Mission Press.

LYNCH, OWEN M.
  1969 *The Politics of Untouchability*, New York, Columbia University Press.
MACE, DAVID AND VERA
  1960 *Marriage: East and West*, New York, Doubleday and Co. Inc.
MAIBI, RAJOO
  1976 *Langol*, Imphal.
MAIR, LUCY
  1969 *Witchcraft*, New York, World University Library.
MANDELBAUM, DAVID G.
  1972 *Society in India*, vols. 1 and 2, Berkeley, University of California Press.
MARRIOTT, MCKIM (ed.)
  1955 *Village India*, Chicago, The University of Chicago Press.
MATTHIASSON, CAROLYN (ed.)
  1975 *Many Sisters*, New York, Free Press.
MEAD, MARGARET
  1935 *Male and Female*, New York, William Morrow and Co.
MEITEI, BHARAT P.
  1977 *Kakching Harouba*, Manipur, M. G. Singh Printers, Kakching Bazaar.
MENCHER, JOAN AND D'AMICO
  1979 'Women and Rice Cultivation in India', *Studies in Family Planning*, pp. 1-13.
MERNISSI, FATIMA
  1975 *Beyond the Veil*, New York, John Wiley and Sons.
MIDDLETON, JOHN (ed.)
  1967 *Magic, Witchcraft and Curing*, New York, The Natural History Press.
MILLER, BARBARA DIANE
  1978 *Sexual Discrimination and Population Dynamics in Rural India*, (unpublished Ph. D. thesis), Syracuse University.
MOIRANGTHEM, KIRTI SINGH
  1971 *Religious Development in Manipur in the Eighteenth and Nineteenth Century*, (unpublished Ph.D. thesis), Gauhati University, Gauhati.
MULLINGS, LEITH
  1976 'Women and Economic Change in Africa', *Women in Africa*, Nancy J. Hafkin and Edna G. Bay, (eds.), Stanford, Stanford University Press, pp. 239-264.
MURPHY, YOLANDA AND ROBERT
  1974 *Women of the Forest*, New York, Columbia University Press.
NADEL, S. F.
  1970 'Witchcraft in Four African Societies—An Essay in Comparison', *Witchcraft and Sorcery*, Max Marwick, (ed.), Harmondsworth, Penguin, pp. 264-279.
NASH, MANNING
  1965 *The Golden Road to Modernity*, New York, Wiley.
NELSON, CYNTHIA
  1974 'Public and Private Politics: Women in the Middle-Eastern World', *American Ethnologist* LXXVI, pp. 551-561.

NELSON, NICE
   1979 'Women Must Help Each Other: The Operation of Personal Networks
        among Buzaa Beer Brewers in Mathare Valley, Kenya', *Women United,
        Women Divided.* Patricia Caplan and Janet M. Bujra, (eds.), London,
        Indiana University Press, pp. 77-98.
NETTING, ROBERT
   1969 'Marital Relations in the Jos Plateau of Nigeria', *American Anthropologist*
        LXXI, pp. 1037-1041.
O'BARR, JEAN F.
   1975 'Making the Invisible Visible: African Women in Politics and Policy',
        Women in Africa—The African Studies Review XVIII, 3:19-27.
OKONJO, KAMENE
   1976 'The Dual-Sex Political System in Operation: Igbo Women and Com-
        munity Politics in Midwestern Nigeria', *Women in Africa*, Nancy J.
        Hafkin and Edna G. Bay, (eds.), Stanford, Stanford University Press,
        pp. 45-58.
ORANS, MARTIN
   1965 *The Santal*, Detroit, Wayne State University Press.
PALA, ACHOLA O.
   1976 *African Women in Rural Development: Research Trends and Priorities*,
        OLC Paper No. 12, Washington, Overseas Liaison Committee, American
        Council of Education.
PATWARDHAN, SUNANDA
   1973 *Change among India's Harijans*, New Delhi, Orient Longman.
PAULME, DENISE
   1971 *Women in Tropical Africa*, Berkeley, University of California Press.
PELLOW, DEBORAH
   1977 *Women in Accra: Options for Autonomy*, Algonac, Michigan, Reference
        Publications Inc.
POTTER, JACK M.
   1974 'Cantonese Shamanism', *Religion and Ritual in Chinese Society*, Arthur
        P. Wolf, (ed.), Stanford, Stanford University Press, pp. 207-231.
RAO, M. S. A.
   1972 *Tradition, Rationality, and Change*, Bombay, Popular Prakashan.
RAPHAEL, DANA (ed.)
   1975 *Being Female—Reproduction, Power, and Change*, The Hague, Mouton
        Publishers.
REITER, RAYNA (ed.)
   1975 *Toward an Anthropology of Women*, New York, Monthly Review Press.
Resistance (IMPHAL)
        December 1973; 13 April, 24 August, 7 and 14 September, 14 December
        1976; 17 May and 14 June 1977.
RICHARDS, AUDREY
        Chisungu, London, Faber and Faber Ltd.
RISLEY, SIR HERBERT
   1969 *The People of India*, Delhi, Oriental Book Reprint Corporation (1915).
RIVERS, W. H. R.
   1906 *The Todas*, London, Macmillan and Co.

ROBERTSON, CLAIRE
  1976 "Ga Women of Socio Economic Change in Accra, Ghana" *Women in Africa*, Nancy J. Hafkin and Edna G. Bay (eds.), Stanford, Stanford University Press, pp. 19-44.

ROGERS, SUSAN CAROL
  1975 'Female Forms of Power and the Myth of Male Dominance: A Model of Female/Male Interaction in Peasant Society', *American Ethnologist* II, 741-54.

ROSALDO, M. Z.
  1974 'Woman Culture and Society: A Theoretical Overview', *Woman Culture and Society*, M. Z. Rosaldo and L. Lamphere, (eds.), Stanford, Stanford University Press, pp. 17-42.

ROY, J.
  1973 *History of Manipur*, Calcutta, Eastlight Book Store.

ROY, MANISHA
  1975 *Bengali Women*, Chicago, University of Chicago Press.

ROY, NIHAR RANJAN
  1980 *Bangalir Itihas, Adi Prabba*, Paschim Banga Nirakharata Durikaran Samity, Dwitiya Khanda, Calcutta.

ROY, SARAT CHANDRA
  1970 *The Mundas and Their Country*, New York, Asia Publishing House [1912].

SANDAY, PEGGY R.
  1973 'Toward a Theory of the Status of Women', *American Anthropologist* LXXV: pp. 1682-1700.
  1974 'Female Status in the Public Domain', *Woman Culture and Society*, M. Z. Rosaldo and L. Lamphere, (eds.), Stanford, Stanford University Press, pp. 189-206.

SCHLEGEL, ALICE
  1974 'Male and Female in Hopi Thought and Action', *Sexual Stratification*, Alice Schlegel, (ed.), New York, Columbia University Press, pp. 245-269.

SCHNEIDER, JANE
  1971 'Of Vigilance and Virgins: Honor, Shame and Access to Resources in Mediterranean Society', *Ethnology* X, 1 : 1-24.

SEN GUPTA, SHYAMALKANTI
  1970 *The Social Profiles of the Mahalis*, Calcutta, Firma K. L. Mukhopadhyaya.

SHAKESPEARE, J.
  1910 'Manipur Festivals', *Folklore* XXI, pp. 79-82.
  1911 'Manipuri Proverbs', *Folklore* XXII, pp. 473-475.
  1913 'The Religion of Manipur', *Folklore* XXIV, pp. 402-455.

SHARMA, F. IBOTO
  n.d. *Meitei Fijet Leilei*, Imphal.

SHARMA, URSULA
  1979 'Segregation and Its Consequences in India: Rural Women in Himachal Pradesh', *Women United, Women Divided*, Patricia Caplan and Janet M. Bujra, (eds.), London, Indiana University Press, pp. 259-282.

SINGH, CH. BUDDHI
  1972 *Fishing Economics of the Thanga* (a lake dwelling peasant community of Manipur, unpublished Ph. D. thesis), Gauhati, Gauhati University.

SINGH, E. NILAKANTA

1977 *Manipuri: The Art of Subdued Eloquence*. Paper presented at All India Sangeeta Natya Kala Conference, Bombay.

SINGH, K. B.

1975 'Slavery in Manipur', *Folklore* XVIII : pp. 7-9.

SINGH, L. IBOONGOHAL

1963 *Introduction to Manipur*, Imphal, Manipur Students' Store.

SINGH, L. JOYCHANDRA

n.d. *Sevel Langols*, (unpublished Master's thesis), Imphal, Jawaharlal Nehru Centre for Post Graduate Studies.

SINGH, N. IBOBI

1976 *The Manipur Administration* (1709-1907), Imphal, Friends and Co.

SINGH, N. R.

1973 'Marriage by Elopement among the Meiteis of Manipur', *Man in India* L III, 2 : 135-152.

SINGH, N. TOMBI

1975 *Manipur: The Mainstream*, New Delhi, Rajesh Printing Press.

1976 *Khamba and Thoibi*, Delhi Rajesh Printing Press.

SINGH, YOGENDRA

1970 'Chanukhera: Cultural Change in Eastern Uttar Pradesh', *Change and Continuity in India's Villages*, K. Ishwaran, (ed.), New York, Columbia University Press, pp. 241-270.

SINHA, S. C.

1966 'Vaisnava Influence on a Tribal Culture,, *Krishna: Myth, Rites, and Attitudes*, Milton Singer, (ed.), Chicago, The University of Chicago Press, pp. 64-89.

SMOCK, AUDREY CHAPMAN

1977 'The Impact of Modernization on Women's Position in the Family in Ghana', *Sexual Stratification*, Alice Schlegel, (ed)., New York, Columbia University Press, pp. 192-214.

SPATE, O. H. K.

1954 *India and Pakistan*, London, Methuen and Co. Ltd.

SPIRO, MILFORD E.

1967 *Burmese Supernaturalism*, Englewood Cliffs, New Jersey, Prentice-Hall Inc.

1977 *Kinship and Marriage in Burma*, Berkeley, University of California Press.

SRINIVAS, M. N.

1952 *Religion and Society among the Coorgs of South India*, London, Asia Publishing House.

1955 *India's Villages*, New York, Asia Publishing House.

1962 'A Note on Sanskritization and Westernization', *Caste in Modern India and Other Essays*, Bombay, Asia Publishing House.

1968 'Mobility in the Caste System', *Structure and Change in Indian Society,* Milton Singer and Bernard S. Cohn, (eds.), Chicago, Aldine Publishing Co., pp. 189-200.

1971 *Social Change in Modern India*, Berkeley, University of California Press.

1978 *The Changing Position of Indian Women*, The T. H. Huxley Memorial Lecture, Delhi, Oxford University Press.

STATHERN, MARYLIN
1972 *Women in Between*, London, Seminar Press.

STEIN, DORCTHY K.
1978 'Women to Burn: Suttee as a Normative Institution', *Signs* (Winter), pp. 252-267.

SUTTON, CONSTANCE, AND BURROW MAKIESKY
1977 'Social Inequality and Sexual Status in Barbados', *Sexual Stratification*, Alice Schlegel, (ed.), New York, Columbia University Press, pp. 292-325.

TIGER, LIONEL
1969 *Men in Groups*, New York, Random House.

TIGER, LIONEL, AND ROBIN FOX
1971 *The Imperial Animal*, New York, Delta Books.

TURNER, VICTOR
1967 *The Forest of Symbols*, Ithaca, New York, Cornell University Press.
1968 *The Drums of Affliction*, Oxford, Clarendon Press.
1969 *The Ritual Process*, Chicago, Aldine Publishing Co.
1973 *Symbols in African Ritual*, A Warner-Modular Publication, pp. 1-6.

ULRICH, HELEN
1977 'Caste-Differences between Brahmin and Non-Brahmin Women in a South Indian Village', *Sexual Stratification*, Alice Schlegel, (ed.), New York, Columbia University Press, pp. 41-66.

VAN ALLEN, JUDITH
1972 "Sitting on a Man: Colonialism and Lost Political Institutions of Igbo Women", *Canadian Journal of African Studies*, vol. 6, no. 2.
1976 'Aba Riots or Igbo Women's War? Ideology, Stratification and the Invisibility of Women', *Women in Africa*, Nancy J. Hafkin and Edna G. Bay, (eds.), Stanford, Stanford University Press, pp. 59-85.

VREEDE DE STEURS, CORA
1970 *Girl Students in Jaipur*, Assen, Koniklijke Van-Varcum and Company.

WHYTE, MARTIN KING
1978 *The Status of Women in Preindustrial Societies*, Princeton, Princeton University Press.

WILSON, MONICA
1957 *Rituals of Kinship among Nyakusa*, London, Oxford University Press.

WISER, W. H., AND C. V. WISER
1967 *Behind Mud Walls*, 1930-1960, Berkeley, University of California Press.

WOLF, MARGERY
1974 'Chinese Women: Old Skills in a New Context', *Woman Culture and Society*, M. Z. Rosaldo and L. Lamphere, (eds.), Stanford, Stanford University Press, pp. 157-172.
1975 'Women and Suicide in China', *Women in Chinese Society*, Margery Wolf and Roxane Witke, (eds.), Stanford, Stanford University Press, pp. 110-141.

WOLF, MARGERY, AND ROXANE WITKE (eds.)
1975 *Women in Chinese Society*, Stanford, Stanford University Press.

YAMBEM, SANAMANI
  1976 'Nupi-Lan: Manipur Women's Agitation, 1939', *Economic and Political Weekly* XI, 8 : 325-330.

YANG, C. K.
  1959 *The Chinese Family in the Communist Revolution*, Boston, The Technology Press, Massachusetts Institute of Technology.

WADLEY, SUSAN (ed.)
  1980 *The Powers of Tamil Women*, Foreign and Comparative Studies Program, Syracuse University.

Glossary

Asprisya	Untouchable
Athenpot	A large tray with fresh fruit and vegetables as offering for the *Lai*
Bamon mandapa	Community hall run by a Brahman
Brahma Sabha	Council of Brahmans
Chak	Rice
Chandan	Sandalwood or white clay paste
Chelhong	A Brahmanic wedding ceremony following a *chenba*
Chenba	Traditional custom of elopement
Choitharol Kumbaba	Royal chronicle
Chong	A huge white umbrella used at a *Lai* temple
Dakhshina	Custom of offering money or cloth to a person as an expression of respect and Vaisnava humility
Eepal lokpa	A team of fishing women
Fanek	Sarong-like cloth for a woman
Firup	A large bulb-shaped ceremonial basket
Hanubi	Matronly or old woman
Heloi	Evil spirit appearing as a beautiful maiden
Hinchabi	Witch
Ibeamma	Address for a younger woman
Iche	Sister
Ihaifu	An earthen pot used in *Lai Harouba*
Ima	Mother, address for an elderly person
Ima Laimaren	Sanamahi's mother, a house deity
Inafi	A large, thinly woven shawl for a woman
Inamma	A woman's address for her brother's wife, real or fictive
Ine	Father's sister
Ipa	Father
Iteimma	A man's address for his brother's wife, real or fictive
Jagoi	Dance
Jagoi Loishang	Council of dance
Kabok Chaoba	Festival of puffed rice
Kainakatpa	A simple traditional wedding ceremony
Kang	An ancient game for young men and women at the community hall
Kasubi	Prostitute

Kei	Family granary
Keirup	Tiger hunting association
Keithel	Market
Khainaba	Separation; divorce
Khudei	Man's loincloth
Khudei matek	A shorter and thicker shawl for a woman's everyday use
Khulong	Women's work team
Khulong Ishei	Song for *Khulong* at rice cultivation
Kithumpuba (*sadhika*)	A holy female
Korfu	A large cooking pot
Lai	Meitei deity
Lai Harouba	"In pleasure of god" : the prime traditional Meitei ritual performed annually
Lai-ibi	The high priestess of the royal Pakhamba temple
Lai-mapu	A temple-keeper
Laipao	An oracle by a *maibi*
Lai Puba	Carrier of the *Lai*
Lairembi	Meitei female deity
Laishabi	"One who moves like a flower": an unmarried maiden or virgin
Laitongba	A *maibi*'s trance
Lallup	Free labour performed for the state (corvee)
Lalmi	"Men of war" : a military organization
Langol	Incarnation of the divine couple
Langsoi	A device to trap and bind wild elephants
Langthrei	Leaves from a bush for *Lai* ceremonies
Lau	Land
Leikai	Ward
Likkol	A game played with cowrie shells
Loi	A Meitei outcaste
Loishang	Council
Loukhotpa	A traditional ceremony to legitimise a *chenba*
Lugun	The sacred thread of a Hindu high-caste man
Luhungba	Brahmanic wedding
Macha nupi	A little woman; a girl
Maharaj kumari	A daughter of a king
Maiba	A male scholar/priest/shaman
Maibi	A ritual priestess/midwife
Maiknaiba fanek	A traditional *fanek* woven in stripes and with an embroidered border
Mandapa	Community hall
Mangani chakoba	A feast given by the bride's family after five days of a Brahmanic wedding
Mangol	Front porch used as a parlour
Mapuroiba	(Her) husband ("her lord")
Marup	Voluntary association

Mayang	A non-Manipuri Indian; a foreigner
Mayang langbam	A foreigner's family
Meimma	Address for a young girl
Mou	A non-virgin woman or wife
Nahutpa	Ear-piercing ceremony for a child
Ningon chakoba	A feast for a daughter or sister
Ningthou	King
Nupi-lan	Women's war
Nupimamal	Compensation paid for an estranged wife
Nupinaongba	Hen-pecked
Nupipala	Women's religious session or group
Nupi-Shingi Numit	Women's Day
Paja	All-women court
Pakhang	A bachelor
Pala	Music and songs
Pala Loishang	Council of musicians
Pana	A revenue division
Pangan	A Meitei Muslim
Pena	A bowed musical instrument
Penakhongba	A *pena* player
Piba	The head of a lineage
Potpang	The custom of a large gift given by close relatives
Poyeng	The custom of a gift of money by neighbours on certain occasions
Pradhan	Head of a *panchayat*
Pukhri	Pond
Pundit Achouba	Chief pundit
Punsinba	Union
Rajkumar	A man of royal blood
Rajkumari	A woman of royal blood
Sagei	Lineage
Sagei Apokpa	Ancestral deity
Salei	Clan
Sanamahi	Meitei house deity
Sankirtana	Religious group singing in Vaisnavite ceremonies
Semjanba	Sorcery
Senmit	Prediction
Shangoi	Detached shed inside a compound used as a multi-purpose room
Shastipuja	A ritual after six days of a baby's birth
Shuddhi	Purification ceremony
Stridhan	Women's wealth
Sumbal	A tool for rice-pounding
Tairen	Leaf used for sprinkling water at a *Lai* ceremony
Thaba	Abduction of a woman
Thabal Chombi	Social dance for men and women during *Lai Harouba* and spring festival

Thang	Sword
Thang-ta	A war game of sword and spear
Thougal	Dedication
Tulsi	Basil plant
Tulsibong	Altar with a basil plant
Vara	Bridegroom (the honoured one)
Yaongingba	Adopted or incoming son-in-law
Yaosong	Spring festival
Yek	Name of the clan
Yektinnaba	In-clan union
Yumnak	Name of the lineage

Index